THE
ROMANIZATION
OF
BRITAIN

An essay in archaeological interpretation

MARTIN MILLETT

Lecturer in Archaeology
University of Durham

CAMBRIDGE
UNIVERSITY PRESS

Published by the Press Syndicate of the University of Cambridge
The Pitt Building, Trumpington Street, Cambridge CB2 1RP
40 West 20th Street, New York, NY 10011–4211, USA
10 Stamford Road, Oakleigh, Victoria 3166, Australia

First published 1990
First paperback edition 1992

Printed in Great Britain at the University Press, Cambridge

British Library cataloguing in publication data

Millett, Martin
The Romanization of Britain: an essay in archaeological
interpretation.
1. Great Britain, 43–410
I. Title
936.1′04

Library of Congress cataloguing in publication data

Millett, Martin.
The Romanization of Britain : an essay in archaeological
interpretation / Martin Millett.
    p.   cm.
Includes index.
ISBN 0 521 36084 6
1. Great Britain – History – Roman period, 55 B.C.–449 A.D.
2. Excavations (Archaeology) – Great Britain. 3. Great Britain –
Antiquities, Roman. 4. Romans – Great Britain – History.
I. Title.
DA 145.M5 1990
936.1 – dc20   89-35682 CIP

ISBN 0 521 36084 6 hardback
ISBN 0 521 42864 5 paperback

WD

Dedicated to the memory of my mother

Contents

Illustrations

Tables

Preface

Some will pick up this volume with the feeling 'oh, not *another* book about Roman Britain'. I have great sympathy with this view as there are too many books with little new to say. It is therefore essential to establish what I have attempted to do in writing this study. To be clear first, I have written an essay in interpretation which aims to present evidence and provide an explanation of it. I trust that it will be judged for the ideas it contains. Where topics are not considered, it is generally because I have not seen them as central to my argument, not because they are irrelevant or uninteresting. I hope to treat some of them and also other parts of the Empire in later works. Here I have attempted to gather a wide range of evidence and provide a series of connected explanations of it. I shall consider the work to be successful if others judge my arguments to be both internally consistent and consonant with all the evidence available to me.

The genesis of this book lies in the late 1970s when I first taught an evening class in Newbury. I soon discovered that the aspects of Roman Britain I wanted to discuss were ill-served by the available literature. Although prolific on the military and political history, the books were limited in their coverage of economy and society. This conclusion was reinforced when I was appointed to Durham University and came to teach the subject to undergraduates. Two elements were missing: first, a synthesis of the results of recent archaeology; not simply the results of the numerous and extensive excavations of the past two decades, but also the artefact studies which now abound. Secondly, we needed a modern commentary on the social and economic development of the province which took some account of information derived from other social sciences. One could find collections of studies on individual topics like towns or villas, but no book since Rivet's *Town and Country in Roman Britain* (1958) has attempted to integrate the results. Even the ubiquitous textbooks which deal with the subject all too often treat the social and economic evidence as appendices to a narrative, text-based history. A review of this evidence seems especially important since members of the post-imperial generation (to which I belong) are seeking new explanations for cultural change in the Roman world: they are unwilling to accept the paternalistic view that 'the Britons did what they were told by the Romans because it represented *progress*'. I have thus attempted to provide one alternative explanatory framework, whilst at the same time gathering and organizing sets of archaeological information which should be of use to students and scholars irrespective of whether they agree with my interpretations. These data illustrate the information explosion which has occurred since the 1960s, and which make Roman Britain a ripe area for research; rarely in archaeology does one find such a rich data-base on which to test ideas.

Whilst the resulting book is partly designed as an 'alternative Roman Britain' it does not aspire to be a 'new orthodoxy'. I trust that those reading it will find it complementary to the better traditional accounts (particularly those in Frere's *Britannia* and Salway's *Roman Britain*), in which they will find the necessary historical narrative which I have not attempted to provide.

Finally, during work on this book I have become intensely aware that some established opinions about the subject are based not on evidence, but on what have been called 'factoids'. These are pieces of information which have been so commonly repeated that they are almost indistinguishable from facts. I have earnestly tried to avoid including or creating these. Indeed, I hope that some of the data presented here may help lay some of their ghosts. If I have unwittingly created new 'factoids', I trust reviewers will unmercifully point them out.

Acknowledgements

Anything one writes reflects the influence of colleagues, and a work like this is particularly prone to contain ideas which have developed imperceptibly through contact with others. I freely acknowledge the ideas and stimulation provided by those who taught me in London and Oxford, my colleagues there and in Durham, and in particular the students I have taught since 1981. I hope any who recognize their ideas unacknowledged will forgive me. A number of people have kindly answered my questions and provided their own data prior to publication. These include Tom Blagg, Jeremy Evans, Paul Harvey, Colin Haselgrove, Ian Hodder, John Mann, Mark Pomel, Steve Roskams, Roger Tomlin and the parents of the late Mark Gregson.

The Department of Archaeology at Durham has provided a stimulating atmosphere in which to think, while the University has provided sabbatical leave which enabled me to put my thoughts on paper. Our departmental illustrator, Yvonne Beadnell, has translated sketches and assorted scraps into artwork with manifest skill and without complaint.

I am most grateful to the following who have read and commented upon various parts of the manuscript: John Casey, Jeremy Evans, Bill Hanson, Colin Haselgrove, Martin Jones, Simon Keay, Chris Scull and J. T. Smith. Their comments have saved me from errors and improved the work. At CUP, Peter Richards and Nancy-Jane Thompson have patiently helped me through the preparation of the text. Most importantly, Simon James has read the whole manuscript and offered very considerable humorous and enthusiastic critical support; any readability owes much to his careful consideration. The remaining errors and infelicities remain my fault. Finally, Victoria Brandon has done much to support me and maintain my sanity throughout.

University of Durham
July 1988

1

THE NATURE OF

ROMAN IMPERIALISM

Romanization

Well over half a century ago, Francis Haverfield (1912) discussed Romanization and defined it both in terms of historical process and material changes in native culture. These alterations were shown to have been brought about by the Roman presence and resulted in native culture more closely resembling that of Rome. Here, in attempting to evaluate these processes again, I intend to build on the foundations laid by Haverfield, but with the considerable advantage of the larger data-base for the understanding of changes in the material culture in the Empire provided by recent archaeological research. In summary, Haverfield stated: 'First, Romanization in general extinguished the distinction between Roman and provincial . . . Secondly, it did not everywhere and at once destroy all traces of tribal or national sentiments or fashions' (1912, 18). This conclusion parallels the idea, developed by Brendel (1979), that 'Roman' culture was by definition a cosmopolitan fusion of influences from diverse origins rather than purely the native culture of Rome itself. We must thus see Romanization as a process of dialectical change, rather than the influence of one 'pure' culture upon others. Roman culture interacted with native cultures to produce the synthesis that we call Romanized. These transformations, and their products, are worthy of examination not simply for themselves, but also as an instance of social, economic and cultural change of wider significance. Of considerable interest are the processes of change and their context within the societies involved. The intensity of archaeological research in Britain makes it a useful province within which to examine these issues.

Britain was finally conquered by Claudius in AD 43 at a comparatively late stage in the growth of the Roman Empire, after the Mediterranean littoral, together with most of western Europe, had already been incorporated. The aim of this book is to examine the integration of Britain into the Empire, thereby exploring more wide-ranging ideas about Romanization. In this it is recognized that Britain is not a typical province, if indeed such existed, but it is equally contended that she should not be seen as exceptional unless sound reasons are found to support such an idea.

Understanding the process of Romanization requires an appreciation of the different societies involved in the interaction which produced the province of Britain. It is essential from the outset to realize that Romanization was a two-way process of accul-turation: it was the interaction of two cultures, such that information and traits passed between them (Slofstra 1983). As such its products were not simply a result of change initiated by the Romans. It is also important to understand that in her expansion, Rome dealt with peoples, not territories. The processes of cultural change which we call Romanization reflect the influences brought to bear by the Roman élite on the different native peoples with whom they were dealing. Thus to understand Romaniz-ation we need to have a view of the protagonists and the systems within which each operated. In this chapter the essence of the Roman system as it affected Britain is intro-duced, before the societies of Iron Age Britain are evaluated in chapter 2.

Roman expansion

Any understanding of the nature of Roman imperialism demands first, an evaluation within a broad historical perspective of the motivation for Roman expansion, and secondly, a brief assessment of the social structure which acquired that Empire. Such an assessment need not be developed in detail here since it has been the subject of a considerable literature elsewhere (cf. Blagg and Millett in press). Nevertheless, with-out this perspective Roman Britain cannot be properly understood, since it did not exist in isolation as a separate entity, but was a small, perhaps insignificant part of a much larger Empire and thus of a broader historical process.

This process began with the expansion of the City of Rome from a local centre, first to hegemony over much of Italy, then to dominion over former Punic territories, and thus to domination of the Aegean. The more far-flung areas of Gaul and central Europe were absorbed before the eventual incorporation of Britain. The process of expansion was neither steady nor planned and some of the Aegean areas incorporated during the Republic were only brought under direct Roman government after failed attempts at indirect rule under the threat of Roman might (Crawford 1978, 62–73). Many areas were incorporated as a result of annexation by individual Roman generals using the excuse of defence as a cover for aggression. Their motivation lay in the necessity to gain victories, which were vital within the competitive social and political system of Rome. Such victories gave or reinforced personal political status and helped to establish a position in the internal power struggles at Rome. The most extreme and celebrated example of this process was Caesar's conquest of Gaul, which brought with it Rome's first direct, if abortive, intervention in Britain. The system also allowed those involved in successful wars to benefit financially from the booty of conquest (Finley 1973, 56) and the subsequent exploitation of the provinces. The scale of this economic benefit seems in some cases to have been enormous (Crawford 1978, 172ff), although it is almost impossible to evaluate its overall scale or impact.

The impetus for expansion was not therefore a simple one derived from a systematic expansionist design. It was rather a complex of motives, the roots of which lay in the highly competitive system of power within Roman society; a system where instability was endemic and power concentrated in the hands of an oligarchy. Moreover, the per-sonal political and economic fortunes of this group were closely bound up with their success in the military sphere. Military service was essential within the social structure of the Roman élite and a *sine qua non* for political advancement (Birley 1981b, 4–35). Indeed, it seems clear that the whole ethos of Roman society and its economic system came to be reliant upon wars of conquest, so that Rome became a truly militaristic society (Hopkins 1978, 1–96).

Power in society was held by a wealthy élite whose status and economic success were defined by land ownership (Finley 1973; Hopkins 1978). This group needed to expend vast resources on public displays of its prestige and on the maintenance of the client networks which exemplified its power base. The élite also increasingly relied upon conquest to bring them both wealth and the slaves who underpinned production on their rural estates and in Rome itself.

Imperialism and economic exploitation

As Hopkins (1978) has pointed out, this influx of wealth led to the evolution of a society in the centre of the Empire which was uniquely reliant upon territorial expansion. This is not to say that the motivation for expansion was economic but simply that, whilst successful, 'the ever increasing need for warfare in the acquisition of personal riches, glory and clients amongst a competitive élite . . . was bound to produce an Empire' (Garnsey and Whittaker 1978, 5). This is a vital point because, as Badian has stressed, the deliberately expansionist interpretation of Roman imperialism is difficult to substantiate (1968). This remains true despite Harris' argument that personal wealth accumulation was a motive in expansion (1979). Although there is undoubted truth in Harris' view, we must not overlook the important distinction between the drive behind the expansion of the Empire and a primarily economic motivation. Whilst the élite in Rome undoubtedly benefited from the expansion, which fed upon itself, neither the administrative structures, nor the rather piecemeal and halting development of territorial acquisition, are consistent with a systematic and conscious expansion motivated by economic gain. The nature of the exploitation within the conquered territories has important consequences for our understanding of the processes of expansion itself.

The mode of exploitation of the overseas territories can be seen as developing through three broad stages up to the period of Britain's incorporation. First, at the height of the Republic, it was apparently largely *ad hoc* and indirect. According to Badian (1968), after the initial prizes from conquest had been taken, a deeply embedded set of social conventions acted as a disincentive to economic excesses for the personal enrichment of the élite. This reflects a tradition whereby the conqueror became the patron and protector of the conquered. This attitude is also related to that which became normal in Roman society, where to be respectable wealth could not be based on anything but the land (Finley 1973, 41–3). This initial phase was followed by one of less restrained exploitation, although this was not organized systematically, but was rather the result of disorganized and perhaps haphazard individual opportunism. There is little doubt that tax farmers (*publicani*) and provincial administrators milked the overseas territories very heavily. The scale of individual exploitation of provincial office became fundamental to the fortunes amassed by the members of the élite who were involved in provincial government. Indeed, it was said of provincial

3

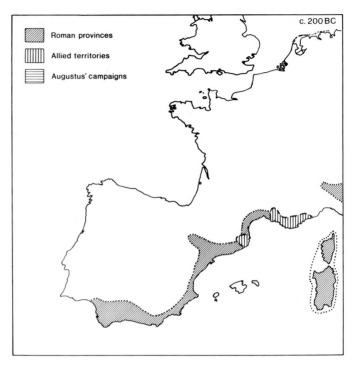

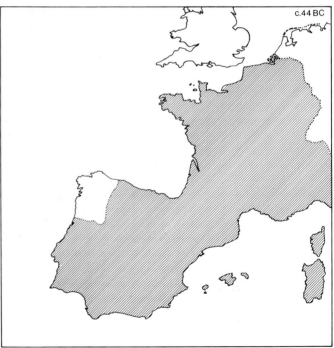

1 The growth and provincial organization of the Western Roman Empire up to AD 14.

c.100 BC

27BC-AD14

GALLIA
LUGDUNENSIS

GALLIA
BELGICA

GALLIA
AQUITANIA

GALLIA
NARBONENSIS

HISPANIA
TARRACONENSIS

CORSICA

LUSITANIA

SARDINIA

BAETICA

governors in the first century BC that they had to make three fortunes from the exploitation of their province, one to recoup their election expenses, the second to bribe the jury at their trial for misgovernment and the third to provide for them thereafter (Crawford 1978, 172). Despite the scale of this exploitation, there was no apparent drive to organize it systematically or to develop the provinces in a way that might have stimulated economic growth. Individual enterprise thus seems not to have resulted in the economic development of the provinces. Indeed if we are to believe some sources, the scale of the expropriations may have been so heavy as to be severely detrimental to the territories.

The third phase of exploitation follows the Augustan settlement which reformed the organization of the provinces (Miller 1935, 400ff) and limited the excesses of provincial exploitation by the élite for their own benefit. The rôle of the *publicani* was curtailed and most taxation was now collected, and thus presumably exploited, locally and through the municipalities (Jones 1974; Mann 1985a, 21). Since the cities were essentially the preserve of the native élites (Garnsey and Saller 1987), the exploitation of taxation was circumscribed by self-regulation and the benefits of tax farming may be assumed to have accrued locally. This seems to have acted as an indirect stimulus to economic growth and civic developments at the provincial rather than the imperial level (Millett in press (b)). The shift in administrative system from Republic to Empire may thus have diminished the centrally exploitative rôle of the imperial system, with consequent benefits for the provinces. The resultant economic disadvantages for Italy may have as much to do with her relative decline in wealth as the effects of her economic dependence on slaves (Hopkins 1978).

Alongside these administrative processes, there was undoubtedly much exploitation through the trade between Rome and the provinces, as shown for instance by the trade in amphora-borne commodities like wine (Carandini and Panella 1981, fig. 29.1). Some of this was exchange demonstrably embedded within the social and political system: the supply of grain to Rome as a prop to the political stability of the City is an outstanding example. The supply of goods like olive oil and wine to the frontier armies also represents a similar large-scale system dependent on motives more complex than free trade. In other cases, like the extraordinary movements of bulk commodities through the western Mediterranean, we suspect a combination of economically motivated trade with exchange resulting from a more complex pattern of land ownership and social obligation. These patterns develop in such a way as to demonstrate that the system was not simply a function of unbridled economic forces. These movements of wealth were thus part of the social and political web which connected the heartland to the provinces in a series of complementary flows (Hopkins 1980; table 6.2).

This background makes it difficult to equate the Roman Empire with any simple world system of exploitation like those recently discussed by Hingley (1981) and Roskams (1986). Such models, derived from Wallerstein's view of a World System, require us to view the Empire as a system which was designed to facilitate economic domination, through flows of both taxes and trade which benefited the centre. This system, it is suggested, was structured administratively and economically to optimize the productive benefit of the Empire to Rome.

This model has some limited use in relation to the late Republic when, as we have seen, there was a period of unbridled although unsystematic exploitation of the conquered territories. Such, however, was not the norm in the Roman world and was significantly curtailed by the Augustan administrative system, which was a re-establishment of the traditional values of the Republic. It is perhaps significant that this period of excessive individualistic enterprise does not seem to have resulted in the growth of the provincial economies that might be envisaged in Wallerstein's model (Roskams 1986).

When one examines the flows of taxes and trade during the Principate, the movement within the Empire seems to have been outward to the provinces rather than inwards to Italy. In this the army acted as the principal mechanism, with the core provinces (excluding Italy, which was largely exempt from taxation) (Miller 1935, 430) providing the bulk of the cash for their pay, which represented the largest single item of state expenditure. This outflow of funds from the core towards the periphery was to some extent mitigated primarily by trade, which returned some of the cash to the core (Hopkins 1980) and perhaps also by the removal of raw materials, particularly bullion, from the provinces (table 6.2). This was of course combined with the once-for-all expropriations of native wealth at the time of conquest, although this is unlikely to have outweighed the longer-term flows in the opposite direction. The nature of the pattern as presently understood cannot be interpreted in terms of any system of world domination based on a conscious economic motivation; such a system is an anachronism based on contemporary views of modern, capitalist imperialism.

Roman imperialism had much more to do with personal power struggles within the oligarchy at the core and this has major ramifications for the structure which comprises the Empire. Its system was far less centralized in administration than is often supposed (Garnsey and Saller 1987), and in essence relied on circumscribed local autonomy with the cities as the fundamental unit. This worked in the interests of the Roman élite, who were not burdened with the expense of directly administering the lands which they controlled. This tradition developed from both desire and necessity in the Republic (Badian 1968). The necessities were, first, that the Roman élite was too small to directly control each incorporated society, and secondly, the scale of territory was so large that the logistics of direct government were probably impossible, even if conceivable, in a pre-industrial era (Millar 1982). Government through the cities was comparatively easy to apply in the territories of the Eastern Empire and the Mediterranean littoral, where there was some tradition of municipal organization going back to the foundation of cities in the period of Greek and Punic colonization in the seventh–sixth centuries BC. In areas without a tradition of *poleis*-type urbanism, the pre-existing tribes were treated as *civitates*, or city states, by Rome. This gave them the same functions within the administration as the Greek cities. Whilst it is clear that they differed both in their territorial extent and in the details of their organization, the Roman system was sufficiently robust to have incorporated them quite satisfactorily into the same administrative framework (Mann 1965). This system meant that Rome governed through the established local élites, whether formerly magistrates or tribal aristocrats, who consequently identified their interests with those of Rome.

7

The net effect of this was an early imperial system of loosely decentralized administration which allowed overall control by Rome while leaving the low-level administration in the hands of the traditional aristocracies. This enabled most areas brought under Roman control to be run without a significant military presence and with a light burden on the conquerors. The corollary of this low input was that the material gain to Rome was negligible by the standards of modern imperialism. Rome's Empire was thus an empire of individual and collective political prestige for the conquerors rather than one of continuing economic benefit. Furthermore, its character was that of a federation of diverse peoples under Rome, rather than a monolithic and uniformly centralized block.

We can draw these strands together to see Roman imperialism as an extension of the competitive structure of the élite in Rome itself. Expansion was not planned in relation to any grand strategy, and was executed piecemeal. Similarly, the advantages accruing from this expansion were not systematically organized and their exploitation was circumscribed because of the moral and ethical constraints of Roman society. These constraints did break down in the late Republic, but the Augustan administrative system deflected any emergence of systematic economic imperialism. This was an indirect result of the formalization of a system of provincial administration which left power in the hands of the local peoples through their own municipalities, thereby removing any necessity for a large central bureaucracy. This administrative structure defused any tendency towards a centralized imperial economy. It did, however, establish within the Empire both a flow of wealth between the core and periphery, and the potential for economic growth in the municipalities which controlled local taxation. In this way the devices of administrative convenience within the militaristic system had become the dominant structuring principles of the Empire when Britain came within her orbit.

2

THE PATTERN OF LATER

IRON AGE SOCIETIES

In this chapter, my aim is to characterize settlement patterns and social organization from the end of the second century BC to the middle of the first century AD in the areas of Britain which became the Roman Province of Britannia. The aim is not to provide a detailed account of the archaeology of the period, for it is already the subject of a considerable and growing specialist literature which deserves a fuller synthesis than space here allows. Instead the salient characteristics are discussed and themes introduced which are to be taken up during the remainder of this volume. These themes are particularly related to the development of the agricultural economy and its productive capacity; regional variations in the settlement pattern, and thus perhaps social formation; and the organization of social power. These aspects will be treated in more detail than has been customary in recent studies of Roman Britain, as to understand its Romanization we must first understand what pre-Roman Britain was like.

One of the principal problems in any appreciation of this period lies in distinguishing long-term processes of change which were fundamentally indigenous from those stimulated by external events, especially the proximity of the growing Roman world. It is difficult to differentiate these strands, but in presenting the archaeological evidence, it is desirable to make an attempt. The fundamentals of the agricultural economy should be seen as the continuation of patterns deeply rooted in prehistory (Bradley 1978; 1984; Fowler 1981). These are thus examined first, before the economy, settlement and social organization are considered, since changes in the latter are more likely to have resulted from short-term events. It is unfortunate that many of the developments in this period have been previously associated with population movements, especially that of the Belgae to Britain, mentioned by Caesar (*DBG* V. 12). This is still often seen as a prime cause of change in the Later Pre-Roman Iron Age (Cunliffe 1984a, 19–20; Frere 1987, 5–6). Whilst there is no doubt that movements of people took place, we may question whether the particular events which have entered the historical record are especially significant. The common cultural traditions shared on both sides of the Channel provide the framework within which these migrations should be seen (Champion 1976). They were almost certainly based on kinship ties which provided the context for regular movements of people as well as the provision of help during periods of warfare (*DBG* IV. 20). Neither migrations nor kinship relationships fully explain the cultural changes that occurred in the Later Pre-Roman Iron Age which have too readily been dated by association with the movements of the Belgae. Explanations for such changes are better sought in the workings of society within the broader historical context.

Cross-channel links place in perspective both the ambiguities in Caesar's use of the term 'Belgae' (Hachmann 1976) and the not-inconsiderable difficulties experienced by those who have tried to relate the material culture directly to Caesar's accounts (cf. Hodson 1962). To avoid prejudging these issues by the use of a particular terminology, my own preference is to avoid the term 'Belgic' in archaeological description. Similarly, the term 'Celtic' has been avoided in the description of social groups because of its ambiguities. Instead, I shall use the convention of Later Pre-Roman Iron Age (LPRIA) to designate the period spanning the introduction of coinage, wheelmade pottery and lowland nucleated settlements, from around the end of the second century BC to the Roman conquest.

The agricultural economy

Fundamental to the understanding of LPRIA societies must be an appreciation of their economies, which were almost exclusively agricultural. Whilst there is evidence for craft specialization, for instance in metal and pottery manufacture, together with the exploitation of mineral resources (principally iron, copper and tin), in addition to the export of slaves (Strabo IV. 5), there is no evidence to support the belief that these were more than marginal to the fundamentals of production.

Agricultural production thus formed the economic basis of society and its understanding is fundamental to an appreciation of the regional variation in the settlement pattern (below, p. 15). Fox's (1983) simple division of Britain into highland and lowland zones, with the former dominated by pastoralism and the latter by arable production, is of limited value in understanding the variations in the economic pattern during this period (Salway 1981). Recent research demonstrates that mixed agriculture was normal throughout the island, but with marked regional variations in microclimate and topography determining the precise exploitation strategies followed. This resulted in considerable regional variations within the archaeological data.

The traditional view of a largely pastoral highland zone is being questioned. Manning (1975) has argued in favour of important pockets of arable production in Wales, while in the north-east of England excavated sites are producing seed assemblages indicative of mixed economies with significant arable components similar to those found in the south (Heslop 1987, 117–20; Van der Veen 1988). Similarly, Grant (1984) has shown that in Wessex techniques of animal husbandry varied, with an LPRIA increase in sheep grazing on the chalklands and a trend towards more cattle rearing in the Thames valley. These pointers illustrate the importance of the pastoral element in the mixed economies of the lowland zone.

There is widespread evidence for a change in the balance and intensity of agriculture in the latter part of the first millennium BC. The period is marked by the maximum utilization of prehistoric field systems which extended over much of the lowland zone (Fowler 1981, 144). Although many of the fields were already of considerable antiquity (Taylor 1987), the extent of their use was at its height in the period after 500 BC, and this points towards significant arable intensification. This is also shown in the extension of agricultural land at the expense of the forest margins in areas like north-east England (Turner 1979) and the Vale of York (Millett and McGrail 1987, 98–101). Increased arable exploitation of heavier soils and damp land has also now been demonstrated in areas from the north-east to the far south (Haselgrove 1984a, 17–22; Jones 1981, 111–21). It is more difficult to identify changes in agriculture through the evidence of animal husbandry, for though there were physically larger breeds of stock in Roman Britain than are seen earlier in the Iron Age, there is a lack of LPRIA material to establish whether these were introduced then, or as a result of the Roman arrival (Maltby 1981). Ryder does suggest that improved breeds of fine-woolled sheep were first introduced before the conquest (1981, 333). Yet more difficult to assess are changes in the ways in which the livestock were exploited. Although Grant (1984, 116) argued that changes detected in Wessex were not entirely the result of increasingly specialized farming in the different ecological zones, it is difficult to escape the conclusion that specialization and intensification of farming was under way.

There is thus sound evidence which points towards a major phase of agricultural intensification in the LPRIA (Jones 1981, fig. 6.4) (fig. 36). This may have been brought about by an increasing population throughout the last millennium BC (Bradley 1978, 123–4). Such growth, within an already densely populated landscape, cannot have been sustained by simply increasing the area under cultivation, even allowing for recourse to hitherto unsuitable wet and heavy lands. More intensive exploitation of existing lands may thus have become vital. However, the stimulus for this probably also came from within the social system, where the increasing hierarchy (see below) implies a rising number of people not primarily engaged in production, yet both consuming agricultural products and requiring further surpluses to meet the demands of their obligations beyond their own tribe.

This evidence should be seen in relation to the results of the Butser experiments, which have indicated that the crops and the farming techniques practised in the LPRIA were capable of producing very substantial yields. Those achieved for emmer wheat average two tonnes per hectare (Reynolds 1979, 61), considerably more than conventional estimates. These experimental figures do not of course mean that LPRIA farmers obtained such yields, simply that their production was not constrained by limitations of crop-type or technology. Given the substantial areas in cultivation (Fowler 1981), it is probable that LPRIA society produced a very considerable surplus (as indicated by Strabo (IV. 5), who refers to the export of corn, cattle and hides). This productive surplus formed the foundation for the sophisticated societies which flourished before the Roman conquest, the patterning and organization of which we will now examine.

Regional groupings in the archaeological evidence

The agricultural evidence shows that there were considerable regional variations within the LPRIA. The material culture is also remarkably heterogeneous; some areas

11

exhibit a rich and varied cultural assemblage whilst others have only a limited quantity of goods within a narrow range. The settlement pattern shows a similarly wide variation from landscapes in which large hillforts are prevalent to those dominated by small farmsteads (Cunliffe 1978a). Recognizing this fragmentation is considerably easier than defining any clear patterning, especially since at least half of Britain seems to have been aceramic (Cunliffe 1978a, fig. 39).

Unless we accept Britain as a unified cultural entity (Hodson 1964), which seems unsatisfactory in view of the fragmentation described, it is necessary to group the available evidence geographically. Collis (1977) has summarized the difficulties in achieving this as the material available does not meet the criteria laid down by Childe (1956) for satisfactorily identifying archaeological cultures. Furthermore, these problems make it difficult to relate any material-culture groupings to distinct populations (Champion 1976). Variations in the quality of evidence which result from the unevenness in the scale, nature and distribution of fieldwork compound these difficulties. To overcome these problems it is appropriate to use the various types of evidence separately to identify different patterns of groupings. Three types of evidence are thus examined here: pottery styles, the coinages, and the settlement evidence.

Pottery has been most widely used to define regional groupings, with the series of style zones defined by Cunliffe (1978a). These style zones must be recognized as imperfect archaeological groupings for several reasons. First, variations in pottery use mean that some areas were aceramic, so pottery is only of value in limited areas. Within the pottery-using areas there were also variations in use; so, for instance, evidence for the long-distance exchange of Glastonbury ware (Peacock 1969) produces a different form of patterning to that generated by the Durotrigian wares. Although centrally produced around Poole, these latter have a more limited spatial and functional distribution and are therefore more appropriate to the definition of population groups (Blackmore et al. 1979). Similar differentials resulting from the use of more prestigious wares within a stratified society may account for the absence of Cunliffe's key types on some sites (for example the absence of Atrebatic ware on farmsteads in the Basingstoke area) (Millett 1983a; Millett and Russell 1984). Finally, we should note that the broad style-zones obscure more localized sets of similar assemblages which may plausibly be related to clan groupings (Lambrick 1984, fig. 11.3), and are thus of considerable potential interest.

Despite these problems we can observe patternings in the LPRIA which change remarkably little through the period (Cunliffe 1978a). A series of regional styles of decorated pottery can be identified around c. 100 BC in south and east England (fig. 2). These ceramic zones could be supplemented by other types of grouping for areas less well served by the pottery, like the tradition of East Yorkshire square ditched barrows (Stead 1979), although we should be wary of mixing different data in this way. The ceramic zones generally conform to sensible regional entities. Later in the period, it is possible to distinguish some sub-divisions within the groups (e.g. Cunliffe 1978a, fig. 7.2), but at present analysis of a full range of assemblages of the period from c. 100 BC to the Roman conquest has not produced such a detailed and systematic picture as that provided by the coinages.

The numismatic evidence provides a valuable contrast with the pottery style-zones based on Cunliffe's original study more than 25 years ago, since the coins have been the subject of a series of recent detailed discussions and sophisticated spatial analyses (Hodder 1977; Kimes *et al.* 1982; Sellwood 1984; Haselgrove 1987a). The most rigorous of the spatial analyses (Kimes *et al.* 1982) is used to provide the coin groupings shown in fig. 3, which shows the principal coin-using areas on the eve of the Roman conquest. The theoretical underpinning of the analysis and the relationship of the coinages to social units have been discussed by Haselgrove (1987a). A comparison

Saucepan pot continuum

Jar continuum

Maiden Castle - Marnhull style

Bowl continuum

Glastonbury style

2 The ceramic style-zones found in Britain around 100 BC (after Cunliffe 1978a). Decorated pottery is generally absent from areas shown as blank.

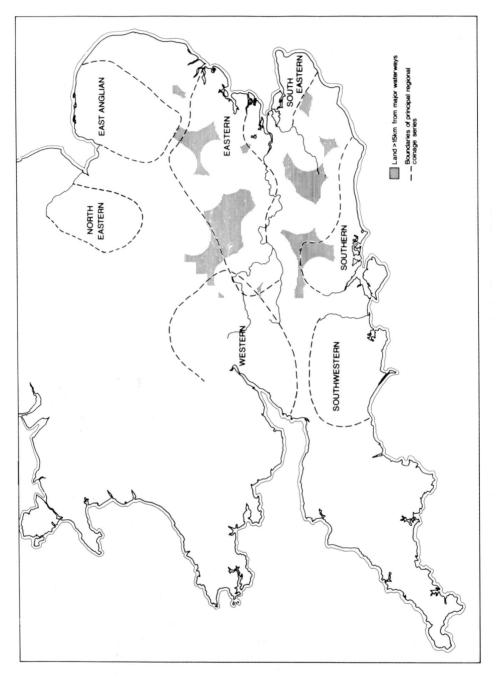

3 Coinage zones in LPRIA Britain, showing the regional nomenclature used (after Haselgrove 1987a). The hatched areas are those further than 15 km from major waterways.

Table 2.1. *Settlement patterns at the end of the LPRIA*

Area*	Major centres		Rural pattern		
	Hillforts	*Oppida*	Enclosed	Unenclosed	'Villages'
SW peninsula	P	A	D		
SW coin zone	D	A	P		
W coin zone	P	P	P	P	
S coin zone	P	P	D	P	
SE coin zone	P	D	P	P	
E coin zone	A	D	P	P	P
E Anglian coin zone	A	A	P		P
NE coin zone	P	P	P	P	P
W Midlands	D	A	P		
Wales	P	A	D		
N Wales	D	A	P		
NW England	P	A	D		
Pennines	P	A	P		
E Yorkshire	A	P	P	P	
NE England	A	P	D		

D = dominant   A = absent
P = present   [blank] = uncertain
*For coin zones see Haselgrove 1987a, and fig. 3.

of these distributions with the pottery style-zones of *c.* 100 BC lends support to the hypothesis that both relate to social groupings. Their strong similarities also suggest a continuity of fundamental groupings through this century and a half. Neither pattern correlates well with the postulated 'socio-economic territories' presented by Cunliffe (1981, fig. 15) on the basis of polygons drawn around supposed centres of power. This may suggest that the social groups were based less on focal sites than some believe.

Sub-divisions also occur in some of the coin distributions. Sellwood (1984, fig. 13.11) has identified a major division between the northern and southern Dobunnic coinages, and a similar division may be suggested by the use of a pair of names on the Corieltauvian coinages (table 2.3; Frere 1987, 36–7). On analogy with the principal groupings, it is possible that these represent social divisions the significance of which are considered further below.

The settlement evidence on the eve of the Roman conquest shows a diversity of pattern which it is extremely difficult to resolve into coherent spatial groupings, especially in the absence of a full set of detailed regional studies. Table 2.1 attempts to codify the available data for the first half of the first century AD from the range of regional studies now available. The regional zones used are based on a combination of Haselgrove's coinage zones (fig. 3) and more generalized geographical regions. These results can be compared with the situation in *c.* 150 BC as mapped by Cunliffe (fig. 4). In both periods there is a marked discordance between the south and east and the north and west. Although partly a function of the nature of the landscape, it seems also to result from differences in social organization. The basic distinction is between the more hierarchical pattern of the south and east, which has a range from large focal sites to small farmsteads, and the less centralized patterns of the north and west. Here settlement is less differentiated with a pattern of more evenly sized settlements, which are generally defended. Systems dominated by hillforts fill an intermediary position in this continuum with a similar rôle presumably played by the nucleated sites, in areas like Lincolnshire, where hilltops are less common. It is certain that a more detailed analysis of settlement types could define a clearer regional patterning and suggest more sensitive correlations with social organization than are possible at present.

Strongly defended homesteads

Hillfort dominated zone

Villages and open settlements

Enclosed homesteads

4 General settlement types in Britain around 150 BC (after Cunliffe 1978a).

The reasonable coherence of the spatial groupings defined in these different ways, combined with the loose correlation between the later groups and the subsequent Roman administrative divisions, lends support to the idea that they relate to social units. A theoretical underpinning to this conclusion is provided by Hodder's (1982) demonstration that material culture styles are used by human groups to define their social identities in certain circumstances. Before this can be investigated further, we must turn to examine the evidence available for understanding the social organization of the LPRIA.

Social organization

The archaeological evidence for the various regional groupings provides ambiguous evidence for the nature of social organization. The problem of its reconstruction is therefore best approached with the aid of the scant literary evidence, which should be examined on its own before being compared with archaeology. We must be acutely aware of the difficulties this entails, especially during such a period of very rapid change, as the literary sources provide their best evidence only for the limited periods of Caesar's invasion and Augustus' reign. However, models built on this evidence form a structure within which the numismatic and archaeological data can be viewed. This static material is thereby placed in context by relating it to changes in the historical context of LPRIA Britain and the dynamics of social power are seen through it.

The classical viewpoint

In contrast to Roman Republican society, the social groupings which formed the contemporary population of Britain are poorly served by the literary sources. Although the islands were known to classical authors, they were a remote and mysterious backwater whose society was of little relevance or concern to the writers, except for providing interesting literary anecdotes. Even during Rome's first direct intervention the information about native social organization in Britain as communicated by Caesar (*DBG* V. 12–14), and later Strabo (IV. 5, 2), was neither detailed nor incisive. These ancient authors' failure to provide the information we desire results from the purpose of their writing, which needs to be understood within the context of its rôle within élite society at Rome. The information central to our interests was little more than embellishment, which must be understood within its literary genre (Woodman 1985). This explains the imprecisions evident, for instance, in Caesar's account of agriculture, which were of no importance to their authors. The background information they provide about the social organization and economies of the native peoples of Britain is therefore of limited value and should not be relied upon too heavily as the basis for generalization. With this in mind we should consider the texts. Caesar states:

> The population is very large, their homesteads thick on the ground and very much like those in Gaul, and the cattle numerous. As money they use either bronze or gold coins or iron bars with a fixed standard of weight. Tin is found inland, iron on the coast, but in small quantities; the bronze they use is imported (*DBG* V. 12).

Of all the Britons, by far the most civilized are the inhabitants of Cantium, a purely maritime region, whose way of life is little different from that of the Gauls. Most of those inhabiting the interior do not grow corn, but live instead on milk and clothe themselves in skins. All the Britons dye themselves with woad, and as a result their appearance in battle is all the more daunting. They wear their hair long, and shave all their bodies with the exception of their heads and upper lips. Wives are shared between groups of ten or twelve men, especially between brothers and between fathers and sons. The offspring on the other hand are considered the children of the man with whom the woman first lived (*DBG* V. 14).

Strabo adds to this:

Most of the island is flat and thickly wooded, though many districts are hilly. It produces grain and cattle, gold, silver and iron. These are exported along with hides and slaves and dogs bred specifically for hunting . . . The men are taller than the Celts, not so blond and of looser build . . . Their customs are in some respects like those of the Celts, in others simpler and more barbaric. As a result, some of them, through their want of skill, do not make cheese though they have no shortage of milk. They are also unskilled in horticulture or farming in general. They are ruled by chieftains. In war they mostly use chariots like some of the Celts. The forests are their cities; for they fortify a large circular enclosure with felled trees and there make themselves huts and pen their cattle, though not for a long stay (IV. 5, 2).

These accounts are not exhaustive and give only a slight basis for understanding the social formations within LPRIA Britain, since they reflect the Roman perspective, expressed by Tacitus that 'one must remember we are dealing with barbarians' (*Agricola* 11). Nevertheless, they have been given undue weight in many past accounts simply because written sources have been given precedence over other types of evidence.

In viewing the archaeological evidence, we must be careful neither to force it into the straitjacket of these rather limited literary sources, nor to expect it to be amenable to the type of particularistic analysis the written evidence allows. We should similarly be wary of using general statements about the similarities between the societies of Britain and Gaul as a basis for transferring better quality information from Gaul to Britain. Nevertheless, the information about social formations in Gaul are of value for comparative purposes as they provide an indication of the forms taken by some developed Iron Age societies in northern Europe.

Nash and Crumley (Haselgrove 1987b, fig. 10.3) have both used Caesar's account to provide slightly different reconstructions of a basically hierarchical Gallic society. This comprised upper classes of nobles, warriors and the learned (including priests), who were bound together, and to whom the lower orders were attached, by social obligations and bonds of clientage. It is clear that, although we may not fully understand the principles by which these societies were organized, there was a relatively highly differentiated and stratified social system in parts of Gaul. This may have relevance to our understanding of contemporary Britain, although we must remain aware that there were considerable variations in social organization across Gaul itself (Haselgrove 1987b).

Some indirect evidence is provided by the literary sources for Britain. In his account

of his expeditions, Caesar makes references which help us to understand the organization of the Britons (table 2.2). He refers to a war leader, Cassivellaunus; a prince,
Mandubracius; various Kentish kings as well as Lugotorix, a noble; and social groups
which may be identified as tribes. These terms show a general correlation with the
social formations described for Gaul, although we should be aware of the danger that
Caesar was rendering an unfamiliar and perhaps ill-understood social system into his
own language and relating it to systems he knew. Allowing for this, we may take it to
provide an outline of the social structures with which he came into contact in
55–54 BC.

5 The LPRIA mirror from Desborough, Northants. The elaborate abstract decoration is
characteristic of high-status display items of the period. (*Photograph by courtesy
of the British Museum.*)

Table 2.2. *LPRIA tribal élites: the evidence of Caesar (DBG) in 54 BC*

Ref.	Content	Text
V.11	Cassivellaunus selected as supreme commander by the Britons	*...imperii bellique administrandi communi...*
V.20	Caesar receives envoys from the Trinovantes, the leading tribe	*...civitas firmissima...*
V.20	Mandubracius' father had been king of the state (the Trinovantes)*	*...in ea civitate regnum...*
V.21	Cenimagni, Segontiaci, Ancalites, Bibroci and Cassi send deputies to Caesar	*...legationibus...*
V.20	Cassivellaunus sends deputies to Caesar	*...legatos...*
V.22	Kent (Cantium) divided into four districts with four kings, Cingetorix, Carvilius, Taximagulus and Segovax	*...regionibus...* *...reges...*
V.22	Caesar captures Lugotorix, a commander of noble birth	*...nobili duce...*

*Possible implication of hereditary succession
Interpretation of social hierarchy
Tribal group probably equivalent to war leader
Tribe probably represented by kings
Clans probably equivalent to the nobility

We may envisage the division of society into a series of comparatively small-scale units, each with its own leader, and aristocratic élite. These clans came together to form larger groups assembled under a single leader at times of stress. We can see these as tribes formed of loosely organized kinship and clientage networks, which were subject to periodic realignments of allegiance, as illustrated by the five sub-groups which apparently split from Cassivellaunus' alliance to surrender to Caesar (table 2.2). This pattern would be consistent with a process in the development of social hierarchies in south-east England analogous to that described in Gaul, although at a less elaborated stage of development.

In 55–54 BC these organizations are seen only under stress and at one stage in their development. We have neither direct evidence of how they changed after this date, nor of the social structures that existed in areas away from the south-east. The archaeological evidence suggests both a development in the scale and elaboration of the south-eastern hierarchies in the following century, and variations in the pattern of organization elsewhere in Britain (below, p. 23). In this context it is unfortunate that the literary accounts of the Claudian invasion are insufficiently detailed to provide full information about native organization in AD 43. In the absence of these we rely on archaeological reconstruction.

The archaeological evidence

If we compare the archaeological evidence for regional groupings with the literary sources we find that the two combine to suggest a pattern of developing social hierarchies in the south and east. The principal material-culture zones (figs. 3 and 4) point to a series of major social groupings which we refer to as tribes. These tribal units, identified in the coin distributions on the eve of the conquest, were composed of smaller sub-units or clans. These are seen in the archaeological evidence through subdivisions in some coin distributions, clusters in the cemetery evidence (Haselgrove 1982, fig. 10.4; Millett 1987a), and the distributions of some decorative motifs on pottery (Lambrick 1984, fig. 11.3). These clans may sometimes have acted as septs to the tribes, each of which had its own leader. This would be consistent with the pattern suggested for some groups more remote from the continent, like the Brigantes, who seem to have been a loose confederation of five such clans (Frere 1987, 42, 46). This particular example highlights the problem of the less materially rich areas, where little can generally be said about the social organization. We should not, however, assume that their society was in any way unsophisticated, since anthropology provides us with numerous examples of complex social networks which leave very little archaeological trace.

In the south and east the pattern suggests that the permanence of these groupings, and the scale of their organization, was changing in the years between the Caesarian expeditions and the Claudian conquest. The best evidence for this comes from the inscribed coinages, which give an indication of their emerging systems (fig. 3). Some of those people named on the inscribed coinages may be equated with individuals mentioned in the classical sources (table 2.3). This lends support to the idea that the minting authorities should be identified as the tribal leaders, who can occasionally be related to particular sites. Indeed, some of those whose names appear on the coins use the latin title *rex*, whether in recognition of status achieved through a treaty with Rome (Frere 1987, 30) or one claimed on the grounds of internal authority. The information the classical sources provide about kings and other nobles leaving Britain (*Res Gestae* 6. 32; Suetonius, *Caligula* 44. 2; Dio 60. 19, 1) suggests that warfare and competition both within and between groups were endemic at this period. These pressures may have provided the stimulus which consolidated the tribal groupings so that they became more permanent, the externally induced stress being the generator of internal cohesion. There are also indications that the emergence of a larger state in the Essex–Hertfordshire area was coming about by similar means. This state, the tribe of the Catuvellauni, had been expanding at the expense of the territory of the Trinovantes. They had become the major force by the end of the LPRIA in Britain. Cunobelinus, perhaps their king, was referred to as *Britannorum rex* (Suetonius, *Caligula* 44), and they were thought of by Rome as her principal target in the Claudian invasion (chapter 3). This group was evolving to a level of sophistication much closer to that of the proto-states of Caesarian central Gaul than that achieved by the adjacent areas of Gallia Belgica on the eve of their conquest (Haselgrove 1987b, 108–11). This is probably the result of the long period of development experienced by Britain independent of, but influenced by, Roman Gaul in the period from Caesar onwards.

Much uncertainty surrounds both the precise character of contemporary changes in the settlement patterns, with the emergence of *oppida*, and the relationship of these developments to the growing social hierarchy (fig. 6). Although *oppida* are commonly treated as a group (cf. Cunliffe 1976) they are heterogeneous. They all comprise large-scale complexes which were often surrounded by substantial but discontinuous dykes.

Table 2.3. *LPRIA tribal élites: the coin evidence*

Date ±10 years	Period/phase	Coinage group						
		Western	South-western	Southern	South-eastern	Eastern	East Anglian	North-eastern
140 BC	– 1							
110 BC	I 2/3							
80 BC	– 4/							
50 BC	II 5/6			COMMIOS[A]				
20 BC	– 7			TINCOMMIOS[B] COMF*	DUBNOVELLAUNUS[B] ADDEDOMAROS	TASCIOVANUS[2] ANDOCO		
AD 10	III 8/	ANTED EISV CATTI		VERICA[E]† COMMIF* TASCIOVANUS EPATICCV[S] TASCIF*	EPPILLUS[1]† COM.F*	CUNOBELINUS[3,D]† TASC.F* SOLIDV	ANTED	AUNCOST ESVPASU VEPCORF DUMN/TIGIRSEN VOLISIOS DUMNOCOVEROS DUMNOVELLAUNUS
AD 40	– 9	CORIO BODVOC		CARATACVS[F]		AMMINUS[C,4]	ECEN PRASTO[G]	CARTIVEL
Roman *Civitas*		Dobunni	Durotriges	Atrebates	Cantii/Trinovantes	Catuvellauni/Trinovantes?	Iceni	Corieltauvi

A = also in Caesar, *DBG* V.1
B = also in *Res Gestae* 6.32
C = also in Suetonius, *Caligula* 44.2 (son of Cunobelinus)
D = also in Suetonius, *Caligula* 44.2 and Dio, 20.1
E = also in Dio 19.1 as *Berikos*
F = also in Dio 20.1, who also mentions TOGODUMNUS as sons of CUNOBELINUS
G = also in Tacitus *Annals* 31

1 = place-name CALLEV[A]
2 = place-name VERLAMIO[N]
3 = place-name CAMVLODVNO[N?]
4 = place-name DVNO[VERNVM?]

* = filial hereditary descent or legitimation device
† = title REX used

Source: after Haselgrove 1987a

As such they appear focal to their regions, representing major communal efforts indicative of social centralization. However, beyond these common factors, they are variable and generally far less organized and imposing than the sites passing under the same term on the continent (Collis 1984). At one extreme, Camulodunum (Colchester) is a complex, multi-functional settlement, with separate foci for religion, craft activity, occupation and perhaps élite residence (Collis 1984, 224–6). At the other, the equally extensive but much less densely occupied site at Stanwick (figs. 7–8) appears to have only a relatively small settlement area where there is evidence for craft activity as well as habitation (Haselgrove and Turnbull 1987). There is also a wide chronological range, with sites like Camulodunum and Calleva (Silchester) starting their sequences around the beginning of the first century AD, and others like Stanwick (Haselgrove and Turnbull 1987) and Bagendon (Trow in press) coming to prominence only in the decade around the Roman conquest of their respective areas (table 2.4).

Despite the apparent focal nature of these sites (fig. 6), these examples illustrate the danger of making too direct an equation between *oppida* and a particular type of social organization or economic sophistication. Some attempt at understanding these settlements in their social context can be made by relating them to the coin evidence. In four cases the *oppida* can be identified as focal sites by using the coin legends which provide the place-names of Callev[a] (Silchester), Verlamio[n] (St Albans), Duno[vernum] *sic.* (Canterbury) and Camuloduno[n?] (Colchester – table 2.3). This is a good reason for identifying them as pivotal and thus relating them both to their tribal territories and to individual social leaders. The precise rôles of the *oppida* are however difficult to evaluate in the absence of extensively excavated examples. Despite these problems some authorities have equated their growth with the emergence of settled proto-urban communities.

The equation of the largest sites with central places focal to society cannot be fully justified in the Iron Age (Haselgrove 1986a), and often relies on the assumption that as they dominated the settlement pattern they were occupied by the most powerful of the élite (Cunliffe 1984b, 559–62). There is little archaeological support for this hypothesis in the middle and later Iron Age, even from the extensively excavated sites like Danebury, where there is little discernible material differentiation between the hillfort and sites in its rural hinterland (Cunliffe 1984b, 559; Collis 1985; Haselgrove 1986b). The range and quality of finds provides equal evidence for élite residence at rural sites. There is, for instance, high-quality smithing debris from the farmstead at Gussage all Saints (Spratling 1979), and most of the high-status burials in both the north Thames (Stead 1967; 1976a) and in Hampshire (Millett 1987a) are associated with rural settlements rather than supposed central sites. Whilst there may be exceptions, like the Lexden tumulus at Camulodunum (Foster 1986), these do not represent the normal pattern. Indeed in the case of Lexden, the burial appears to relate to a settlement phase before the development of the *oppidum*.

We must thus be careful not to confuse the two variables of settlement centralization in *oppida* with élite residence at focal sites, for whilst social power remained essentially personal it was vested in the leader rather than at a particular central place. The two variables should be separated although they may be related to each other

Table 2.4. Oppida *and related sites (fig. 6)*

Site	Roman civitas	Cunliffe (1976) classification	Establishment date	Reference
Stanwick	Brigantes	Territorial *oppidum*	Claudian–Neronian	Haselgrove & Turnbull 1987
North Ferriby	Parisi	Port-of-Trade	Claudian–Neronian	Crowther 1987 Didsbury n.d.
Dragonby	Corieltauvi	Nucleated settlement	c. 100 BC	May 1984
Old Sleaford	Corieltauvi	Nucleated settlement	uncertain	May 1984
Ancaster	Corieltauvi	Nucleated settlement	early first century BC	May 1984
Leicester	Corieltauvi	Territorial *oppidum?* Place-name *Ratae* means 'ramparts'	Augustan	Clay & Mellor 1985 Rivet & Smith 1979, 443
Cambridge	Catuvellauni	Nucleated settlement	uncertain	Cunliffe 1978a
Colchester *Camulodonum*	Trinovantes	Territorial *oppidum*	site starts c. 20 BC; *oppidum* c. AD 10	Fitzpatrick 1986; Haselgrove 1987a
Baldock	Catuvellauni	Nucleated settlement	Main phase c. 20 BC	Stead & Rigby 1986
Braughing- Puckeridge	Catuvellauni	Nucleated settlement	Main phase c. 20 BC	Partridge 1981
Wheathampstead	Catuvellauni	Enclosed *oppidum*	Caesarian	Wheeler & Wheeler 1936
St Albans *Verulamion*	Catuvellauni	Nucleated settlement	Augustan on coinage	Frere 1983
Dyke Hills	Dobunni	Enclosed *oppidum*	uncertain	Hingley & Miles 1984
Grim's Ditch	Dobunni	Territorial *oppidum*	uncertain	Cunliffe 1978a
Salmonsbury	Dobunni	Enclosed *oppidum*	Claudian	RCHM 1976
Bagendon	Dobunni	Territorial *oppidum*	Augustan–Tiberian?	Trow in press
Silchester *Calleva*	Atrebates	Territorial *oppidum*	Main phase before c. 20 BC	Fulford 1985; 1986
Winchester	Belgae	Enclosed *oppidum*	First century BC	Biddle 1975
Hengistbury	Durotriges	Port-of-Trade	Starts c. 100 BC, declines after 50 BC	Cunliffe 1987
Chichester Dykes/ Fishbourne	Regni	Territorial *oppidum*	Late Augustan–Tiberian?	Haselgrove 1987a, 458
Loose	Cantiaci	Enclosed *oppidum*	uncertain	Cunliffe 1978a
Bigberry	Cantiaci	Enclosed *oppidum*	Second-century BC; abandoned mid-first century BC	Thompson, F. H. 1983
Canterbury *Dunovernum?*	Cantiaci	Nucleated settlement	Early Augustan	Arthur 1986

Note: several of the sites listed by Cunliffe (1976) have been omitted on the basis of more recent data, whilst two sites have similarly been added.

indirectly, via the permanence and significance of the tribal group in relation to its constituent clans. We may propose the following hypothetical sequence of development for the *oppida*. The increased permanence and importance of the tribal organization defined an increasing rôle for its leaders and an enhanced need for a tribal focus. That focus may have developed in one of two ways. At sites like Camulodunum there already seems to have been an élite settlement which formed the nucleus around which the centre grew. Evidence from Bagendon (Trow in press) and Silchester (Fulford 1987) suggests that this may have been the usual pattern. Elsewhere the sites might have begun as temporary or periodic meeting places, perhaps even in a normally unoccupied and neutral location. The rôle as a place where clans came together allowed the development of ritual functions, where the gods oversaw the activities. This coming together at a meeting place further encouraged the development of exchange activities; meanwhile clan and temporary tribal leaders may have main-

6 The distribution of sites known as *oppida* in LPRIA Britain. For details see table 2.4.

tained normal residence at their rural home bases. Whether or not permanently occupied, the focus of the tribe became identified with the central location, and functions like the production of coinage became established. The place thus symbolized the tribal identity, acting as a communal centre as much as the focus for any particular individual. Only with the stimulus towards more permanent tribal or even proto-state organization under a powerful élite or individual need the centre have combined the symbolic with the residence function to become the tribal town. This phase, identified with the apparent presence of the élite residential enclosures at Verulamium (Frere

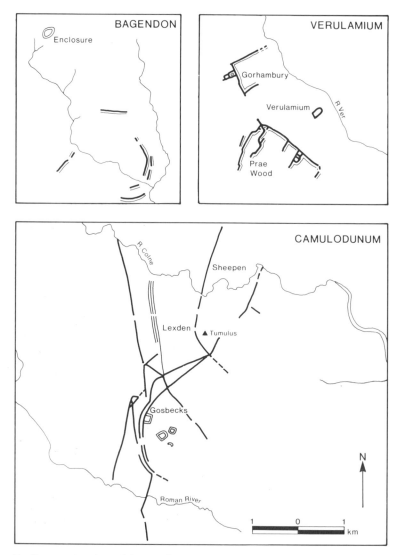

7a Comparative plans of the *oppida* at Bagendon, Verulamium and Camulodunum. For details see table 2.4.

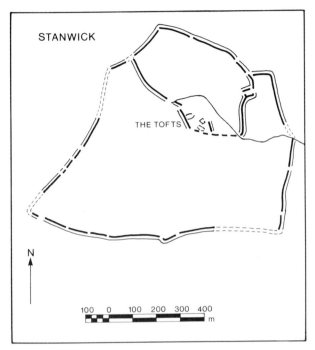

7b Comparative plan of the *oppidum* at Stanwick, North Yorks. For details see table 2.4. Note the settlement enclosures revealed by geophysical survey within The Tofts (after Haselgrove and Turnbull 1987).

8 Air photograph showing part of the LPRIA *oppidum* at Stanwick, North Yorks from the east (see also fig. 7b). The principal focus of settlement (The Tofts) lies to the left of the circular churchyard at the centre of the picture. (*Photograph by courtesy of Dept. of Archaeology, Durham University.*)

Table 2.5. *Tentative division of* oppida *according to variables of élite residence and tribal centralization*

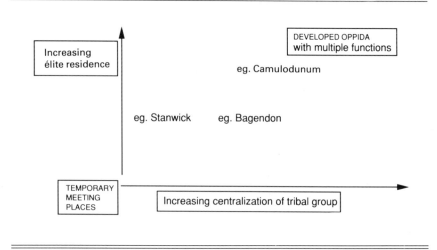

1983, fig. 2), Silchester (Fulford 1985, fig. 3) and Camulodunum (Collis 1984, fig. A23), need not have been achieved by all the *oppida*. With the changes in alliance and power evident in the LPRIA, shifts in importance of these sites which are now beginning to be observed thus become more explicable (Haselgrove 1987a, appendix 5).

This model of differentiation is useful in examining areas where the variability in the settlement pattern is considerable (table 2.4). We may use it to define the organization of focal settlements as positions on a continuum defined by the dual variables of élite residence pattern and centralized power (table 2.5). Thus in the south-west peninsula, where the pattern is dominated by enclosed homesteads without apparent regional foci, we may envisage a system of clan groups who rarely came together, at times of warfare for instance, or for purposes concerned with the enhancement of the group's social identity. These groups may have been without a leader in ordinary circumstances. At an intermediate level the Durotriges have a strongly defined territorial identity (Blackmore *et al.* 1979) and a multifocal settlement system based on hillforts, and appear as a strongly defined alliance of clan groups. Their main centre seems to have been the largest hillfort at Maiden Castle, which did not develop in a neutral place and was perhaps the residence place of the leader of the most powerful clan, whose rôle was that of war leader for the whole tribe. Fragmentation of power is indicated by the multiple hillforts which probably represent the centres of a set of powerful clan leaders. This organization contrasts with the strength of the group identity, but may relate to the absence of an inscribed coinage and the inferred absence of a single permanent and all-powerful tribal leader.

These variables are tentatively explored in table 2.5. The model summarizes only some of the possible range of social forms. It is perhaps influenced too strongly by areas with the best evidence, although it forms a reasonable framework within which to view the emergence of *oppida* in relationship to the developing social hierarchy, but the process highlights the interconnected changes which seem to characterize the period from *c.* 100 BC onwards. We now turn to examine these developments and attempt to present a framework within which they can be understood in relation to the history of the period.

The dynamics of social change

The century and a half before the Claudian invasion are marked by a series of changes in the settlement pattern which we have argued are accompanied by an increase in social differentiation, especially within the groups of the south and east. This is accompanied by shifts in the composition of the material culture assemblage, most notably with the introduction of coinage and the appearance of a wider variety and number of imports. Additionally, technological change is shown by the introduction of the potter's wheel and agricultural intensification. Finally, the imports show an increase in contact with Gaul and Rome. These trends begin during the later second century BC with the widespread importation of Gallo-Belgic gold coinage (Haselgrove 1987a) and Italian wine represented by Dressel 1A amphorae (Fitzpatrick 1985; Cunliffe 1987). After the middle of the first century BC the range increases with the presence of Central Gaulish Mica Dusted jars (Tyers 1981) and a range of Italian bronze and silver items. The scale of the flow increases around the end of the first century BC, when we see a wider range of metal and ceramic imports (including Arretine and Gallo-Belgic table wares), and an increased variety of commodities like olive oil and fish sauce transported in amphorae from around the western Mediterranean (Peacock 1984; Sealey 1985).

To understand the pattern, we need first to define the periods of change, and second to establish their European context. Dividing the LPRIA into periods is artificial, since the matrix of Iron Age society was evolving with the consequences already discussed. Thus the patterning defined at any particular point in time should be seen simply as a convenient snapshot taken for comparative purposes. The difficulties are increased by the imprecision of archaeological chronologies and the consequent danger of being too heavily influenced by the classical framework. For the purpose of our analysis it does, however, seem appropriate to divide the LPRIA into phases which relate to events on the continent.

The base line for this study must be the last part of the second century BC. Prior to this date most of Gaul lay outside the Roman sphere of influence, although from the end of the second Punic War in *c.* 206 BC Rome's annexation of Spain had led her to control the Mediterranean coast to the west of the Rhone (Ebel 1976). The allied territory of Massalia (Marseilles) then stretched eastward to the Alps (fig. 1). This phase of the Roman presence had only a visibly minor impact on the area and there is little sign of exploitation of the adjacent areas.

With the intensification of Roman influence in France after *c.* 128 BC, the date traditionally associated with the foundation of the Gallia Transalpina, there is increased influence on adjacent communities. Increased trade and external political influences began to stimulate the development of settlement centralization and state formation amongst some of the central Gaulish tribes. The process of their social evolution (as described by Nash 1978a) also had an indirect effect on the development of groups far beyond Roman territory to the north (Haselgrove 1987b). Changes in settlement patterns throughout Gaul have been seen as the result of two related processes. Economic exploitation of the whole of Gaul by those supplying the Roman province stimulated changes in production and distribution (Nash 1987). Such exploitation included the removal of slaves and this enhanced raiding and intertribal warfare. Rome took advantage of the results of this when forming alliances or buying the services of mercenaries, thereby introducing a monetary system to the areas. The stresses of this caused political pressure in the tribes affected, stimulating political and settlement centralization. Roman influence thus provides the context for both the trade, represented in these areas by Dressel 1A amphorae (Fitzpatrick 1985), and the emergence of base-metal coinages (Nash 1978b).

In southern Britain, the period sees an acceleration of change which is a pale reflection of that seen in related parts of Gaul. Contacts with the Roman world through Gaul, and particularly via Armorica, were concentrated in the south, with the site at Hengistbury Head being the major known port of entry (Cunliffe 1987). Here we see a concentration of Italian Dressel 1A amphorae, Armorican pottery and continental glass and metalwork. It is therefore held that the site was a Port-of-Trade (cf. Polanyi 1963), via which Roman entrepreneurs exploited the barbarian lands, albeit through native Gallic intermediaries (Cunliffe 1987, 340). This is seen as the catalyst for social and economic development of southern Britain analogous to that just described in Gaul.

We must be cautious in our interpretation of the significance of this material. First the imported goods have been shown to have only a comparatively local impact in their distributions (Cunliffe 1987, fig. III. 233–6). Secondly, changes in the settlement pattern within this area are very localized, even if one accepts that the end of occupation at Danebury was as a result of the dislocation caused by the emergence of this trade (Cunliffe 1984b, 554; cf. Haselgrove 1986b, 365).

Although the quantity of amphorae from Hengistbury is large in comparison with that from other British sites (a total of 69.6 kg; 1,019 sherds of Dressel 1), this represents only a minimum of 30 vessels (Williams 1987, 271), the equivalent of about 720 litres of wine over fifty years (Sealey 1985, table 2). This pales into insignificance beside the quantities regularly found throughout the western Mediterranean on even the smallest rural sites, let alone the 24,000 vessels from the Saône at Châlon (Tchernia 1983, 88–90), or the contents of Monte Testaccio in Rome. The conclusion may reasonably be drawn that Britain lay on the very edge of the distribution of this wine at a time of exceptional production, perhaps even glut. The ripple which affects it is of only the most minor significance in Rome's trade, especially when it is considered in relation to the scale of wealth involved in Roman expansion (chapter 1).

The absolute figures do not necessarily belittle the impact of the imports in Britain, because, however valueless they were to a Roman trader, the very scarcity of wine in LPRIA Britain probably made it highly prized and thus prestigious (Hodder 1982). Indeed it is clear from Cicero that there was a significant increment in the value of commodities like wine as they passed from Transalpine Gaul into native society

(Cicero, *Pro M. Fronteio*, 19–20). Nevertheless, their limited distribution in Britain suggests that the effects in the first half of the first century BC were more marginal and localized than some allow, and their significance to Roman wealth accumulation through trade has been exaggerated.

Increased inter-tribal warfare in Gaul was probably a consequence of the social and political changes which occurred during this period of rapid change. That unrest provided the context for Caesar's politically motivated intervention in the region in his conquering campaigns of 58–51 BC (*DBG* I). These led to the total subjugation of Gaul beyond the existing province and to his expeditions to Britain in 55–54 BC, which may have brought Britain formally under Roman control by the imposition of tribute (*DBG* V. 22; Stevens 1951). The campaigns and the subsequent upheaval probably had important consequences for Britain, but it seems impossible to distinguish adequately between these and those already in progress as a result of previous contacts via Gaul.

The period following Caesar's conquest of Gaul was dominated by civil war at Rome, so the newly conquered Gallic territories were left very much alone, with a resultant slow development of new institutions or archaeologically visible changes (Drinkwater 1983). We may therefore see the period from *c*. 50 to 20 BC as a lull before more intensive Romanization began in Gaul.

In Britain this period sees a movement in the axis of contact with Gaul as a consequence of changes there. A disruption occurs in the links between Hengistbury and Gaul, which is most likely to result from the Caesarian conquest destroying the networks which had tied Armorica with the Mediterranean. At approximately the same time we can detect an increase in contact between the areas north of the Thames and the continent. This is seen in the emergence of the rich cremation burials of the Welwyn tradition, which show Italian links (Stead 1967; 1976a). These burials should be viewed in the context of the wider introduction of the cremation rite, known as the Aylesford tradition, into the region. The widespread distribution of Dressel 1 wine amphorae in this area (Fitzpatrick 1985) similarly relates to the introduction of the La Tène III pottery tradition formerly associated with Belgic incursions (Birchall 1965). Fitzpatrick has also drawn attention to the occurrence of these amphorae on rural settlement sites in central southern England. Here they have attracted less attention, as they are more fragmentary than the grave finds from the Thames area (fig. 9). This evidence thus illustrates a shift in the focus and a broadening of the range of contacts, although the absolute number of amphorae remains very small (Fitzpatrick 1985, appendix).

The imprecise chronology makes it difficult to distinguish the changes which follow Caesar's conquest of Gaul from those occurring slightly earlier or later, as activity in Gaul intensified. In Gaul the Augustan period sees two major changes which have an effect on the LPRIA societies in Britain. First, the peace, following the civil wars, marks the beginning of the organization of Gaul into fully administered provinces. The road system, which reached the Channel, was established by Agrippa (perhaps as early as 39–37 BC) (Drinkwater 1983, 125) and formed the basis for opening up the conquered territory. Furthermore the foundation of the provinces of the Three Gauls and the formalization of their *civitas* organization (which may have its origins before the census of 27 BC) (Drinkwater 1983, 104) formed the basis for their economic development. Whether this was the result of intensive, externally stimulated trade and exploitation, or a by-product of the administrative centralization set in motion by Augustus (Millett in press (b)) is debatable, although there seems little doubt that the origins of the Romanization of Gaul lie in this period.

Secondly, from 16 BC Augustus looked towards military expansion into Germany and established the first permanent military presence along the Rhine. Between 12 BC and AD 9 Roman forces moved eastwards to reach the Elbe. In AD 9 military defeat, with the loss of three legions and nine auxiliary units (Wells 1972, 237–45), halted this and led to the decision to fall back to the Rhine, which became a firmly defended frontier (Schönberger 1969) with a substantial garrison including eight legions along it. The Augustan military build-up for the campaigns and the subsequent continued

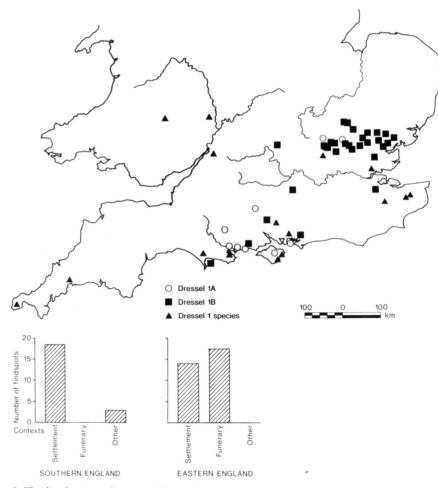

9 The distribution and context of Dressel 1 wine amphorae in LPRIA Britain (after Fitzpatrick 1985).

military presence along the Rhine brought additional wealth and resources to this hitherto remote area of Belgic Gaul.

It has been suggested that this activity in Germany stimulated the further developments in Britain, where the Augustan period witnessed a further enhancement of contact with the Roman world and a perceptible increase in the social and settlement hierarchy. This is the view taken by Cunliffe (1984a, 15), who relates the intensification of contacts between Britain and Gaul to the military situation. Against this, however, we may point to the relative scarcity of Italian amphorae on the Augustan frontier in Germany, which may result from the bulk of that trade being earlier. The alternative possibility is that too much stress has been laid on the importance of the military market during the campaigning period, and that the British material was arriving via the Gaulish networks throughout the period, because of the Romanization of the civil population (Fitzpatrick 1985, 312–13).

It is difficult to evaluate the importance which should be attributed to the military as opposed to the civil developments in Gaul as stimuli for changes in Britain. Although the military presence accounts for more than 48,000 men, who required supplies, the scale of the market represented by the native Gallic population is more difficult to assess but should not be underestimated. There is thus a tendency to credit the military with more importance than they perhaps deserve, although we know that the supply routes to the German frontier were important and well maintained (Middleton 1979). Romanization and growth in the Low Countries does not seem to have been rapid at this stage (Bloemers 1983; in press), and McGrail (1983) has pointed out that the Channel crossing from the Rhine mouth is more hazardous and less likely to have been used than that across the narrower Straits of Dover, connecting with the civil rather than the military networks. This points to a greater impact of Gallia Belgica on the LPRIA Romanization of southern Britain. The origins of the goods arriving here support this, as do the kinship links previously discussed. In addition to the wider range of amphorae, which contained various commodities in addition to wine, we see the arrival of a variety of ceramics which are largely Gallic. These included Arretine and its provincially manufactured copies from southern Gaul (Dannell 1981), a range of central Gaulish vessels (Tyers 1981; Rigby and Freestone 1986), together with Gallo-Belgic table wares (Rigby 1981). The last are particularly likely to have been transported direct from their place of production to Britain, rather than moving via the Rhine army. All these types began to have a wider distribution in the south-east than that achieved by the earlier Italian amphorae.

Whatever the cause of this detectable increase in the variety and intensity of contact between Britain and Gaul, its origins can probably be dated to c. 15–10 BC, when the coinages show a major phase of Romanization (Haselgrove 1987a, fig. 5.5 and p. 201). This may relate to the possible establishment of formal treaties between the British tribes and Augustus, since he was perhaps consolidating his territorial control by the renewal and formalization of such contacts.

This intensification of contact coincides approximately with the emergence of some of the *oppida* in the south and east (table 2.4). The chronology of these is far from clear as some of the sites developed on earlier settlements and the excavated evidence is of variable quality. It may be that arrival of imports is exaggerating the apparent change in the *oppida* at this period, although at present the evidence supports the idea of a major phase of change in the settlements around this time.

The continental contacts seem to have involved activity in a variety of forms of exchange. Diplomatic gift exchange is suggested by the goods from the Lexden tumulus at Camulodunum, which include a ceremonial Roman stool used by those in authority (Foster 1986). We should note the suggestion that some such exchanges result from British tribes being clients of groups in Gaul (Haselgrove 1987a, 196) rather than direct dependents on Rome.

The nature of possible commercial contacts is more difficult to assess as there does not seem to be sufficient material to justify its interpretation as the result of large-scale Roman trade. The presence of Roman or Gallic traders certainly cannot be ruled out as they appear in other areas just outside the Empire (Alföldi 1974). However, the evidence which is taken to support their presence at Braughing (Skeleton Green) (Partridge 1981, 351) is insufficient to be satisfactory. Latin graffiti are not enough to prove the case, since literacy is attested by the contemporary coinages, and the building types are not diagnostically intrusive. We should be certain that the criteria for the identification of such groups are made clear and the evidence more satisfactory before their identification can be accepted. In the absence of evidence for such traders we should be wary of putting too much stress on the importance of exploitative trade relationships, seen by some as the prime cause of changes at this period. Furthermore the general evidence of the Roman world renders implausible the development of such a highly directed economic system (see chapter 1). An explanation which interprets the bulk of exchange within the social context of native society is more satisfactory, since it is more consistent with both the scale and distribution of the evidence.

This should be compared with the model put forward by Luttwak (1976), who identified the development of areas beyond the Roman frontiers as critical to Roman

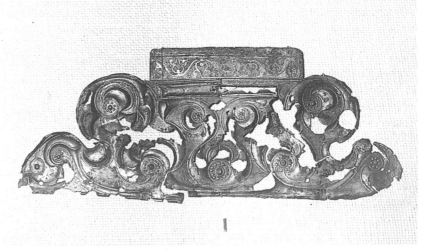

10 A panel of decorated bronze, probably a casket mount from Elmswell, East Yorks. The elaborate LPRIA decoration also shows some classical influence. (*Photograph by courtesy of Hull City Museums.*) The object is approximately 26 cm long.

strategic interests and thus the subject of diplomatic efforts and political intrigue. The diplomatic skills employed by Rome were designed to divide and dominate. By lending support to one tribal group against another they enhanced inter-tribal stresses and thus prevented the emergence of any overt external threat, while also providing a zone of allies beyond the frontier whose accelerated development made them into natural targets for eventual incorporation. We may doubt the presence of any conscious Roman strategy in the development of the 'zone of inner diplomatic control' (Luttwak 1976, 7–51; cf. Mann 1979) which encompassed Britain in the first half of the first century AD. However we cannot deny the analytical value of the concept, even though these emergent pro-Roman states in the south-east cannot have been true client states, but were raither loosely allied. The concept of an 'outer zone of Roman influence' (Luttwak 1976, 7–51) lacks the same value in explaining the British data, as it is very difficult to find any sound evidence for even indirect Roman impact outside the coin-using south and east before the arrival of the Roman army. Sites like Stanwick (Haselgrove and Turnbull 1987), North Ferriby (Crowther 1987) and Bagendon (Trow in press) lie on or beyond the edges of the zone of direct contact and appear at first sight to show the expected pattern of development. However, these are now known to have their floruit in the decades around the conquest of their respective areas, thus seemingly emerging as the 'zone of inner diplomatic control' expanded to incorporate them. The circumscribed distribution of Romanized Iron Age centres is paralleled by the distribution of Romanized material culture, which is limited to the same inner zone until the conquest. The general absence of such material from areas beyond the south and east makes it impossible to go beyond tentative conclusions about the organization of contacts based on the settlement patterns.

Warriors, art and power

This survey of change in the LPRIA has been essentially descriptive, with the patterns defined in relation to the evolution of overseas contacts. In this sense the patterns owe much to the analyses of Haselgrove (1982; 1984b; 1987a), Nash (1978a; 1978b; 1987) and Cunliffe (1984a). Such description does not explain how power was articulated within the societies as they underwent such drastic alteration. We cannot doubt that they were sophisticated organizations with developing social hierarchies and internal differentiation, based on tribute networks. Where there is room for considerable debate is over the question of how power within the societies was maintained and organized.

In his discussion of these problems, Cunliffe (1978a, 334–43) has stressed the martial elements in LPRIA society. Both the inter-tribal warfare and the ubiquity of defended settlements in this period suggest that physical force lay not far behind social power. This is likely to be true in both inter-personal and inter-group relationships. However, the sophistication of organization and the underlying stability of the tribal groups (compare figs. 2 and 3) suggest that any stage during which warfare had regularly been used to establish the social hierarchies had passed at least in the south and east. What remained was the military symbolism founded in this form of dominance which is apparent in both the art and ritual of society.

Table 2.6. *The occurrence of the categories of LPRIA metalwork (percentages in brackets)*

Category	A Southern Britain (Spratling 1972)	B Northern Britain (Macgregor 1976)	A + B	Ritual deposits from the Thames* (Fitzpatrick 1984)
Horse & cart trappings	232 (50)	136 (39)	368 (45)	8 (8)
Martial equipment	79 (17)	53 (15)	132 (16)	72 (76)
Mirrors	25 (5)	5 (1)	30 (4)	—
Drinking equipment	68 (15)	26 (7)	94 (11)	4 (4)
Others (including personal ornaments)	56 (12)	133 (38)	189 (23)	11 (12)
Totals	460	353	813	95

*To ensure comparability coins and fibulae have been excluded from Fitzpatrick's data.

One of the most characteristic sets of material from this period is the decorated metalwork which was produced for the élite (figs. 5, 10 and 11). An examination of this as the product of élite display reveals some marked patterns (table 2.6). We should see this high-quality material as inappropriate for everyday use and a product of the way in which the social élite demonstrated and symbolized their domination over the rest of their groups. The range of material is thus of considerable interest, for it indicates that the principal arenas for display were in the equestrian sphere, which was probably associated with warfare and perhaps hunting. Martial equipment itself was of less numerical importance, comprising the most spectacular objects, which seem to represent the highest social and craft investment. There are regional differences, also seen in the plausibly ritual pattern of deposition of material in the Thames (Fitzpatrick 1984), where weaponry is the most frequent category found. This pattern of disposal should be equated with the conspicuous consumption of valuables, and is thus also related to demonstrations of élite social domination. In this respect the prevalence of martial equipment in the pre-conquest deposits at the Hayling Island temple in Hampshire reflects the same pattern (Downey *et al.* 1980). A similar picture is seen in the disposal of the dead. In East Yorkshire the most prestigious burials are warriors associated with carts (Dent 1984; 1985; Stead 1987). A few warrior burials have also been noted elsewhere in Britain by Collis (1973), illustrating the same symbolism and supporting the hypothesis that warrior display was one of the ways in which the dominance of the social élite was maintained. The ritual and spectacular character of the material also supports the idea that display rather than active warfare was the underlying principle of social dominance (fig. 11).

We must clearly be aware of the biases in this material. These include the lack of good chronological control and the absence of material obviously related to other elements in the social hierarchy (such as the priests – Druids), whom we may assume to have had a major rôle in the social order (Tacitus, *Annals* 14. 29). Nevertheless, the

11 The Battersea Shield is one of the finest items of warrior equipment decorated in the characteristic style of the LPRIA. Such objects were probably used to display and define the status of the élite in a society in which warfare was institutionalized. (*Photograph by courtesy of the British Museum.*)

pattern is strong and thus has a value which would undoubtedly be enhanced by more detailed research. We should note the potential importance of the mirrors (fig. 5), especially those occurring in burials (which are not geographically widespread) (Cunliffe 1984a, fig. 8), and perhaps indicate women with the same major leadership rôle in the Durotriges and Dobunni as are well known from Boudicca and Cartimandua among the Iceni and Brigantes.

Of equal interest is the comparatively small contribution made by the drinking equipment which is often given a prominent position, particularly in discussions of the Welwyn phase of cremation burials where a strong link with the Roman wine trade is made (e.g. Cunliffe 1984a, 15). Thus Nash (1987, 101) has stated that 'the Celts everywhere were notoriously eager to import wine, whose consumption at princely feasts generated a continuous demand for more'. The quantity of surviving art objects, together with the small absolute numbers of wine amphorae, undermine the arguments which stress the importance of alcoholic consumption in Britain. This returns us to the rôle of external contacts in the developments we have seen.

The most cogent arguments have been put forward by Haselgrove (1982; 1984b), who sees the intensification of Roman trade contacts with the south-east providing foreign materials which allow power to be controlled in the British societies by the maintenance of a prestige goods system. Thus, the social leaders of the south and east held a monopoly of trade in raw materials passing to the Empire from their territories and those further inland. Through their trade contact with Rome they acquired scarce imported goods for themselves, which were held as a monopoly. They thus attained additional value as symbols of prestige. The monopoly of such goods enabled the élite to maintain and enhance their power over society through control of these prestige goods, their conspicuous consumption and their disposal to clients within or beyond the social system.

This model fits the concentrated distribution patterns of Roman material within Britain, but is a less satisfactory explanation where it relies on a strongly exploitative Roman trade network through which Roman goods were obtained and to which raw materials were exported. It has already been argued that the quantity of Roman goods arriving was really small, whilst a highly exploitative economic network is inappropriate in the Roman Empire (chapter 1). A more satisfactory context for the Roman material coming into circulation would be through the related functions of kinship, client status and diplomatic contact with Gallia Belgica. This would be consistent with the relatively low intensity of supply evident and the common cultural tradition connecting the zones (Champion 1976). These types of contact between the tribal élites of the areas allow the same prestige function for the goods arriving in Britain, whilst also permitting for some movement onwards of exports to Rome to join profit-making networks. These exchanges would, however, have acted through, rather than outside, the social order. Such an alternative model is impossible to substantiate, but does provide an explanation for all the available evidence. In particular it explains the rather circumscribed distribution of Roman goods and influence in the south-east, which fails to extend to the ends of Haselgrove's proposed procurement axes (1982, 83–4). This limitation in distribution is difficult to understand if one invokes a fundamentally economic motivation like that which Haselgrove has proposed. Thus the limited but significant contacts between Britain and Gaul are seen here as inwardly focused, strengthening the social networks through which they passed within the area that Luttwak (1976) calls the 'inner zone of diplomatic control'. Beyond it they had only a very limited effect in the areas which were to prove the least susceptible to Romanization after the conquest. Thus, on the eve of Claudius' conquest, these islands were not for the last time divided geographically into two nations.

3

THE INVASION STRATEGY

AND ITS CONSEQUENCES

The background to the Claudian invasion

The emerging tribes of LPRIA in southern and eastern Britain had a long history of contact with the Roman world and were heavily influenced by Roman attitudes and actions because Rome saw all her neighbours as within her sphere of influence. Whether or not the British tribes still paid tribute, some of them had been subject to Roman control following the invasion of Julius Caesar in 55 and 54 BC (*DBG* V. 22). This precedent meant, for the Roman emperors, that the island lay within their legitimate sphere of interest. This interest had already been shown by both Caligula (Suetonius, *Caligula* 44; 46) and Augustus (Dio 49. 28, 2; 53. 22, 5; 53. 25, 2), who had contemplated and prepared for invasion. Such direct intervention following a long period of indirect contact had precedents, for the general pattern of Rome's expansion saw her first taking an indirect interest, then a successively more active rôle before assuming absolute control. In the case of Britain this process was slow, since annexation had been delayed first by the civil wars, next by Augustus' interests in Germany and elsewhere, then by Tiberius' static frontier policy and finally by the troubles of Caligula. Notwithstanding this, the question should not be why Claudius invaded Britain, but why it had not happened earlier (Collingwood and Myres 1937, 76).

We should not, however, seek any grand strategy behind Rome's expansion, as the motivation for each successive conquest lay in the primarily personal nature of power at Rome and with the particular political circumstances of the times (chapter 1; Mann 1979). The élite social system of the Roman Empire relied on a power base which combined control of the military with the support of the rich landowning senatorial aristocracy, who held vestiges of their power from the traditional structure. At the time of Claudius' accession this power balance was still poised, so an emperor needed control of both the army and the senate. The power of both these vested interests had developed a reliance on the expansion of Rome's overseas territories (chapter 1). The system of political power had come to rely on militaristic exploits; thus to control power emperors had to show their own legitimacy through military prowess. The careers of most prominent Romans had included a period of service as a military tribune (*tribunus laticlavius*) in a legion at about the age of 24, and sometimes as a legionary legate or commanding officer (*legatus legionum*) after the age of about 32, provided they had achieved praetorian rank. This service had given them that legitimacy (Birley 1981b, 8–24).

Claudius had become emperor as a compromise; he had been put forward by the Praetorian Guard as a member of the Julio-Claudian house, unlikely to present a threat to their interests, but acceptable to the senatorial élite. His weak political position had given him power but meant that he was in great need of military prestige to reinforce his position, as he lacked any such experience. Fulfilment of this need was offered by the prospect of a military triumph, which was best achieved by the conquest of Britain. Although we are told that this campaign was of no great importance (Suetonius, *Claudius* 17.1), Britain remained an island which held a certain mystique, lying beyond the ocean and having the additional advantage of previously being the object of campaigns by Julius Caesar, founder of the dynasty. The prospect of a British expedition was further favoured as Caligula had begun the logistical preparations for it (Suetonius, *Caligula* 46. 1), and a ready excuse for intervention, which enabled the campaign to be presented as defensive, could be found in the inter-tribal disputes characteristic of LPRIA Britain that had most recently brought Verica to Rome seeking Claudius' help (Dio 60. 19, 1). We need not, however, see this as any more than a convenient pretext for invasion, as similar incidents previously had not led to Roman intervention (*Res Gestae* 6, 32).

Some would argue that there was a major economic motive for the Roman conquest but there seems little justification for this hypothesis. Whilst Tacitus suggests Britain's mineral wealth made her worth conquering (*Agricola* 12), Strabo's view (II. 5, 8) was that although the customs dues from commerce were worthwhile, the cost of military conquest would be higher than any gain from such conquest. This shows some consideration of the problem, but we may suggest that there was a lack of detailed information available to contemporaries. The army of conquest was itself a major expense, the magnitude of which was known (below, p. 58). Nevertheless, however much Rome may have known about Britain, she seems unlikely to have had either the motivation or the detailed knowledge of the territory reliably to estimate either the likely wealth to be obtained or any balance of cost against the benefit of invasion. Secondly, while there is no doubt that wealth accrued from the conquest and its immediate aftermath (both in booty and in the benefits of subsequent mineral exploitation and trade), there is nothing in the contemporary sources (even those of scurrilous intent) to suggest that there was any major economic motivation for Claudius' intervention in Britain. In this context the passage in Tacitus (*Agricola* 12) seems to have little significance beyond setting the scene for the author's narrative. Furthermore, there is little to suggest that the conquest was followed immediately by any substantial or systematic economic exploitation of the conquered territories, although such would surely be expected if any major economic motive lay beyond the project. Modest exploitation of silver deposits began around 49 (Frere 1987, 276–7; cf. Whittick 1982). However, the fact that some of the mines were in the hands of civilian contractors by 60 suggests that little bullion of significance was extracted. For these reasons we should conclude that the economic benefits were incidental to the political motives. It is best to view the Claudian conquest primarily as a function of the emperor's insecure political position within a system which had territorial expansion embedded in it and which required its leader to have military stature.

This hypothesis is supported by the way that Claudius himself used the campaigns, deciding to be present in person to lead his army in taking Camulodunum, the capital of the Catuvellauni, the principal state against which the first stage of the campaign had been launched and the major centre in Britain (Dio 60. 21, 1). This personal leadership entitled him to a legitimate Triumph (rather than the purely formal one which he had been offered on achieving the Purple (Suetonius, *Claudius* 17. 1; Dio 60. 22)). He took full advantage of this honour: a monumental arch, voted by the senate, was built in Rome to commemorate the triumphal procession (*CIL* VI. 920); he took the title *Britannicus* and struck coins commemorating the conquest. These practices are similar to those followed by other victorious emperors, although Suetonius' account suggests that they were taken to an unusual extreme. As such they are significant in legitimating Claudius within this lineage.

The invasion tactics

Much has been written about the course of the Claudian invasion and subsequent campaigns on the basis of the accounts in the surviving literary sources. Full discussion of this evidence (Dudley and Webster 1965; Salway 1981; Frere 1987) will not be repeated here although the substance of the sources is summarized in table 3.1. Instead, it is the intention to examine the archaeological evidence against the LPRIA background, and compare it with the literary sources to expand upon the basic approach taken by the Roman army and to explore how this is informative about the structure of native society. This consideration will be confined to the period from the invasion of 43 until the Agricolan campaigns, which have been the subject of recent re-evaluation (Hanson 1987), and after which it became clear that the whole island was not to fall directly under Rome's control. Because of the varying quality of the literary sources and the information about the spatial patterning of LPRIA societies, it is inevitable that more can be said of the campaigns in the midlands, south and east than elsewhere.

Before any consideration of tactics is developed, it is essential to begin by attempting to examine the aims of the army of invasion, for without some understanding of these there is no possibility of establishing the methods used to achieve them. There is little doubt that the initial aim was to control the whole of the island, as at this period there was an underlying optimism associated with Rome's expansion; although temporary halts, delays and setbacks might occur, in the long term is was clear to contemporaries that Rome could control the known world of which Britain was only an insignificant part (Mann 1974, 509–10). In her expansion Rome had accumulated a great wealth of experience both in military invasion and in diplomatic manoeuvring to obtain the maximum gain of territory and prestige with minimum cost. In Britain, she was faced not with a single undifferentiated land mass, but with a series of independent political units whose varying histories and social organizations led to different relationships both with each other and with Rome herself. We see only glimpses

Table 3.1. *Basic literary sources for the Roman invasion of Britain (AD 43–83)*

Year	Events	Source
43	Invasion army of three legions under Aulus Platius to aid Berikos (= Verica).	Dio 60.19
	Defeated Caratacus then Togodumnus, winning over Bodounni (= Dobunni).	
	Battle at river crossing (Medway?).	Dio 60.20
	Platius sent for Claudius; he arrived and captured Camulodonum, capital of Cunobelinus, and won over a number of tribes before returning to Rome.	Dio 60.21
	Senate voted Claudius a triumph and title Britannicus.	Dio 60.22
43–47	Vespasian legate of IInd Augusta.	
	Fought 30 battles, subjugated 2 warlike tribes, and captured more than 20 towns besides the Isle of Wight.	Suetonius, *Vespasian* 4
47–52	P. Ostorius Scapula arrived to find revolt, disarmed and reduced territory as far as Trent. Iceni revolted, but were defeated.	
	Army struck against Decangi (= Degeangli).	
	Campaign interrupted by Brigantian revolt, which subsided.	
	Silures not subdued, so territory garrisoned.	
	Veteran colony founded at Colchester before invasion of Silurian territory.	
	Resistance led by Caratacus, who was defeated and fled to Brigantia, where handed over by Cartimandua, and sent to Rome.	
	Silurian territory garrisoned, but resistance continued.	Tacitus, *Annals* 12.31–39
52–57	Ostorius Scaplua died; replaced by A. Didius. Gallus appointed to take over.	
	Silures revolted during the interregnum.	
	Venutius divorced from Cartimandua, fought her and revolted against Rome; Rome came to Cartimandua's aid.	Tacitus, *Annals* 12.40
57–58	Quintus Veranius succeeded Gallus as governor.	Tacitus, *Agricola* 14
58–61	G. Suetonius Paulinus appointed new governor.	Tacitus, *Agricola* 14
	He mounted campaign against Druids on Mona (= Anglesey) with success. Whilst doing this Iceni revolted under Boudicca.	Tacitus, *Annals* 14.29–39
61–63	Consolidation under new governor, P. Petronius Turpilianus.	Tacitus, *Agricola* 16
63–69	M. Trebellius Maximus, the new governor, remained militarily inactive as there was an army mutiny.	Tacitus, *Agricola* 16; *Histories* 1.60
69–71	Maximus' successor M. Vettius Bolanus continued same static policy.	Tacitus, *Agricola* 16
	Brigantian client kingdom fell apart, with Roman military aid to Cartimandua against Venutius.	Tacitus, *Histories* 3.45
71–74	Q. Petillius Cerialis appointed governor by Vespasian, and conquered Brigantes.	Tacitus, *Agricola* 17
74–77	S. Julius Frontinus succeeded him, and subdued Silures.	Tacitus, *Agricola* 17
77–83(78–84)	G. Julius Agricola conquered remainder of Britain.	Tacitus, *Agricola* 18–40

of these relationships through the historical sources, but this must not blind us to the fact that these were the realities which faced the Roman invader. It was these which determined the diplomatic and military tactics employed by her envoys and army commanders before, during and after the invasion.

The scant literary evidence for the invasion, together with our general information about the expansion of Rome elsewhere, suggests that she dealt with the British tribes by a combination of threat, promise and military action. If we begin from the premise that Rome dealt separately with each individual people, we should view the pattern of the invasion as one of picking off individual tribal units with one or more of these tactics. Thus the reward for those who remained pro-Roman was a form of continued, although circumscribed, independence. Thus some of the British peoples, which certainly included the Iceni (Tacitus, *Annals* 14, 30), and the group that became the Civitas Regnorum (*RIB* 91; Bogaers 1979), were treated as client kingdoms, retaining many of their rights and privileges – including initially the right to bear arms (Tacitus, *Annals* 12, 30) – in return for their help to Rome (Braund 1984).

Other groups, initially antagonistic to the invaders, were bribed or threatened by the superior force of the massive invasion army and sued for terms at an early stage, before they had to face battle (Dio 60. 19; 60. 22). These groups would have been treated less harshly than those who went to war, but presumably had to give hostages to ensure their remaining loyalty and eventually received a less favourable constitutional settlement than the groups who began as clients. Finally, those peoples who went to war and eventually lost received harsher treatment, although Rome was rarely punitive with defeated peoples; their co-operation would be required in the administration of the provinces (chapter 4).

Against this background we need to examine the process of the conquest, not as a problem of gaining and controlling ground, but as one of winning over the peoples of LPRIA Britain. In this respect most previous analyses of the invasion have been poor because they have sought to trace campaigns largely independently of what we know of the political geography of the LPRIA. The literary sources which talk of tribal leaders and peoples rather than territories, together with the general hypotheses just presented, show that any analysis which treats LPRIA Britain as a single undifferentiated unit misses the essential point.

In addition to the historical sources we have the evidence of the archaeology of the forts occupied by the invading army. To arrive at a sensible interpretation of military tactics we need to relate these to the LPRIA tribal groupings (chapter 2). As we have seen, there are difficulties in identifying the boundaries of these territories, but some tentative conclusions can be drawn from their relationships with the fort distribution. The military sites also present serious difficulties, since despite the fact that much energy has been spent on their examination they are inherently difficult to date. This is especially true in the crucial period late in Claudius' reign and early in that of Nero (to 64), when regular bronze coinage was not being supplied to Britain so the precise dating of sites is extremely difficult (Reece 1987, 16). A series of attempts has been made at establishing the course of the various invasion campaigns using the archaeology of the forts (e.g. Webster 1970; 1980), but the quality of the evidence has meant that these have been far from satisfactory, especially when the basic data are subjected to close critical scrutiny.

One specific chronological problem which emerges from attempts to compare the historical and archaeological evidence is a systematic difference between the dates provided by the forts and those suggested by the historical sources. This has previously been noted, and argued away for specific sites, such as Lincoln (M. J. Jones 1985). However, the pattern of the archaeological dates appearing later than those derived from the historical sources is so consistent that it deserves further consideration. For instance, the accepted reading of Suetonius (*Vespasian* 4; Salway 1981, 92–4) identifies the two tribes that Vespasian defeated when leading *Legio II Augusta* between 43 and 47 (Birley 1981b, 227) as the Durotriges and the Dumnonii. However, the archaeological evidence from the forts in the territory of the latter suggests that Roman occupation began *c.* 50 at the earliest (Fox and Ravenhill 1972, 86–7; Bidwell 1979, 3–9). This may be the result of a systematic error in the archaeological dating but is more likely the result of the difference between the invasion by a mobile army and the establishment of a settled garrison. The supplies for the former comprised mainly robust hardware (for instance *paterae*: metal cooking utensils) unlikely normally to be deposited as rubbish and thus reach the archaeological record. In contrast, settled garrisons used materials like pottery which provide useful dating evidence when rubbish is recovered in excavation. This pattern should certainly explain the total absence of archaeological evidence for the military presence in North Wales before the Flavian period (Davies 1980, maps 17.2–3), although Tacitus reports campaigns fought against the Degeangli as early as 48 (*Annals* 12. 31). This limitation should be carefully considered before attempts are made to use fort distributions to reconstruct military campaigns.

In addition to the problem of obtaining a precise chronology for the sites it is often less easy to establish the nature of the sites than has sometimes been assumed, for many lie beneath later settlements and are generally only available for small-scale exploration. In the past, distribution maps have been confused by their authors succumbing to the temptation to identify as forts many sites occupied in the conquest period, on which coins, samian ware or military equipment have been found. Since there is a series of mechanisms by which such objects may have reached the archaeological record, we need to be far more circumscribed in the conclusions that we draw from their discovery. In the compilation of the map used here (fig. 12), rather stricter criteria have been applied (below). Structural evidence alone has been accepted as indicating a certain military presence. The rash of sites found by aerial photography over the past few years, although certainly military, is largely undated and the problems already referred to mean that those sites occupied for only a short period will probably remain undated. Although some can be related to an overall understanding of the campaign strategy, this cannot be used to support any precise dating. In this study these sites, together with those where military equipment has been found without structural evidence, are included only as possible sites (fig. 12; table 3.4).

Much detailed evidence about the nature of the size and type of the military forces which occupied these sites can be drawn from their archaeology, although in many cases the details are not clear enough for a general pattern to emerge. The only information which is widely available concerns the size of the forts. It has often been generally accepted that the military equipment found on fort sites indicates the type of units that occupied them. Maxfield (1986) has now demonstrated that the problem is more difficult than has often been assumed, so the garrison types listed here should be treated with some caution. Six basic categories of size and type have been identified in the compilation of the map (fig. 12). The largest are the full legionary forts, with a size around 17–18 ha; next there are the much debated vexillation forts (8–12 ha), which perhaps held garrisons drawn from the legions sometimes mixed with auxiliary troops. The majority, the remaining forts, were generally around 2.5 ha and conventionally held auxiliary units, although some may have contained mixed garrisons rather than integral units. In addition to the regular forts there are first a few fortlets (around 0.4 ha) which can only have held parts of units. Secondly, a small but increasing number of Iron Age hillforts have been identified as bases used for whole or part units of auxiliaries and sometimes legionaries (Todd 1985a). Finally, we have one or two certain examples of coastal supply bases together with a number of other similar locations where such sites have tentatively been identified. Although garrisoned, these were for strategic supply rather than part of the tactics of conquest of the target territory.

It is absolutely clear from the recent work on sites of the invasion period that Rome's conquering strategy was pragmatic and did not rely on stock solutions to the problems. This is demonstrated by the variations in size and unit type seen in the forts of the period, which contrast with the more rigid approach seen in the regimented and uniform layout of the forts of the later first and second centuries (Collingwood and Richmond 1969, 29ff). These variations in site type and distribution relate to the pattern of treatment of the tribes suggested by the historical evidence.

We should begin by looking at the tribes which we know submitted to Rome without any significant struggle. The identification of these peoples presents a problem, for both the inscription on the Arch of Claudius at Rome (*CIL* VI. 920) dedicated in 52 and that on the arch at Cyzicus (*CIL* III. 57061) state that eleven kings formally submitted to Claudius. Some of these are generally identified as the leaders of the Iceni, the Brigantes, the Atrebates, the Cantiaci and at least part of the Dobunni (Dio. 60. 20). The remainder present a problem, and it may be suggested that a number of these kings were the leaders of tribal septs. The distribution of forts in the identified territories shows little military activity. This is probably because occupation was either of a short duration, or was never required in areas which became client states and were thus satisfactorily pro-Roman. The installations seen in some of the client states should be viewed as strategic, either for supply purposes (for instance at Chichester and Fishbourne, or Richborough and Canterbury), or for the control of important routes (such as Silchester, Staines and Winchester). Alternatively some of these forts may have been carefully placed at centres of political power, where there was either a requirement to oversee the allies (Millett 1984) or a desire to have a secure base at a friendly location. Whichever the case, the occupation of these forts was generally shortlived, rendering them difficult to date satisfactorily. The client state of the Dobunni does, however, have a significant military presence, although the coin and samian evidence currently suggests that this occupation can be dated to the period from *c.* 55 onwards (Millett 1983b, 204–8, *contra* Wacher and McWhirr 1982, 57–60), when the attention of the army was already focused on the Silures (Tacitus, *Annals* 12. 29–37). We should therefore explain the military presence in the territory of the Dobunni by the strategic necessities of campaign support and supply, not for their own subjugation. Indeed the confusing evidence of the garrisons at Cirencester

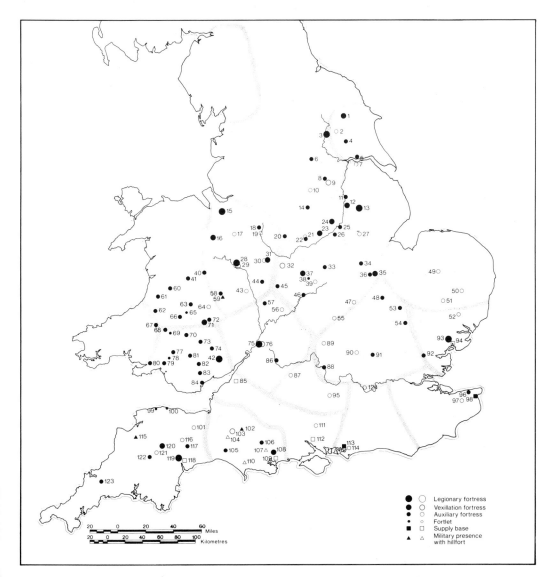

12 The Roman military sites of the period to AD 75 in Britain. For the identification of the sites see table 3.4 (p. 61), and for the later *civitas* boundaries see fig. 16. Open symbols represent possible sites, those in black are certain.

47

(Wacher and McWhirr 1982) is perhaps more consistent with their being bases for units moving forward and back from campaign rather than for an occupying garrison. The fort distributions in these territories thus tell us little about the native societies, except by perhaps indicating which centres were perceived by the Romans as political foci.

The tribes which initially presented a problem to the invaders were the Catuvellauni, the Trinovantes and the Durotriges. The two former represented the main centre of power in the pre-Roman period and were clearly the focus of Rome's initial campaign, although there are relatively few certainly identified military sites within them. It is probable that by the time of the invasion the Catuvellauni were part of the larger state ruled from Camulodunum (fig. 3), and subsequently split from it, becoming pro-Roman. Thus the primary focus of Claudius' own campaign was Camulodunum, which, once taken, was used as the location for both a fortress for *Legio XX* and a small auxiliary fort (Crummy 1977, figs. 13–14) (fig. 13), although Crummy has pointed out that both these sites are set to one side of the native centre, and seem thus to show some respect for it (Crummy unpublished). The focus of both campaign and fort locations on Colchester is significant as it demonstrates that Rome was taking control of a sophisticated and centralized state whose people and territory could be taken and held by wresting control at that single centre, thereby taking advantage of the pre-existing concentration of power (fig. 14).

The other forts within these tribal territories are difficult to assess given the possibility, in the absence of better dating evidence, that some relate to the period after the

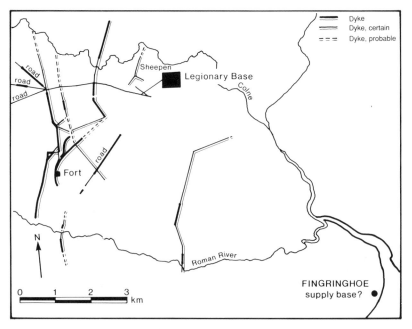

13 Outline plan of the *oppidum* at Camulodunum showing the location of Roman military sites of the invasion period.

Boudiccan revolt of 60/61. Some may focus on subsidiary political centres, such as, for instance, that at Verulamium, although this fort seems more shortlived than the five or six years suggested by Frere (1983, 5). This is perhaps because the Catuvellauni did not need to be watched over since they were by now pro-Roman, as their acquisition of municipal status for Verulamium before 60/61 suggests (Frere 1983, 26–8; cf. Bogaers 1967). The remainder of the forts were strategically placed to control the communication network, especially along the road towards Longthorpe, which was of importance during the campaigns against the Corieltauvi. This route clearly remained important, explaining the continuing occupation of sites along it well into the reign of Nero, despite the movement forward of *Legio XX* in 49 (Tacitus, *Annals* 12. 32), which implies that the area had been satisfactorily pacified.

This contrasts markedly with the Durotriges, whose territory can be characterized as a confederation, comprising a series of small centralized units. Each had its own centre, usually a hillfort, which presumably formed the focus for a sept of the tribe, whether or not it was permanently occupied at the time of the conquest. It was in this area that *Legio II Augusta* (under the future Emperor Vespasian) encountered a series of difficulties in the conquest, having to take twenty *oppida* (meaning hillforts), according to Suetonius (*Vespasian* 4). Here, the archaeological evidence shows a pattern which we see repeated later.

A vexillation fort at Lake Farm near Wimborne (fig. 12, no. 108) lies just inside the territory near the boundary with the Belgae to the east. This location makes tactical sense, as the base for the launch of the invasion by mobile forces. Such a boundary

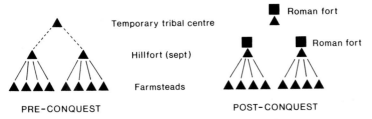

14 Alternative responses of the Roman army to centralized and decentralized native societies. The two models serve only to summarize two extremes; alternative native organizations probably also existed.

location, close to a coastal supply base, can be seen as a recurrent pattern in the conquest of the British tribes. At Lake Farm the fort, occupied by part of a legion, was situated so that the reserve dominated the area of the campaign, perhaps suggesting that the auxiliary units undertook most of the forward action, whilst the legionaries were held in reserve for specialist activities like the sieges of Hod Hill (Richmond 1968) and Maiden Castle (Wheeler 1943). There is a series of forts across the territory together with several hillforts garrisoned by Roman units (fig. 15; table 3.4). These almost certainly relate to the immediately post-conquest garrisoning of the area largely by auxiliary troops, but imply that military activity in the campaign was concentrated on the centres of the tribal septs. Suetonius' account, together with the archaeology of the sieges of several hillforts, demonstrates how such a loosely federated state, with multiple political nuclei, proved more difficult both to conquer and then control than a highly centralized state like that of the Catevellauni (fig. 14). Once conquered each sept had to be supervised by a separate military detachment, thus requiring a comparatively heavy garrison, which the archaeological evidence shows remained into the Neronian period. We can therefore see again something of the structure of the LPRIA tribe through its conquest by the Roman army.

The other tribe apparently tackled by Vespasian was the Dumnonii, although the archaeological evidence from their territory is as yet less clear. The campaign base is unknown, and indeed the forts within the conquered area are all rather later than the conquest date given by the literary sources (cf. above, p. 45). The fortress of *Legio II Augusta* established at Exeter in *c.* 55 dominates the territory (Bidwell 1979, 14). This, taken with the continuing occupation of other forts into the Vespasianic period, gives the impression again of a tribe difficult to conquer and subdue (table 3.4). The general indications are of a decentralized LPRIA settlement pattern (Todd 1987, 155–72), and with the exception of Hembury (Todd 1984; 1987) the known Roman forts seem not to relate to pre-existing centres. We may therefore be seeing, for the first time in Britain, Rome placing forts to oversee territorial gains because centres of LPRIA political power were absent (fig. 6). This explains the long duration of the military phase in the south-west. The difficulty in rapidly removing forces anticipates the problems experienced by Agricola and later governors in defeating wholly decentralized tribes whom they found it almost impossible to pacify. We do, however, need to be aware that this interpretation is based on the absence of archaeological evidence for centralization, for there is no doubt that sophisticated political structures could have existed without permanent settlement centres.

In the absence of literary sources giving details of the campaigns against the tribes further north, we rely on the archaeology of the military sites to arrive at an understanding of native attitudes to the conquering forces. Whilst acknowledging that this presents problems, we can suggest first that the Corieltauvi, initially anti-Roman, were taken by military action since there is a comparatively dense distribution of forts in their territory. Some of these relate to the subsequent conquest of the Brigantes early in the Flavian period. However, the location of the vexillation fortress at Longthorpe, on the boundary of the Corieltauvi with the Iceni and Catuvellauni (fig. 12, no. 35) is reminiscent of the location of Lake Farm in relation to the Durotriges and suggests that it was the campaign base for their conquest.

The forts within Corieltauvian territory are mostly post-Claudian on the archaeological evidence, and may indicate a prolonged garrisoning. Nevertheless, most are located as a network to control supply lines. These can be related to two campaigns. One route led to the vexillation forts as Osmanthorpe and Newton-on-Trent, surely bases for the assault on the Brigantes. The other road (Watling Street) led to the vexillation forts at Wall and Kinvaston, which presumably fulfilled a similar rôle in the attack on the Cornovii. The other forts exhibit a comprehensible pattern, for there is a military presence at the LPRIA centres of Leicester (Clay and Mellor 1985) and Ancaster (Todd 1975), although not beside that at Bourne. This supports the idea that forces were focused to oversee several centralized septs of the tribe.

The establishment of the base for *Legio IX Hispana* in *c.* 60 on a navigable section of the River Witham at Lincoln (M. J. Jones 1981, 86) seems part of a system established to oversee Brigantes from positions within Roman controlled ground. There is little evidence for a substantial pre-Roman presence at Lincoln. Indeed Lincoln lies on the edge of the core distribution of the Corieltauvian coinage (fig. 3), and may thus be positioned on the boundary between tribal septs. This location may have been strategic, although the simple convenience of its siting beside a navigable river should not be ignored.

We have already seen that there were vexillation forts possibly at Wall and certainly at Kinvaston, which can be interpreted as bases for the conquest of the Cornovii, who may thus have been hostile to Rome. There are sufficient auxiliary forts within their territory to have held a garrison, but most are positioned on the supply routes needed for the later campaigns to west and north. The other large forts can also be connected with these campaigns. The location of the full legionary base at Wroxeter in relation to the Ordovices can be compared with that of Lincoln, whilst the vexillation fort at Rhyn Park is near the boundary with the Degeangli and may be the campaign base for their conquest in 47 (Tacitus, *Annals* 12. 32). The territory of the Cornovii has provided little evidence for centralization in the LPRIA (Webster 1975), and consequently any interpretation of the fort distribution in relation to its political organization is presently impossible. As with the Dumnonii it is likely that the absence of discernible native foci led the army to locate its forts to oversee territorial zones rather than established political foci. Indeed, Hanson (1986) has suggested that many of the forts in this *civitas* were positioned to oversee the extraction of minerals.

The campaigns against the Silures were costly and took a considerable time, stretching from *c.* 49 to 74 (Tacitus, *Annals* 12. 32; *Agricola* 32. 17); this alone indicates the scale of the opposition that Rome faced. It has already been argued that the forts in the territory of the Dobunni were established as part of the strategy for their conquest. The basic pattern is familiar; the main legionary vexillation for the campaigns was first based at Kingsholm (Hurst 1985), then at Usk (Manning 1981), just beyond the border with the Dobunni. A similar fort at Clyro-on-Wye may represent another such base for this campaign, although it may equally be the base for that against the Ordovices. Beyond these, the forts which line the routes through the territory suggest a decentralized society which continually plagued the Romans with guerrilla warfare and which could only be held down by a large garrison placed to oversee blocks of territory rather than to control political centres (cf. Lawrence 1939). The placing of

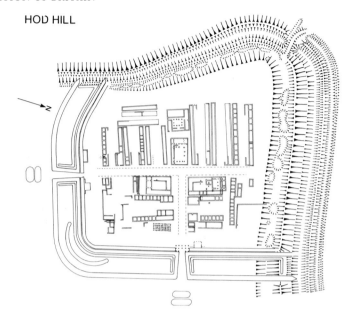

HOD HILL

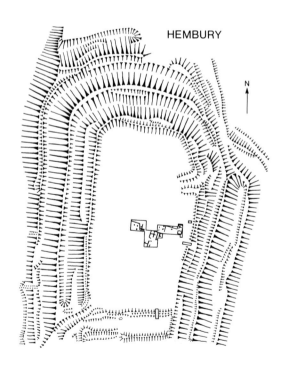

HEMBURY

15 Roman invasion-period military sites located
within hillforts. For details see table 3.4, p. 61.

52

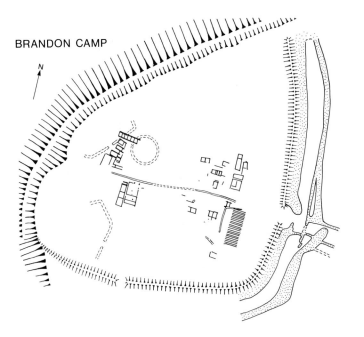

BRANDON CAMP

N

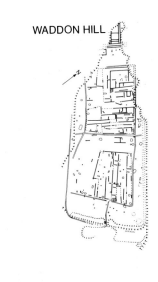

WADDON HILL

50   0   50   100
                    m

Legio II Augusta at Gloucester just after *c.* 65 (Hurst 1974; 1985, 122) shows that a strategic reserve was required to watch over this troublesome area even after the closure of the conquest base at Usk. The nature of the protracted and heavily contested campaign in South Wales forms the model for the later occupation of territories further north, typified by Agricola's campaign, and it is in these areas that some form of direct military government may have been needed, perhaps with centurions (*centuriones regionarii*) (cf. Bowman and Thomas 1983, 107–10) administering territory in the absence of a sufficient local élite on whom this task could be devolved (chapter 4).

In the north-east the Parisi seem to have been incorporated easily. The pre-Flavian trading site on their southern border at Redcliff, North Ferriby (Crowther 1981) perhaps suggests that they had previously been allied to Rome. It is not impossible that they were amongst the tribes who submitted to Claudius and became a client kingdom, although we lack any specific evidence to support this hypothesis. Although their territory lacks major foci in the LPRIA (Millet in press (c)), its incorporation seems to have been straightforward as there is no evidence for any campaign against them. The forts in their territory are located along the supply roads vital for the campaign against the Brigantes in the early Flavian period. To this period we can attribute the establishment of both the vexillation fort at Malton and the base of *Legio IX Hispana* at York (table 3.4). Both these conform to the now familiar pattern, being based on borders of the target territory. The remaining forts in the lands of the Parisi are all along the routes leading to these two bases from the sheltered harbour at Brough-on-Humber (fig. 12).

The distribution of the bases for the campaigns against the huge territory of the Brigantes indicates a remarkable concentration of forces around their borders, with full legionary bases on the flanks at York and Chester plus a series of vexillation fortresses around their southern and eastern limits (cf. Tacitus, *Agricola* 13). These legionary bases, like those previously founded, are well placed for supply from the sea, and clearly anticipate the two-pronged attack on the north mounted by Agricola (Frere 1987, 90). The conquest of Brigantia and the subsequent northern campaigns were against societies about whom we are comparatively ignorant (Hanson 1987). The settlement evidence shows that they were heterogeneous and that the pattern was generally not focused on major sites (Breeze 1982, 36–41), with exceptions like the Romanized *oppidum* at Stanwick (Haselgrove and Turnbull 1987) and some of the hillforts of southern Scotland, such as Eildon Hill and Traprain Law (Hanson 1987, 90–2). The Brigantes themselves appear to have comprised a confederation of tribal septs. Indeed one interpretation of their name as 'the hill-people' (Rivet and Smith 1979, 279) reinforces the idea that they lacked real social cohesion. This is reflected in their division into pro- and anti-Roman factions under Cartimandua and Venutius respectively in the face of Roman expansion (Tacitus, *Annals* 12. 36; 12. 40). These divisions, together with their size, mean that they presented a problem for military conquest when it came under Petillius Cerialis in 71–74 (Tacitus, *Agricola* 17). Although this impression may be altered by future work, it is supported by the presence of the garrison which is concentrated on strategic routes rather than native centres. These routes formed the launch pad for Agricola's campaigns to the north, which culminated in what Tacitus saw as total conquest, subsequently thrown away (*Histories* 1. 2). An examination of the installations of these campaigns (Hanson 1987, fig. 18) makes it clear that they too were strategically located to oversee territory rather than to control polities. This is presumably the result of the general lack of existing centralization in these territories (below, p. 76).

In summary we can see that the method of warfare and subsequent territorial control relied upon an understanding of the political geography of the area. Its success was closely related to the degree of centralized political development, with the more developed societies being taken more quickly and requiring a smaller and more temporary post-conquest garrison than those with a less developed settlement hierarchy. In many of the former areas any military presence after the conquest was to secure supply lines for campaigns in areas hitherto unconquered. In this context, we should reconsider the hypothesis that following the Boudiccan revolt there was a reoccupation of areas in the south and east which had been affected by the fighting (Frere 1987, 73–4). Whilst this is plausible, we should note that few sites can certainly be dated to this postulated phase; almost all that have been so interpreted are better seen within the supply network already in existence. An absence of forts specifically relating to this period should not occasion too much surprise as we have already seen that temporarily occupied campaign bases are exceedingly difficult to find and date. Thus the small number of forts known in the territory of the Iceni should not be taken as an indication of the real pattern of occupation at the end of the Boudiccan revolt.

This pattern also undermines the concept of a Claudian frontier along the Fosse Way (Collingwood 1924; Webster 1970). First, the concept itself is anachronistic, as there is no evidence for any idea of fixed frontiers this early in the first century – the expectation was for continued expansion by a mobile and victorious army (Mann 1974, 510–11; Breeze and Dobson 1987, 11–12). Secondly, the Fosse Way cuts across a series of tribal territories and all the evidence suggests that these were tackled as separate entities by the Roman army; the fact that those in the south and east were the first conquered cannot be taken to suggest that their north-westward-facing boundaries formed any perceived limit to Claudian expansion. Finally, a critical analysis of the evidence of the forts along the line of the supply road known as the Fosse Way supports neither the idea of any regular spacing of forts nor any contemporaneity of foundation for those that lie on its line. Most of those known are Neronian, and the evidence seems most consistent with a pattern of piecemeal development between *c.* 55 and 65, when the legionary forts at Exeter and Lincoln were both in occupation. This evidence provides little basis for seeing the Fosse Way as any more important than the other garrisoned supply routes already discussed.

In the early years of the conquest the tactics of the military seem to have been flexible, perhaps with mixed units and the occupation of native centres reflecting this. Although there can be no doubt that the momentum of conquest relied in the ultimate on the political will of the emperor, the tactics on the ground clearly relied on an assessment and an appreciation of not only the terrain but also the organization of the enemy. The selection of a suitable governor was thus of the utmost importance (Birley 1953, 1–9). Their knowledge of the native tribes was also to prove crucial in the development of the conquered territory as a Roman province (chapter 4).

Supplying the invaders

The size of the invasion army can be reasonably estimated at *c*. 40,000 men (Frere 1987, 48). This army required a wide range of supplies, initially food, later other necessities including timber, leather and other hardware (Breeze 1984). It is generally contended that fulfilment of this demand was a significant determinant of change in the conquered areas. Although the supply bases at Richborough (Cunliffe 1968) and Fishbourne (Cunliffe 1971) show that facilities were built for stockpiling imported grain to supply the invaders, the logistics of supplying this number of men, with grain alone amounting to *c*. 8–20,000 metric tonnes a year (table 3.2), probably prevented any total reliance on either imported material or even the large-scale overland movement of bulky foodstuffs. This is, indeed, the reason for the location of all but one of the legionary bases near an estuary where maritime transport would guarantee more economical and rapid supply. Nonetheless, the logic of necessity leads us to believe that army supplies were as far as possible drawn from the local area.

The hypothesis of local supply in the immediately post-conquest period is illustrated by the pottery evidence. Where this had been produced in the LPRIA, local supplies were generally exploited by the army. Specialist wares, like samian ware, *mortaria*, and other fine wares were imported, whilst some of these together with flagons were also manufactured by potters beside forts like Longthorpe (Dannell and Wild 1987) and Colchester (Hull 1963). However, in the previously aceramic areas like the territory of the Silures, military workshops produced the full range of goods for army needs; the rarity of this pattern suggests that the army preferred to use local supplies (Greene 1973; Hurst 1985, 123).

The complexities of supply were even greater if we are correct in assuming that the conquerors tried to ensure that unnecessary discontent was not created by making excessive demands on the native population. The self-interest in this is evident and would have combined with the desire not to antagonize native populations, whether allied or defeated, with an imperative not to over-exploit the supply base and thus threaten future years' harvests by lack of seed corn. These considerations suggest that native supplies would have been carefully exploited and supplemented by imports where necessary. We should not however overlook the corruption which probably undermined this policy. Thus Decianus Catus (Tacitus, *Annals* 14. 32) is said to have abused his position, fermenting some of the discontent which lay behind the Boudiccan revolt.

The principal military requirement was for food and, although the available evidence shows a mixed diet, the bulk of demand was for grain (Breeze 1984). Estimates suggest that this requirement was probably in the range 8–20,000 metric tonnes per year (table 3.2). This is a substantial quantity of grain, but working from the premise that it was acquired by requisition (Mann 1985a, 272), we can establish the approximate area of land needed to produce it, assuming the crop yield was at the lower end of the range established at Butser (Reynolds 1979). This shows that the requirement was the product of a 10 per cent yield requisitioned from 200,000 ha at maximum – a square of arable land *c*. 45 by 45 km (Millett 1984, 70–2, adjusted to the first-century army size). This calculation takes little account of the complexities of

Table 3.2. *Burden of the Roman army of conquest*

The Roman army used to conquer Britain comprised approximately 40,000 men. *If* these men were fed on the produce of the conquered territory, then we may make the following calculations:

Garnsey (1983, 118) gives the level of the corn dole at Rome as 30 *modi* per annum = 200 kg of grain. This is a minimum figure for consumption as it represents subsistence. Thus the minimum army requirement would be 200 × 40,000 = 8,000,000 kg = 8,000 tonnes.

Davies (1971, 123) suggests that a Roman soldier required 3 lb (1.36 kg) of corn per day, the annual equivalent of 496.4 kg. Thus, using his figures we can estimate the military requirement as 496.4 × 40,000 = 19,856,000 kg = 19,856 tonnes.

This suggests a range of need from 8,000 to 20,000 tonnes.

Reynolds (1979, 61) has shown that yields of emmer wheat may have averaged around 2 tonnes per ha. If we take the pessimistic view, and divide this yield in half, the corn needed by the army could have been produced on between 8,000 and 20,000 hectares. Taking taxation at 10 per cent, this represents the tax yield of 80,000–200,000 ha, or 800–2,000 km^2.

This is the equivalent of the tax product of a square of ground 28 × 28 km to 45 × 45 km.

the agricultural system, but demonstrates that this burden could be borne by the agrarian societies of the LPRIA without excessive stress being imposed (above, p. 10). This is reinforced if the army formed less than 2 per cent of the total population as my estimates suggest (below, and table 8.5). The suggestion that the burden of the conquering army was heavy is thus untenable. However, in the early stages after the conquest the problem was the organization of supply, which could most conveniently have been arranged through the social and political system of the conquered peoples where this was sufficiently evolved. Thus military requisition became a burden similar to that of any previous tribute (chapter 4). The concentration of the burden during the short period of military occupation may have been inconvenient but as the situation became settled after strategic forts had been established this burden was limited as it was spread thinly over wide areas.

That the logistics of supply were well organized is demonstrated by the bone assemblage from the legionary fortress at Exeter. Animals were driven there on the hoof and slaughtered beside the defences (Maltby 1981). Detailed evidence about the food supply and processing at other military sites is not yet available, but it seems a reasonable assumption that the demands of occupation remained modest; to quote Tiberius on provincial taxation, 'a good shepherd shears his sheep, he does not skin them' (Suetonius, *Tiberius* 32).

The indirect impact of the army

Although we have argued that the direct impact of the army on the native economy was not substantial, their presence had a number of indirect influences on the population and its organization. In the long term these had a major influence on the development of the province. Their rôle in the incorporation of the conquered peoples into the administrative framework of the Empire will be dealt with in chapter 4; only indirect structural influences will be considered here.

First we should consider their impact on wealth distribution and thus power within

Table 3.3. *The cost of the Roman army of conquest*

---

(1) The army comprised approximately 20,000 legionaries and 20,000 auxiliaries. Watson (1969, 89–102) gives legionary pay as *c*. 225 *denarii* per annum and basic auxiliary pay may be estimated as *c*. 100 *denarii* per annum.*

Reece (1987, 39) gives the mid-first-century *denarius* as the *equivalent* of 0.2908 g of gold.

Combining this data we can estimate the cost of the army as:
$$20,000 \times 225 \times \frac{0.2908}{1,000} \text{ g of gold} = 1,308.6 \text{ kg of gold}$$

plus
$$20,000 \times 100 \times \frac{0.2908}{1,000} \text{ kg of gold} = 581.6 \text{ kg of gold}$$

= 1,890.2 kg of gold for pay alone

(2) This compares with the much more approximate figures based on later estimates of the total cost of the army:

Dio's figures are interpreted as giving the total cost of the army at 210 million *denarii* after Caracalla's pay increase (Birley 1981a).

Working back through the pay increases (Watson 1969) to the mid-first century:
Caracalla = 210 million
Severus = 140 million
Domitian = 105 million
Pre-Domitianic = 78.75 million
– although we must recognize that this does not account for changes in the size of the army or the proportion of cost taken by pay.

Given that the army of conquest represents approximately 10 per cent of the total army, their cost would be
$$78.75 \text{ million} \times \frac{10}{100} = 7,875,000 \text{ denarii}.$$

This represents $7,875,000 \times \frac{0.2908}{1,000}$ kg of gold

= 2,290.05 kg of gold

Given the uncertainties in the second calculation (which is for the total cost of the army) the two estimates seem reasonably consistent.

---

*Watson (1969, 100–1) shows that there were various rates for auxiliary pay; that of 100 *denarii* used here is an arbitrary figure scaled down from the Domitianic pay scales, and in the middle of the range of basic pay. It is almost certainly an underestimate of the average.

Britain. It will be argued that although the administrative system essentially reinforced the power of the native élite, the 40,000 men in the army brought a very substantial inflow of coinage, amounting to a total of approximately 6.5 million *denarii* per year, the equivalent of 1,890 kg of gold (table 3.3). This money, together with that paid for requisitioned food, was a major input of wealth which acted as a honey pot for camp followers and traders. According to Hopkins' model (1980), the trade so stimulated accounted for the substantial quantities of Roman goods that arrived in Britain soon after the conquest (below). These goods, together with the soldiers' pay, may have had a destabilizing effect on native society, in that they will have devalued a number of commodities (such as wine) which had hitherto been scarce and had fulfilled a rôle as a prestige commodity maintaining individuals' power within their tribes. This dislocation, combined with the disarming of the native élite in 47 (Tacitus, *Annals* 12.

30), was perhaps a major cause of the shift in the methods of expressing social position after the conquest (chapter 4).

By analogy with some of her other conquests, there was initially a substantial out-flow of captured wealth to Rome. We have no way of knowing the magnitude of this, but the volume of bullion circulating in LPRIA coinages (Haselgrove 1987a, especially table 3.1) shows that a large outflow can be accounted for by this source alone. Except in the case of defeated leaders and tribes, the direct effect of this seems unlikely to be significant as Rome does not seem to have systematically stripped the conquered peoples of their wealth. Nonetheless, the indirect impact of the army with its own inde-pendent wealth would have been substantial. This would have undermined the social order and also released people from social control in the native power structure as they became dependent on the wealth of the invading army. This effect was greatest in areas where native opposition led to confrontation and hence a larger-scale and longer-term military presence. In areas which transferred peacefully to Roman rule, we shall see that the result was a reinforcement rather than a dislocation of the power structure (chapter 4).

The presence of the army was also felt in the confiscation of lands for settlement. This is particularly obvious at Colchester where the *colonia* was established in 49. The large new population planted on the former native capital must have had a destabiliz-ing effect on both native power and the balance of wealth, while also depriving natives of their land. The impact of this may have been substantial, although only obvious at those forts like that of Camulodunum which were placed on native sites. We have little evidence for the *territoria* which should have existed around each fort.

Outside the realm of wealth and resources, we can identify three main influences on LPRIA society. First, the army had a rôle in the administration of the conquered areas, although it is argued here that this was limited, except in the hitherto decentralized societies where centurions administered the captured territories. Whenever power was transferred from the indigenous structure this had a destabilizing effect on the social order (chapter 4). Secondly, the military presence provided a new means of social advancement for some young males recruited into the army. *Ad hoc* recruitment into units serving in Britain was already happening by the 80s (Tacitus, *Agricola* 29) and continued, although the numbers involved are impossible to evaluate (Dobson and Mann 1973, 198–205). More easy to quantify are the fourteen auxiliary units raised in Britain down to the reign of Trajan, totalling *c.* 9,500 men for their initial manning. Recruitment came from the allied or friendly tribes, soon after their con-quest in the pre-Flavian or early Flavian periods (Holder 1980, 110 and 217). Although only a small number – far less than 1 per cent of the total population (table 8.5) – recruits may represent a significant proportion of particular societies. They will not have been drawn evenly from the conquered states and will presumably have been from the warrior élite, so the effect on individual tribes may have been disproportion-ate. Unfortunately, British units were presumably raised after 69 and so not taken from individually named tribes, but instead bear the name of the province. Amongst the origins of specific known recruits we have *civitates* listed for only three: two from the Belgae and one from the Dobunni, whilst another comes from the city of Ratae

[Corieltaunorum] (Holder 1980, 129). These isolated incidences offer little help in assessing the impact of manpower loss and social change.

Nevertheless, the significance of recruitment should not be underestimated as it enabled some to bypass the native hierarchy to achieve wealth, and a status not otherwise available to them, through the grant of citizenship which they received on completion of their twenty-five years service (Watson 1969, 136–7). In addition, it may have brought a Romanized group into the population, in the form of those who returned after military service. This is, however, comparatively unimportant in the case of the units drawn from Britain which would have served abroad and are unlikely to have returned to their homes. Those who joined units stationed here may have returned home afterwards making an important impact on the social structure and speeding up the incorporation of the province. This pattern of service with the Roman army is also important for the interpretation of the items of military equipment from many native sites like those in the territory of the Dobunni at Lechlade (Miles and Palmer 1982, 11), The Ditches (S. T. James pers. comm.) and Kingscote (Wilson 1969, 227). These may have arrived with returning veterans or through the circulation of 'army surplus' and not through the presence of any garrison (cf. Webster 1970).

Finally, and of equal social importance, were the 40,000 or so foreign soldiers based in Britain, many of whom probably became involved with native women. Although they could only be unofficially married while serving (Watson 1969), they will still have had a major social impact. The removal of any large number of younger women would have had a significant impact on the sex ratio in society with a resultant destabilizing effect. Furthermore, the women when Romanized may have been a very significant force in the acculturation of the remainder of the native population over whom they had a fundamental influence. These changes in the British tribes, brought about by the presence of the army, should be seen as integral in the longer-term development which the conquest stimulated and to which we now turn.

Table 3.4. *Invasion period forts to c. AD 75 (fig. 12)*

No.	Site name	*Civitas*	Fort type	Reference
1	Malton	Parisi	Vexillation	M. J. Jones 1975, 164–5
2	Stamford Bridge	Parisi	Possible auxiliary	Breeze & Dobson 1985
3	York	Parisi/Brigantes	Legionary	Breeze & Dobson 1985
4	Hayton	Parisi	Auxiliary	Breeze & Dobson 1985
5	Brough-on-Humber	Parisi	Auxiliary	Breeze & Dobson 1985
6	Castleford	Brigantes	Auxiliary	*Current Archaeol.* 109
7	Winteringham	Corieltauvi	Possible auxiliary	Stead 1976b
8	Doncaster	Corieltauvi/Brigantes	Auxiliary	Breeze & Dobson 1985
9	Rossington Bridge	Corieltauvi/Brigantes	Possible vexillation	M. J. Jones 1975, 176
10	Templeborough	Brigantes	Possible auxiliary	M. J. Jones 1975, 178
11	Littleborough	Corieltauvi	Auxiliary	M. J. Jones 1975, 161
12	Newton-on-Trent	Corieltauvi/Brigantes	Vexillation	M. J. Jones 1975, 170
13	Lincoln	Corieltauvi	Legionary	M. J. Jones 1985
14	Chesterfield	Corieltauvi/Brigantes	Auxiliary	*Britannia* 9, 387
15	Chester	Cornovii/Brigantes	Legionary	M. J. Jones 1975, 142
16	Rhyn Park	Cornovii/Degeangli?/Ordovices?	Vexillation	*Britannia* 9, 436–7
17	Whitchurch	Cornovii	Possible auxiliary	Webster 1970, 190
18	Chesterton	Cornovii/Brigantes	Auxiliary	M. J. Jones 1975, 143
19	Trent Vale	Cornovii/Brigantes	Possible auxiliary	M. J. Jones 1975, 180
20	Rocester	Cornovii/Corieltauvi/Brigantes	Auxiliary	M. J. Jones 1975, 175–6
21	Strutts Park	Corieltauvi/Brigantes	Possible auxiliary	M. J. Jones 1975, 178
22	Littlechester	Corieltauvi/Brigantes	Auxiliary	M. J. Jones 1975, 161
23	Broxtowe	Corieltauvi/Brigantes	Vexillation	M. J. Jones 1975, 133
24	Osmanthorpe	Corieltauvi/Brigantes	Vexillation	*Britannia* 11, 330; 15, 290
25	Thorpe by Newark	Corieltauvi	Auxiliary	Wacher 1966, 28, fig. 1
26	Margidunum	Corieltauvi	Auxiliary	M. J. Jones 1975, 166
27	Ancaster	Corieltauvi	Possible auxiliary	Webster 1970, 184
28	Wroxeter	Cornovii	Legionary	Webster 1987
29	Leighton	Cornovii	Possible vexillation	Frere 1987, 56
30	Stretton Mill	Cornovii	Possible auxiliary	M. J. Jones 1975, 177–8
31	Kinvaston	Corieltauvi/Cornovii	Vexillation	*Britannia* 5, 427
32	Wall	Corieltauvi/Cornovii	Possible vexillation	M. J. Jones 1975, 181–2
33	Leicester	Corieltauvi	Auxiliary	Clay & Mellor 1985
34	Great Casterton	Corieltauvi	Auxiliary	Todd 1968
35	Longthorpe	Corieltauvi/Iceni/Catuvellauni	Vexillation	Frere & St Joseph 1974
36	Water Newton	Corieltauvi/Iceni/Catuvellauni	Auxiliary	Wild 1974, 142–3
37	Mancetter	Corieltauvi	Vexillation	Webster 1970, 194–5
38	Wigston Parva	Corieltauvi	Fortlet	M. J. Jones 1975, 184
39	High Cross	Corieltauvi	Possible auxiliary	Webster 1970, 184

Table 3.4 (*cont.*)

No.	Site name	*Civitas*	Fort type	Reference
40	Forden Gaer	Cornovii/Ordovices	Auxiliary	Davies 1980
41	Caersws	Ordovices	Auxiliary	Davies 1980
42	Usk	Silures	Legionary	Manning 1981
43	Walltown	Cornovii	Possible auxiliary	Jones 1975, 182
44	Greensforge	Corieltauvi/Cornovii	Auxiliary	Webster 1970, 190–1
45	Metchley	Corieltauvi/Dobunni/ Cornovii	Auxiliary	*Britannia* 2, 263
46	Lunt	Corieltauvi/?Dobunni/ ?Catuvellauni	Auxiliary	Hobley 1969
47	Irchester	Corieltauvi/ Catuvellauni	Possible auxiliary	M. J. Jones 1975, 157
48	Godmanchester	Iceni/Catuvellauni/ ?Trinovantes	Auxiliary	*Britannia* 13, 363
49	Saham Toney	Iceni	Possible auxiliary	*Britannia* 17, 1–58
50	Scole	Iceni	Possible auxiliary	Webster 1970, 193
51	Ixworth	Iceni/Trinovantes	Possible auxiliary	*J. Roman Stud.* 43, 82; *Britannia* 61, 294–5
52	Coddenham	Iceni/Trinovantes	Possible auxiliary	Webster 1970, 193
53	Cambridge	Iceni/Catuvellauni/ Trinovantes	Auxiliary	*Britannia* 15, 296
54	Great Chesterford	Trinovantes/ Catuvellauni	Auxiliary	M. J. Jones 1975, 153
55	Towcester	Catuvellauni/ Corieltauvi	Possible auxiliary	*Northants. Archaeol.* 15, 35–118
56	Alcester	Dobunni/Corieltauvi	Possible auxiliary	Webster 1970, 183; *Britannia* 13, 361
57	Droitwich	Dubonni/Cornovii	Auxiliary	M. J. Jones 1975, 148
58	Leintwardine	Cornovii/Ordovices	Auxiliary	Davies 1980
59	Brandon Camp	Cornovii/Ordovices?	Within hillfort	*Britannia* 18, 1–48
60	Caer Gaer	Ordovices	Auxiliary	Davies 1980
61	Trawscoed	Ordovices	Auxiliary	Davies 1980
62	Llanio	Ordovices/Demetae	Auxiliary	Davies 1980
63	Castell Collen	Ordovices	Auxiliary	Davies 1980
64	Walton	Ordovices	Possible auxiliary	Davies 1980
65	Pen-min-caer	Ordovices/Silures	Fortlet	Davies 1980
66	Beulah	Ordovices/Silures	Auxiliary	Davies 1980
67	Pumsaint	Silures/Ordovices/ Demetae	Auxiliary	Davies 1980
68	Llandovery	Silures/Ordovices/ Demetae	Auxiliary	Davies 1980
69	Y Pigwn	Silures/Ordovices	Fortlet	Davies 1980
70	Brecon Gaer	Silures	Auxiliary	Davies 1980
71	Clyro-on-Wye	Silures/?Ordovices	Vexillation	Davies 1980
72	Clifford	Silures/?Ordovices	Auxiliary	Davies 1980

Table 3.4 (*cont.*)

No.	Site name	*Civitas*	Fort type	Reference
73	Pen y Gaer	Silures	Auxiliary	Davies 1980
74	Abergavenny	Silures	Auxiliary	Davies 1980
75	Gloucester	Dobunni	Legionary	Hurst 1974
76	Kingsholm	Dobunni	Possible vexillation	Hurst 1985
77	Coelbren	Silures	Auxiliary	Davies 1980
78	Hirfyndd	Silures	Fortlet	Davies 1980
79	Neath	Silures	Auxiliary	Davies 1980
80	Loughor	Silures/Demetae	Auxiliary	Davies 1980
81	Penydarren	Silures	Auxiliary	Davies 1980
82	Gelligaer	Silures	Auxiliary	Davies 1980
83	Caerphilly	Silures	Auxiliary	Davies 1980
84	Cardiff	Silures	Auxiliary	Davies 1980
85	Sea Mills	Dobunni	Supply base	Ellis 1987
86	Cirencester	Dobunni	Auxiliary	Wacher & McWhirr 1982
87	Wanborough	Atrebates/Dobunni	Possible auxiliary	*Britannia* 11, 117
88	Dorchester-on-Thames	Catuvellauni?/Atrebates	Auxiliary	Frere 1984b
89	Alchester	Catuvellauni/?Atrebates	Possible auxiliary	Rowley 1975, 115–23
90	Cow Roast	Catuvellauni	Possible auxiliary	*Britannia* 7, 338–9
91	Verulamium	Catuvellauni	Auxiliary	Frere 1983, 33–44
92	Chelmsford	Trinovantes/Catuvellauni	Auxiliary	Drury 1975, 159
93	Colchester	Trinovantes	Legionary	Crummy 1984
94	Fingringhoe Wick	Trinovantes	Supply base	Willis 1986
95	Silchester	Atrebates	Possible auxiliary	Fulford 1985
96	Reculver	Cantiaci	Auxiliary	*Britannia* 1, 304
97	Canterbury	Cantiaci	Possible auxiliary	Bennett *et al.* 1982, 28–9
98	Richborough	Cantiaci	Supply base	Cunliffe 1968
99	Martinhoe	Dumnonii	Fortlet	Webster 1970, 186
100	Old Barrow	Dumnonii	Fortlet	Webster 1970, 186
101	Wiveliscombe	Dumnonii	Possible auxiliary	M. J. Jones 1975, 185
102	South Cadbury	Durotriges	Within hillfort	Todd 1984, 265
103	Ilchester	Durotriges	Possible vexillation	Leech 1982b; Casey pers. comm.
104	Ham Hill	Durotriges	Possible within hillfort	Webster 1970, 181
105	Waddon Hill	Durotriges	Within hillfort	Webster 1979
106	Hod Hill	Durotriges	Auxiliary	Richmond 1968
107	Spettisbury Rings	Durotriges	Possible within hillfort	Webster 1970, 181
108	Lake Farm	Durotriges	Vexillation	*Britannia* 13, 384
109	Hamworthy	Durotriges	Possible supply base	Webster 1958, 57

Table 3.4 (*cont.*)

No.	Site name	*Civitas*	Fort type	Reference
110	Maiden Castle	Durotriges	Possible within hillfort	Todd 1984, 265
111	Winchester	Belgae	Possible auxiliary	Biddle 1975, 296–7
112	Bitterne	Belgae	Possible supply base	*Antiq. J.* 27, 165
113	Fishbourne	Regni	Supply base	Cunliffe 1971
114	Chichester	Regni	Possible auxiliary	*Britannia* 14, 333
115	Hembury	Dumnonii	Within hillfort	Todd 1984
116	Tiverton	Dumnonii	Possible auxiliary	*Britannia* 14, 323
117	Cullompton	Dumnonii	Auxiliary	*Britannia* 16, 303
118	Topsham	Dumnonii	Supply base	Webster 1958, 56
119	Exeter	Dumnonii	Legionary	Bidwell 1979
120	Bury Barton	Dumnonii	Auxiliary size	Todd 1985b
121	Taw	Dumnonii	Possible auxiliary	*J. Roman Stud.* 48, 98
122	Okehampton	Dumnonii	Auxiliary	*Britannia* 8, 415
123	Nanstallon	Dumnonii	Auxiliary	Fox & Ravenhill 1972
124	Staines	Atrebates/?Regni/ Catuvellauni	Uncertain	Crouch & Shanks 1984, 2–3

Table 3.5. *Movements and bases of the legions to the end of the first century*[*]

Date	Legion				
	II Augusta	*IX Hispana*	*XIV Gemina*	*XX Valeria*	*II Aduitrix*
43	From Strasbourg	From Pannonia	From Mainz	From Neuss	
	SW England	E Midlands	W Midlands	Colchester	
49				Kingsholm	
c. 55	Exeter		Wroxeter		
c. 58				Usk	
c. 60		Lincoln			
c. 65/6	Gloucester		Withdrawn to East	Wroxeter	
69			Returned to Britain		
70			Withdrawn to continent		
71		York			From Rhine to Lincoln
c. 74/5	Caerleon				Chester
83				Inchtuthil	
87–92				Chester	To Moesia

[*]Where no single base is shown before 60, the legions were probably divided into vexillations.

4

THE EMERGENCE

OF THE 'CIVITATES'

Rome's activities in other provinces and the way she acquired her overseas territories indicate how she worked towards circumscribed self-government in provincial administration. In the western and north-western provinces the development of the *civitas* system enabled Rome to fulfil her requirements by the incorporation of conquered tribes in a way analogous with the *polis* (Mann 1965). Although the geographical areas covered by these *civitates* were larger than those of the territories of the Mediterranean city states, they could be treated like units of government with each *civitas* representing a unit of population, inhabiting a territory. This was administered by a council (*curia*), comprising landowning aristocrats (*decuriones*), which met at a town within the territory. This settlement was the administrative capital, and thus the focus for the population. The essence of the concept of the *polis* was thus also the essence of the *civitas*: town and country were subsumed within the same constitutional concept which, in the case of Britain, was normally equated with the tribe.

In archaeological terms this process presents a series of problems, since the constitutional concept is not directly reflected in the archaeological record and Rome's attitude to the incorporation of provinces was inherently flexible. It is widely assumed that social development during the LPRIA was limited, so that civilian rule in Roman Britain was artificially created through Roman coercion or encouragement over at least a generation (Wacher 1975a). This thesis has given rise to the concept of a 'military zone' cutting across the tribal divisions of the LPRIA, followed by a period of control by military officials (*praefecti civitatum*), culminating in the establishment of the *civitates* by official action (Wacher 1975a, 27; Rivet 1977, 121). According to this scheme the chief towns generally grew from the *vici* of forts abandoned as the army moved north and westwards (Webster 1966).

Such a model is difficult to reconcile with the nature of the conquest and takes insufficient account of the variations within the LPRIA discussed in chapter 2. These seem certain to have led Rome to a flexible approach in arriving at its preferred constitutional arrangements with the different tribes: those defeated in battle being dealt with differently from those who had been allies or who had surrendered without resistance. On analogy with Gaul we might therefore expect the development of *civitates liberae et immunes*, *civitates stipendiariae*, *civitates foederatae* and *civitates*

peregrinae (Abbott and Johnson 1926), depending upon the attitudes of the conquered tribes to Rome. In Gaul tribes generally became *civitates* without any process
of restructuring and the variations in their status had a direct bearing on their liability
to taxation, at least in the early stages following the invasion (Drinkwater 1983). We
suggest that the same pattern is widely identifiable in Roman Britain. The evidence
from other provinces supports this view. *Praefecti civitatum* do not seem to have fulfilled the rôle envisaged by Wacher (1975a, 27). They are only attested either from
areas where social evolution was minimal, such as parts of Dalmatia (Wilkes 1969,
169, 174) or where disloyalty had required the replacement of the tribal élite (Drinkwater 1983, 123). In Britain the problem encountered by Rome in areas devoid of
apparent centralization may have been overcome by centurions supervising territory
from forts, but this should also be seen as the exception rather than the rule. Similarly,
the forced removal of native towns from hilltops to new cities on the plains as attested
in north-west Spain is an exceptional result of their intransigent resistance to Rome
(Sutherland 1939, 135). We must therefore reject any model which postulates an
active reorganization or a 'military zone' as the norm. We should rather attempt to
understand the fundamental processes which led to the emergence of the *civitates* in
Britain.

If we accept that Rome's general practice was to adapt what was already there, we
should assume that the first *civitates* established in Britain, in the south and east, were
based on the social groupings of the LPRIA (fig. 16). Although *civitates* as an insti-
tution were not uniform throughout the Empire and their constitutions are not well
known in detail, the general principles can be outlined. These were based on Rome's
constitution, with the landowning classes (*decuriones*), defined by a property qualification, controlling power in a senate (*ordo*) from which were elected the council
(*curia*), as well as annually elected magistrates (usually in pairs – *duoviri*) who exercised power within the *civitas*. There is known to have been considerable variation in
the local practice of these institutions, and although it is sometimes assumed that there
had to be one hundred members of the *ordo* there is little evidence to support the idea
that this was applied universally (Abbott and Johnson 1926).

The application of the system to Britain means that the incorporated tribal élites
transformed themselves into the *decuriones* of the *civitates*. In this way they were
rewarded by retaining power, control of their tribe and wealth, thus continuing a *de
facto* hereditary system. Power within the new structure brought its burdens.
Municipal government was strongly paternalistic so some of the wealth controlled
by the aristocracy was redistributed through private patronage and civic benefactions.
The wealth displays and social hierarchies of the developed societies of the LPRIA
imply that they had taxation or tribute which helped maintain the wealth of the social
élite (Cunliffe 1983, 168). Working through the native hierarchy, Rome would have
taken advantage of this existing structure, as during the Principate the *ordo* was
responsible to the provincial administration for tax collection. The assessment was
made through the imperial census and any shortfall had to be met by those serving on
the *ordo* (Jones 1974; Mann 1985a). By using the existing system in this way, Rome
simultaneously reinforced the position and power of the native aristocracy and
ensured the cheap and effective collection of taxes without the outlay needed for direct

collection. The extent to which the weight of taxation fell on the native population is uncertain, but given the size of the population in relation to that of the army it is unlikely to have been as severe as has sometimes been assumed. Whatever the burden on the population, the net effect was to reinforce the position of those in power, thereby increasing their reliance upon Roman control to maintain and enhance their own social positions. Access to the new system in the early years after the conquest may have been eased by such things as involvement in trade or military service, which allowed increased upward social mobility. These opportunities may themselves have provided an impetus for the status competition seen in the archaeological record (below, p. 80) and on which the whole Roman system was founded.

The application of this model to Britain is unlikely not to have required changes in the existing structure, for it has already been argued that the LPRIA tribes were in a state of change whilst the conquest itself may have encouraged septs to band together

16 The *civitates* of Roman Britain. The boundaries shown generally follow those suggested by Rivet (1958). Their limits are uncertain and were themselves probably fuzzy, but the map forms a reasonable working hypothesis which is used as the base for many other maps in this book.

to fight. This forced social change, which may have encouraged the emergence of more centralized proto-states like that led by Cunobelinus (Dio 60. 21). The importance of this process should not be underestimated, as constitutional arrangements were as much a function of the Roman perceptions of the social groups as of their own. Roman treaties with the native states were undoubtedly arrived at through the tribal aristocracy who would, at this stage, have been the war-time leaders. Thus, small social units who had banded together in reaction to the Roman invasion were likely to be treated as a group within the Roman constitutional settlement, not through design as much as through the Roman perception of them as the prevailing groups. Roman society was oligarchic and recognized the practical effectiveness of arrangements made with those in other societies who also had a vested interest in stability. Thus, for instance, the Civitas Durotrigium, the Civitas Corieltauvorum and the Civitas Cantiacorum (Rivet and Smith 1979, 299) may have their origins as a unified whole in this way. The other likely process is the taking of larger septs and treating them as tribes, so that they became independent *civitates*. This may explain separate treatment of the Catuvellauni and the division of the kingdom of Cogidubnus into the *civitates* of the Regni and Belgae. In such cases it would be most consistent with Roman attitudes to follow existing sub-divisions rather than making arbitrary divisions (cf. Haselgrove 1984b, 34–5).

Apart from those tribes which created particular problems during the invasion, the constitutions of the *civitates* aimed at securing the agreement of the tribal aristocracies and incorporating them into the new system. This principle could also be applied to the troublesome tribes both inside and outside the conquered territory, where sympathetic aristocrats could be used as instruments of Roman interest. This exploitation of intra-tribal rivalries through rewards for allies ensured future loyalty, while perhaps having a destabilizing effect on the social structure of the tribes concerned. We can see this, for instance, in the Brigantian clan led by Cartimandua (Tacitus, *Annals* 12. 36; 12. 40). The aim with both existing and promoted tribal leaders was to encourage an identity of interest between conquered and conqueror. Once achieved, both stability and Romanization could be assured without coercion.

To understand how this could be achieved we need to re-examine the structure of LPRIA society. Social status and power within these societies was maintained by a combination of control of access to scarce resources and by the emergence of an aristocracy whose position was maintained through status competition. Under the new circumstances of defeat and incorporation into the Empire, the social status of those at the top of the hierarchy was defined as much in relation to Roman power as by dominance within the tribe. Within the social system, however, status could no longer be maintained by virtue of military power since the *Lex Julia de vi publica* (*Digest* 48. 6, 1) forbade conquered peoples to bear arms. Further, some of the prestige goods, such as wine or Roman table wares, used to emphasize social status in the LPRIA became more prolific and therefore began to lose their power as status indicators.

Political positions within the new structure may have conferred their own status both through access to the new supra-tribal source of power and the knowledge of Roman ways, together with the associated material attributes. This access to things

Roman, both materially and in the abstract, would fulfil an important rôle in social competition. The Romanization of institutions and possessions of the aristocracy should thus have played an active part in the process of social change and not simply have been a reflection of it. In the early years after the conquest this process was vital, as shown in the words of Tacitus (*Agricola* 21): 'competition for honour proved as effective as compulsion . . . ' Although the process of portraying oneself as Roman – wearing the *toga* and speaking latin – became a 'prestige good' in its own right, the material reflections of that Romanizing process are more difficult to understand with clarity.

Urban development

The most characteristic phenomenon related to Romanization is the emergence of towns of a particular character, which are seen right across the Empire (Ward-Perkins 1974). These towns, many of which acted as the administrative centres of *civitates* in Britain, were characterized by a series of features (fig. 17): organized planning on a street grid and a suite of substantial Roman-style public buildings, notably the *forum* (public square and meeting place), *basilica* (town hall and law courts), public baths, temples, amphitheatre and theatre. These towns were different in form from the nucleated settlements of the LPRIA which they replaced, although some of these fulfilled similar social and administrative functions (chapter 2). There is no doubt that the new form directly resulted from Roman influence, and that their construction was a result of native aristocrats emulating Roman ways.

In the words of Tacitus:

> Agricola had to deal with people living in isolation and ignorance, and therefore prone to fight; and his object was to accustom them to a life of peace and quiet by the provision of amenities. He therefore gave private encouragement and official assistance to the building of temples, public squares and good houses. He praised the energetic and scolded the slack; and competition for honour proved as effective as compulsion (*Agricola* 21).

These are some of the most commonly quoted words which refer to Roman Britain. They have generally been interpreted to support one particular model (Frere 1987, 98–9; Wacher 1975a), despite the fact that they come from the only passage in ancient literature which claims that the Romans had a policy of urbanization (Mann and Penman 1978, 61). It is argued that there was a deliberate and actively supported policy of Romanization by the Roman administration with the extensive use of army personnel to undertake construction work in the towns. This is seen as the result of indigenous societies lacking the skills, resources and motivation to undertake such work for themselves. The most eloquent exposition of this view has been presented by Frere in his analysis of the structures excavated in Insula XIV at Verulamium. He argues that the row of shops excavated there were dissimilar to pre-Roman traditions, and so closely similar in plan and construction technique to military barrack blocks that military architects and craftsmen must have been lent by the government to construct them (Frere 1972, 9–11). He further suggested that, at this early date (*c.* 49), only the military would have had the necessary supplies of wood for this type of construction. This example has been used as the basis for generalizations about the development of Romano-British towns and is so frequently cited to support arguments in favour of official involvement that it deserves careful examination.

A reappraisal of the evidence casts considerable doubt on Frere's conclusions. First, although it was suggested that the buildings were planned and roofed as a single unit (Frere 1972, fig. 5), a detailed analysis of the plan (fig. 18) shows that the absence of a continuous rear wall parallel with the frontage makes such roofing impossible.

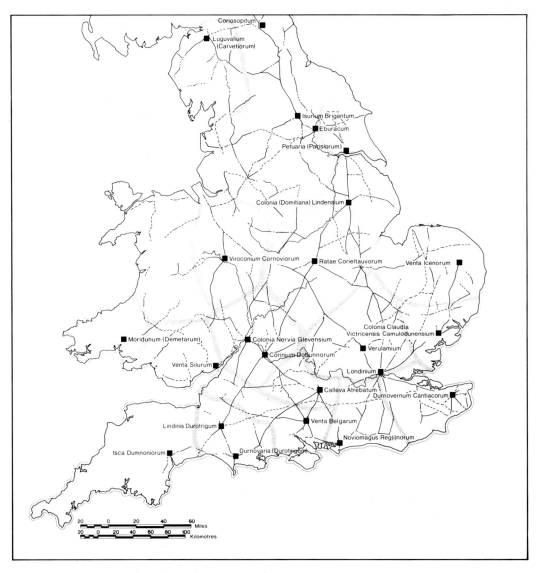

17 The Public Towns of Roman Britain. For details see table 4.4 (p. 102).

70

Furthermore, a detailed comparison with the Valkenburg barrack blocks cited as parallels shows that the similarities are superficial and can be taken neither to indicate an identity of structural type, nor to support the conclusion that the same craftsmen and architects were concerned. Although Frere draws a contrast between LPRIA structures and those in Insula XIV, these comparisons oversimplify the problem. There is now a series of rectangular structures which illustrates the emergence of new, perhaps Romanized, architectural styles in the LPRIA. Examples can be seen beneath Insula XVII at Verulamium (Frere 1983, 102–5) and at Skeleton Green nearby (Partridge 1981, 34–6), where the form of the plan is not dissimilar to the buildings under discussion. Although the details of the structure preserved in the Boudiccan fire at Verulamium cannot be paralleled precisely because preservation has been less fortuitous, there are examples of closely similar joinery preserved by waterlogging at Glastonbury (Bulleid and Gray 1911, pl. LVIII). The probable first-century BC date of these demonstrates that a sophisticated technology was available prior to the arrival of the Roman army and that native social organization was sufficient to provide suitable supplies of timber for these buildings. Given this evidence, it is most

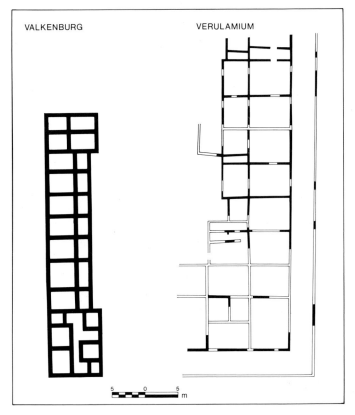

18 Comparative plans of a barrack block from Valkenburg Z.H. (The Netherlands, after van Giffen) and the pre-Boudiccan structures at Verulamium, Insula XIV (after Frere 1972).

improbable that the military was the source of the technology and materials for the construction of the buildings.

The other case commonly put forward to favour official assistance in the layout and construction of towns has been the observed similarity between the plans of Romano-British *fora* and fort headquarters buildings (*principia*). This has been taken to suggest that the former were constructed by the military (Atkinson 1942, 345; cf. Goodchild 1946). The majority of the British *fora* differ from those of the Gallic type common on the continent. The main difference lies in the absence of one important functional element: the temple (fig. 19). This difference, and indeed the unity of plan amongst the British examples, cannot simply be explained as an architectural form borrowed from the military. As Blagg (1980) points out, even if constructed by the army, a *forum* without a temple would have been unsatisfactory to its users if they required a religious building. The difference in form between the types must therefore have been a result of differences in their patrons' needs. The British towns generally had their temples separately located, sometimes in tight clusters as at Silchester Insula XXX (Boon 1974), showing how their different religious requirements were met. Given the difference, Ward-Perkins (1970) has noted that the form adopted for both the *principia* and the Romano-British *forum/basilica* has a strong continental pedigree; it was adopted for both building types because it was appropriate to needs which were indeed similar. Throughout the history of architecture satisfactory forms have often been used in this way for different purposes (for example, basilicas for christian churches) without the same architects or builders having been employed.

Of more general significance is the relationship between military and civilian craftsmen in the early years after the conquest. Blagg (1980; 1984) has shown that the use of military craftsmen, architects, surveyors and workmen on civil projects is difficult to substantiate. There is little evidence that skilled stonemasons were always present with the legions at this period, as the Gallic affinities of the Flavian quadrifrons arch at Richborough show (Strong 1968). Their loan to civic authorities is thus problematical. Further, where evidence is available, civilian building work was not undertaken by military craftsmen. The study of the detail on first- and second-century buildings has shown that the column capitals from civilian sites form a group distinct from those found on military sites (Blagg 1980). Civilian architecture is also closely related to that of civic buildings in the northern and western provinces (for example, the Temple of Sulis-Minerva at Bath (Blagg 1979), and Fishbourne (Strong 1971)). This suggests that inspiration and expertise were drawn from those areas, rather than from the army. Finally, the documented military campaigns, together with the construction of forts and roads, are unlikely to have left the army in a position regularly to loan troops and specialists to the municipalities. Where such military aid is attested in other provinces it is generally later, when wars of conquest had stopped (MacMullen 1959, 216, 218).

Tacitus' words on the assistance to communities clearly require an alternative interpretation. Blagg (1980) suggests that this took the form of the governor allowing tax remissions to free resources for building or using contacts and clients to secure funds or architects and builders from other provinces. The latter may either have been loans or grants from the imperial *fiscus* or private individuals; both sources are

AMPURIAS

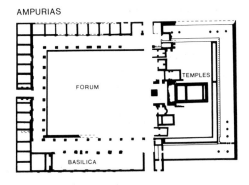

AUGST

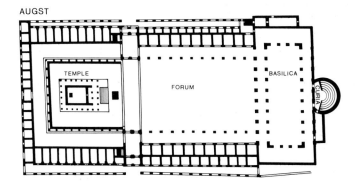

SILCHESTER

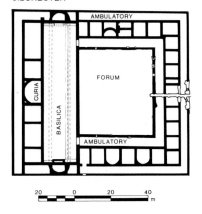

19 Comparative plans of the *fora* at Ampurias (Spain),
Augst (Switzerland) and Silchester (Hampshire).

attested by Dio (62. 2). The initiative for any of these may have lain with the *civitates* rather than any central authority, although governors like Agricola took credit.

If we accept that the establishment of the towns was largely a result of the native élites' desire to participate in a Roman style of life, then the pattern will provide information about native society. To examine this we need a broad understanding of the speed of change in the different tribal areas, which is not easily obtained since the archaeological evidence is variable and many of the most important sites lack good data. Despite these limitations it is possible to propose explanations which elaborate the model, evidence being best summarized in table 4.4 below.

The first crucial issue is the origin of the towns, and until recently the favoured interpretation envisaged their foundation as the result of official action, with the widespread use of fort sites, abandoned as the army moved forward (Webster 1966) (fig. 20). The hypothesis is that the army presence had stimulated economic activity and the growth of associated settlements (*vici*), and that these remained to form the nuclei of the towns after the military withdrawal. There are two objections to this model. First, it provides no explanation of why those living in the *vici* (the *vicani*), who were economically dependent on the army, chose to remain behind rather than follow the army forward, and secondly, the need to seek an explanation for urban origins at this period lies in the idea that the LPRIA lacked any developed urbanism. Since it has already been argued that the forts of the conquest were located in relation to the pre-existing political geography, which included proto-urban centres, the need for a mechanism to explain their foundation is redundant. Any rôle of the army as a stimulus to urban growth is thus unnecessary. Furthermore, as Rome adopted the native taxation systems, an alternative spur to urban growth may be suggested since modest taxation is likely to have encouraged extra production (Hopkins 1980). Similarly, its collection through the *civitas* centres will have consolidated their importance as territorial centres. This continuity both in taxation and social foci from the pre-conquest tribes to the *civitates* emphasizes the conservative nature of the Roman power, which reinforced existing structures within the conquered societies.

It is thus suggested that the forts were located in relation to pre-existing political centres because of their continued importance in the *civitates*. This is particularly the case for that focus in each *civitas* which became its chief town. The development of certain towns perhaps owed something to the army, and this debt must be seen in relation to the whole pattern of change. Thus, for instance, at locations like Cirencester and Dorchester, there is a minor shift in the location of the centre, from Bagendon and Maiden Castle to the site of the later town (Wacher 1975a). There may have been some deliberate policy behind such moves but the Gallic precedents (Drinkwater 1983, 130–1) suggest that the shift resulted from changes in geography brought about by the establishment of the Roman roads. Thus, although the people and institutions may have marginally moved their social focus to a new location, there remained a continuity of personnel and power. The normal pattern in areas of pre-Roman development was a direct continuity of site rather than any shift. This contrasts markedly with some other areas, in the north and west, where a less developed tradition of centralized authority has been noted. Here *civitas* capitals like Exeter (Bidwell 1979) and Wroxeter (Webster 1987) show a pattern of development which contrasts with those in the south and east. Limited traces of military occupation best interpreted as evidence for a very short-term military presence are found at many southern cities like Verulamium. At centres further north and west some were the sites of substantial military bases (fig. 12). At both Exeter (fig. 21) and Wroxeter (fig. 22), the towns reused military bases in a way comparable with the *coloniae* at Gloucester and Colchester (below, p. 85). The fact that both sites were also former legionary bases, rather than simply auxiliary forts, may be significant as they were perhaps more permanent and substantial. Such reuse of bases need have been no more than an expedient to enable a native community to have a settlement centre without construct-ing it from new. This passive encouragement is similar to the other aid already dis-cussed. We can only speculate about the early development of the towns in other areas

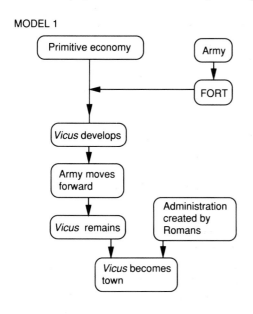

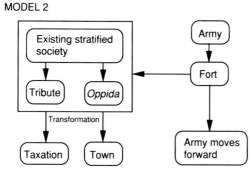

20 Alternative models for the relationship of forts to town origins in early Roman Britain. Model 1 (based on Webster 1966) emphasizes the active rôle of the military, whilst Model 2 (Millett 1984) stresses the continuity of native political systems and centralization accentuated by the taxation system.

without centralized LPRIA communities, as we have too little evidence available (table 4.4).

In the north, there is considerable doubt about the constitutional status of the settlements (Salway 1967, 41). Recent excavations in Carlisle (Luguvalium [Carvetiorum]) show that the civilian centre (although not a *civitas* at this stage) developed to the south of the Flavian fort, where the excavators have drawn attention to military-style structures (McCarthy 1984). There is some doubt about the status of these buildings and the site itself at this date. It has also been suggested that a *civitas* was centred on Corbridge (Coriosopitum) (Rivet and Smith 1979, 322) in the latter part of the second century (Daniels 1978, 94), although the evidence for this is ambiguous. If we accept the case together with the identification of the 'store building' on site XI as a *forum* complex, we can contrast it with the pattern observed at Wroxeter and Exeter. The abandonment of the fort at Corbridge led to the demolition of the barrack blocks and some other military works, which was followed by a substantial replanning of the site. This did not result in it remaining entirely civilian, since both the later military compounds and the epigraphic evidence demonstrate a continued military association. This, the adjacent Hadrian's Wall garrison, and the late development of both Carlisle and Corbridge as urban centres, suggest that they fit into a different framework from

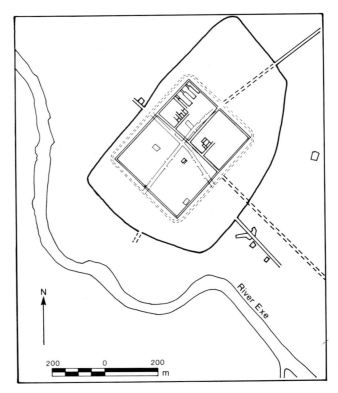

21 Simplified plan showing the relationship between the legionary fortress at Exeter (ditches in dashed outline) and the later *civitas* capital (after Bidwell 1979).

the other towns, which were in areas of less sustained military occupation. Indeed, Corbridge may well have been the centre of a *pagus* of the Civitas Brigantum rather than a *civitas* capital itself. This administrative status is suggested by its *Corio-* place-name, which signifies the centre of a tribal sept (Rivet and Smith 1979, 318) and Frere (1987, 46 n. 8) interprets the corrupt text of the *Ravenna Cosmography* as indicating that it was the centre for a group known as the Lopocares (cf. Rivet and Smith 1979, 323).

The areas of short-lived military occupation themselves present problems, as the evidence of military activity is by its nature very limited. In centres such as Verulamium (Frere 1983) or Silchester (Fulford 1985; 1986), where we have com-paratively good evidence for early history, military activity seems peripheral to the main development of the site. In both cases the *fora* overlie LPRIA enclosures, perhaps the foci of the pre-existing *oppida* (figs. 23–4) (Frere 1983, 3; Fulford 1987), and these may be compared with those within The Tofts at Stanwick or at Gosbecks, Camulodunum (fig. 7). In contrast, the military evidence suggests low intensity, short-

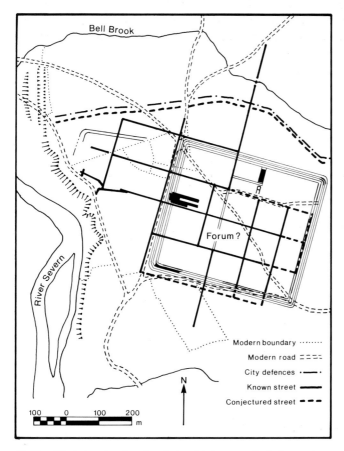

22 Simplified plan showing the relationship between the legionary fortress at Wroxeter (rectangular ditches in outline) and the later *civitas* capital (after *Current Archaeology* 107).

lived activity. Fulford's suggestion (1985, 57) that the large timber structure beneath the Silchester *forum* might have been the *principia* of a post-Boudiccan fort is excluded now that more of its plan is clear (Fulford 1986, 3). The nature of the military evidence on these sites is problematical as there is rarely any structural evidence, which would be difficult to identify and interpret in small-scale, deep excavation beneath later towns, especially as temporary camps leave little structural trace. When structures are absent, military equipment alone does not point to the presence of a base (above, p. 60); such explanations for the 'drift' of military equipment perhaps reduce its importance in explaining the early development of the towns. Where evidence suggests several phases of forts (for example, Cirencester) (Wacher and McWhirr 1982), a rôle as winter quarters for a sequence of campaigns may emphasize the importance of the already emergent administrative centres. This function might explain the forts at Chichester (Down 1978) and Winchester (Biddle 1975, 296–7), which are within the client kingdom of Cogidubnus, both legally quasi-independent and self-governing.

The pattern of urban development contrasts with much of the remainder of the Empire; the British towns are more impoverished in public buildings, statuary and inscriptions. Nonetheless, the evidence indicates that the towns at *civitas* centres did develop within the same framework of munificence (Frere 1985), and that there was not the same concept of public expenditure in the Roman world as we see in the West today (Duncan-Jones 1985). The bulk of central government expenditure raised by

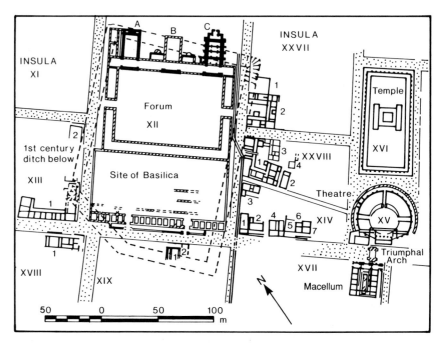

23 The *forum* at Verulamium, showing the ditches beneath (dashed lines). These perhaps defined a high-status enclosure within the LPRIA settlement (after Frere 1983).

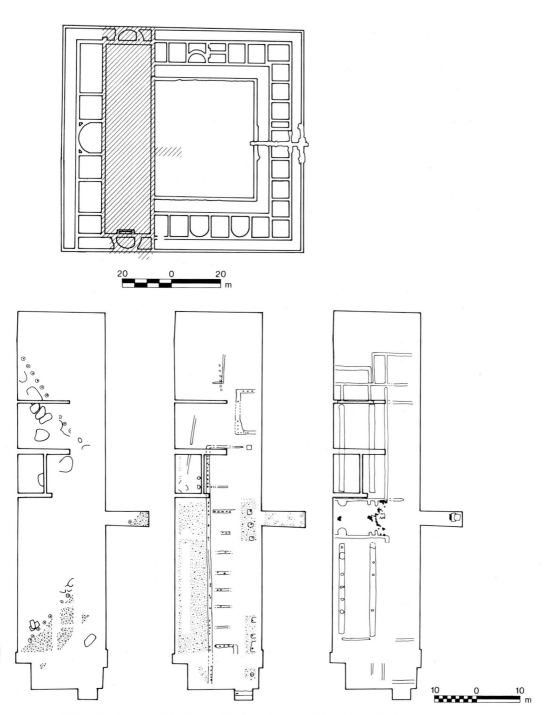

24 The development of the *forum* at Silchester. The trench beneath the *basilica* (top, hatched) revealed a sequence starting with an LPRIA enclosure (*left*), followed by successive timber structures – probably *fora* – built *c.* 55/60 (*middle*) and *c.* 80/90 (*right*) before the construction of the stone version (*top*) *c.* 150 (after Fulford 1985; 1986; 1987).

taxation was used for a limited set of purposes, with an estimated 55 per cent spent on the army alone in the first century AD (Hopkins 1980, 119, 125). The levels of taxation have been seen as low (Jones 1974, 178 and Hopkins 1980, 119 takes it at *c.* 10 per cent gross), and as the system was not progressive (Jones 1974, 172–3), wealth could be rapidly accumulated by the powerful, like the few enormously rich people known to us from the ancient sources (Finley 1973, 99–102).

The accumulation of money and power was institutionalized in the Roman system. It required those undertaking public office both to fulfil a property qualification in order to serve and to use those resources for the public good through the provision of games, feasts and endowment of public buildings. As Hopkins (1983a) has shown, this did not result in the fossilization of power in the early Empire; indeed the process led to a steady replacement of the families at the top of the pyramid in Rome as fortunes waxed and waned. There was a strong reliance on a desire and an ability to compete; elections to magistracies in Rome were contested and fortunes expended on competition for them. Within the local municipality a similar process can be seen, at least in the major communities of the Mediterranean. The *sine qua non* was a series of wealthy families willing to compete, and many public buildings, statues and inscriptions are a permanent memorial to this process (Mackie in press), although feasts and games were perhaps more popular amongst some citizens. Self-advertisement and munificence sometimes got out of hand and through the Principate governers were progressively forced to restrict their extravagance (Lewis and Reinhold 1955, 341). Nonetheless, competitive munificence was central to the functioning of government in the early Empire.

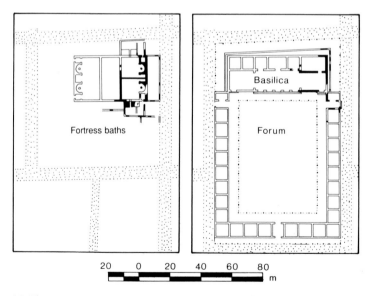

25 The monumental baths of the legionary fortress at Exeter (*c.* 70), demolished to make way for the *forum-basilica* (*c.* 80/85). Fulford (1985) has pointed to a possible phase of timber public building between the two (after Bidwell 1979).

In the later Empire the urge to compete was lost (chapter 6), but in the *civitates* of Britain we can perhaps suggest that other factors affected the pattern of munificence. The epigraphic evidence (Biró 1975) (fig. 26) clearly demonstrates that by the standards of the central Empire the 'epigraphic habit' (MacMullen 1982; Mann 1985b) failed to catch on, while there are also comparatively few public buildings (below, p. 104). An analysis of inscriptions recording dedications has recently been prepared by Blagg (forthcoming), who has compared the British evidence with that from other

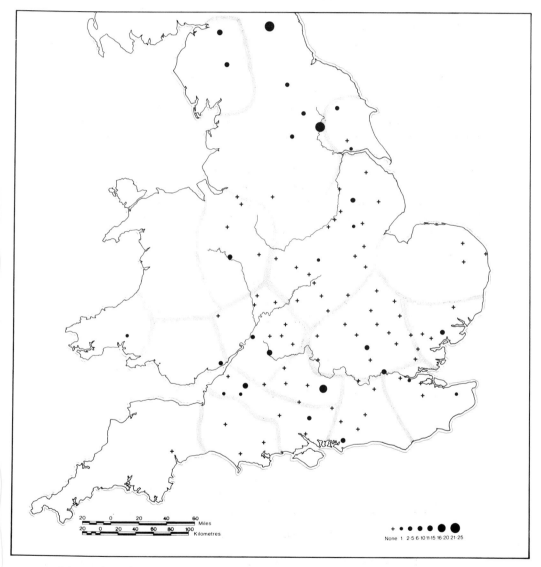

26 Distribution of monumental dedicatory inscriptions from Roman Britain (data drawn from *RIB* and the 'Roman Britain' reports up to and including *Britannia* 14).

81

Table 4.1. *Numbers of inscriptions recording architectural benefactions from Britain and adjacent provinces (percentage in brackets)*

Type of construction	Gallia Aquitania	Gallia Belgica	Gallia Lugdunensis	Germania Inferior	Germania Superior	Britannia
Sacred building	11 (18.5)	12 (26)	23 (24.5)	27 (64)	66 (41.5)	50 (63.5)
Statues	1 (1.8)	2 (4.3)	17 (18)	1 (2.5)	32 (20)	9 (11.8)
Sacred, total	12 (20.3)	14 (30.3)	40 (42.5)	28 (66.5)	98 (61.5)	59 (75.3)
Public squares	7 (11.8)	4 (8.8)	10 (10.5)	1 (2.5)	9 (5.5)	3 (4)
Enclosed buildings	8 (13.8)	5 (11)	4 (4.3)	3 (7)	5 (3.3)	2 (2.5)
Baths etc.	10 (17)	7 (15.2)	6 (6.5)	2 (5)	11 (7)	—
Places of entertainment	2 (3.5)	4 (8.8)	8 (8.5)	1 (2.5)	3 (2)	1 (1.2)
Public, total	27 (46)	20 (43.8)	28 (29.8)	7 (17)	28 (17.8)	6 (7.8)
Highways & miscellaneous	20 (33.8)	12 (26)	26 (27.8)	7 (16.5)	33 (20.8)	13 (17)
Grand total	59	46	94	42	159	78

Sources: Blagg forthcoming; Frézouls 1984.

north-western provinces compiled by Frézouls (1984) (tables 4.1 and 4.2). These figures demonstrate a series of consistent patterns. As might be expected, a high proportion of inscriptions record gifts by soldiers in all the heavily garrisoned provinces. Less expected is the small number of civic benefactions by individual donors, whose activity was central in the Mediterranean cities (Mackie in press). In contrast, a high proportion mark donations by corporate bodies, as also occurs in Gallia Belgica (table 4.2). If we exclude the military, British inscriptions clearly show limited munificence, dominated by the provision of sacred structures rather than other public buildings, whilst individual gifts were less common than those donated collectively. This compares with other northern provinces, especially the Germanies which also show a paucity of civic building inscriptions, contrasting with the more Mediterranean pattern in the provinces of central Gaul.

These patterns cannot simply result from an absence of money, as the wealth of the villas illustrates. They must be viewed instead as a result of social organization and aspirations. The best model is one where effective power remained in the control of a small oligarchy, comprising the leaders of the pre-Roman tribes and their descendants. There was thus little need to compete; power was already theirs and remained with their families. The wealth they wished to invest in social display could be used to provide the towns with basic Roman facilities, perhaps indicating competition with adjacent *civitates*. Such a display of *Romanitas* could be collective rather than individual, but served to reinforce the power of the controlling élite within its own society. The absence of serious competition for power meant that the facilities constructed were not frequently replaced or duplicated in the wasteful manner seen in the central Empire. Although this general lack of status competition shows some variation within Britain (Blagg forthcoming) (fig. 26), the main contrast is between the northern and the core provinces. The northern European pattern indicates a social organization in which power was both largely personal and limited to a small social group. It was thus

Table 4.2. *Numbers of known benefactors recorded on inscriptions for Britain and adjacent provinces (percentage in brackets)*

Benefactor	Gallia Aquitania	Gallia Belgica	Gallia Lugdunensis	Germania Inferior	Germania Superior	Britannia
Emperor or representative	—	1 (2.8)	1 (1.7)	2 (5.9)	3 (2.0)	6 (7.6)
Corporate body	1 (2.6)	9 (25)	2 (3.4)	1 (2.9)	9 (6.1)	14 (17.8)
Civic magistrates	4 (10.3)	1 (2.8)	6 (10.3)	1 (2.9)	19 (12.9)	2 (2.5)
Priests	6 (15.4)	2 (5.6)	6 (10.3)	1 (2.9)	3 (2)	3 (3.8)
Holders of priesthood plus civic position	4 (10.3)	1 (2.8)	1 (1.7)	—	2 (1.4)	—
Military	3 (7.7)	—	3 (5.2)	15 (44.1)	32 (21.8)	26 (33)
Freedmen notables	2 (5.1)	5 (13.9)	2 (3.4)	—	3 (2)	2 (2.5)
Presumed members of civic community	10 (25.6)	5 (13.9)	20 (34.5)	8 (23.6)	38 (25.9)	12 (15.2)
Foreigners	—	—	—	—	1 (0.7)	—
Other freedmen	—	2 (5.6)	2 (3.4)	1 (2.9)	4 (2.7)	1 (1.3)
Slaves	—	—	—	1 (2.9)	1 (0.7)	—
Indeterminate	9 (23.1)	10 (27.8)	15 (25.9)	4 (11.8)	32 (21.8)	13 (16.5)
Total	39	36	58	34	147	79

Sources: Blagg forthcoming; Frézouls 1984.

not the object of the same inter-family rivalry that led to competitive munificence in the socially unstable climate of Mediterranean society.

The pattern in those *civitates* which had formerly been client kingdoms is of particular interest. At Chichester we have two building inscriptions (*RIB* 91 and 92) which show that public monuments were dedicated in a Roman fashion before the tribe was legally incorporated within the Empire. We lack excavated evidence for these buildings, although the villa at Fishbourne (fig. 35) (Cunliffe 1971) and the temple at Hayling Island (fig. 27) (Downey *et al.* 1980) illustrate the level of *Romanitas* they are likely to have achieved. Recent work at Silchester, also ascribed to the client kingdom of Cogidubnus, shows the types of public building constructed in the crucial period in the mid-first century. Around 55/65 a substantial timber courtyard building was constructed. It is interpreted as a *forum* since its form is closely comparable with that of the later timber and stone structures (Fulford 1986) (fig. 24). The significance of this is considerable, since, although a *forum* need not have been built immediately a *civitas* was legally constituted, as government could be run from another structure, it was almost certainly an important symbol of civic pride. Most *civitates* are thus likely to have constructed one soon after their status was formalized. The significance of the *forum* at Silchester and the Romanized structures at Chichester lies in the clear evidence they provide for an indigenous impetus to Romanization under leaders like Cogidubnus. This is evident from their precocious construction while the territories were still legally independent (provided we accept that Cogidubnus did not die until the 70s) (Bogaers 1979, 254). Some Roman involvement in these developments is hinted at by the Neronian stamped tiles from Silchester (Fulford 1985, 57).

Fulford (1985, 58) has recently drawn attention to a possible timber predecessor to the stone-built *forum* at Exeter (fig. 25) (Bidwell 1979, 73, fig. 20), significantly and perhaps symbolically replacing the legionary baths. Such timber buildings are difficult to trace beneath monumental stone structures, and we might expect them elsewhere, as pre-existing unenclosed *fora* have been identified in London (Marsden 1987, 19–22) and Leicester (Hebditch and Mellor 1973, 7–8). The comparatively late date of the stone construction of known *fora* (table 4.4) may be explained by the more widespread occurrence of timber predecessors. This would be unsurprising, as there are few stone buildings in first-century Britain and the native tradition employed timber. The use of wood does not imply any lack of architectural pretensions as the Flavian timber *basilica* at Silchester shows (fig. 24). However, the problem of identifying such buildings beneath later *fora* makes it difficult to assess the speed of urban growth in the province, and to discuss the character of the towns until the later first century, when stone building becomes more common. By this stage the towns in the south and east were already well established (chapter 5).

The geographical pattern of urban growth is not yet entirely clear. That postulated

27 Air photograph showing the early Roman temple at Hayling Island, Hants. This unusual form of round Romano-Celtic temple within a square *temenos*, or sacred enclosure, overlay a timber predecessor of the LPRIA. Excavation has demonstrated that the stone structure was similar in style and date to the nearby villa at Fishbourne (fig. 35). (*Photograph by courtesy of G. Soffe.*)

by Wacher (1975a), in which phases of urban growth are directly correlated with moves forward by the army in step with a conscious programme of urbanization, is not borne out by the evidence. It would be more satisfactory to classify the *civitas* centres into groups by the periods and rates at which they grew, and the pattern suggested is comparatively simple (table 4.3), based on the status and development of areas in the LPRIA. The hypothesis is that Rome incorporated existing systems, and transformations occurred accidentally as a result of interaction between Rome and the *civitates*, not as a consequence of any deliberate policy.

The coloniae *and London*

Apart from the *civitas* capitals (with which Verulamium has been included as the *chef-lieu* of the Catuvellauni), we have five further major towns in Roman Britain: London and the four *coloniae*. These centres occupy an anomalous position within the settlement system as all are alien additions to it. The foundation of the *coloniae*, with the exception of York (to which we will return), represents deliberate acts of policy by the Roman administration. Tacitus wrote that Colchester was founded to protect the country against revolt and to familiarize the natives with law-abiding government (*Annals* 12. 32), and emphasis is commonly placed on their rôle in encouraging the Britons to follow a Roman way of life through example (Frere 1987, 65). Of equal importance was the necessity of providing land grants to retiring Roman legionaries in lieu of a cash gratuity (Watson 1969, 147–8). Provision of this grant presented emperors with a problem, as it was in their interest to keep retired soldiers away from

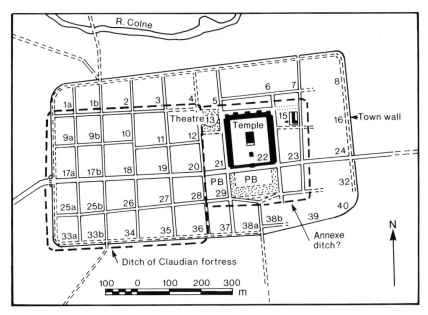

28 The *colonia* at Colchester, showing the location of the Temple of Claudius in relation to the ditches of the Claudian legionary fortress and its annexe (after Crummy 1984).

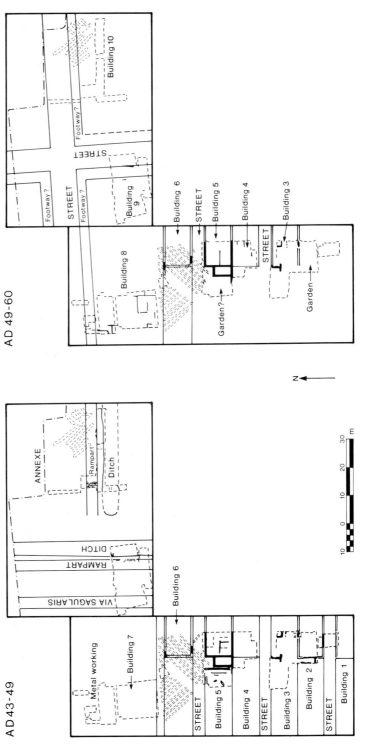

29 Comparative plans of the Lion Walk excavations in Colchester, illustrating the transformation of buildings of the legionary fortress to those of the *colonia* (after Crummy 1984).

the land-starved centre of the Empire (Hopkins 1978), where they might also constitute an alternative political force (Salmon 1969). The solution adopted, both economical and beneficial to the government, was to settle legionaries on the sites of former legionary fortresses in the recently conquered provinces. The sites were already in Roman hands and fulfilled the veterans' requirements at minimal cost, while also providing a loyal reserve of men in potentially hostile areas (although this proved to be of little use in the Boudiccan revolt). The value of veterans' *Romanitas* in stimulating native Romanization seems likely to have been a secondary purpose, especially as most of those settled by this date were themselves provincial in origin (Mann 1983). Nevertheless, as colonists they were Roman citizens, whose legal rights and privileges were superior to those enjoyed by the inhabitants of the *civitates* (Abbott and Johnson 1926, 3–9).

In Britain the three veteran *coloniae*, founded at Colchester in 49 (Tacitus, *Annals* 12. 32), at Lincoln in c. 90–6 (*CIL* XII. 6679) and Gloucester in c. 96–8 (*CIL* VI. 3346), are comparatively well documented. The sites were taken over almost intact from the legions, the streets and buildings used in the early stages of the town (figs. 28–9) (Crummy 1982a). Thus, although superior in legal status to the *civitas* capitals, initially they were little more than converted army camps. At Colchester the legionary fortress was planted next to the major LPRIA centre and may have been intentionally developed as a provincial focus. Similar centres at Condate by Lugdunum (Lyons) in Gaul (Drinkwater 1983, 111–14) and Tarraco (Tarragona) in Spain (Keay 1988) included temples of the provincial cult and the meeting places for their provincial councils. Lack of space within the former fortress at Colchester meant that its annex had to be cleared for the construction of the major public buildings (fig. 28), including the Temple of the Deified Claudius, a *basilica* and theatre (Crummy 1982b; Drury 1984). This complex is comparable to the provincial centre at Tarraco, with its own *forum* separate from that of the town (Keay 1988, 121). At Colchester the provincial centre (fig. 30) is similar in form to the so-called Gallic *forum* (cf. fig. 19). Monumental buildings were first constructed before 60/61, although the developed buildings are post-Boudiccan. The temple itself cannot have been dedicated to Claudius until after his death in 54, but was in existence at the time of the revolt (Fishwick 1972). This *colonia* was significantly at the LPRIA capital, and its development at Colchester was a matter of Roman policy, which caused some of the stresses on native society manifested in the Boudiccan revolt (Tacitus, *Annals* 14. 31). The provincial centre so designed was, however, eclipsed by the development of London in the post-Boudiccan period.

The cities of Gloucester (Hurst 1974) and Lincoln (M. J. Jones 1985) are dissimilar to Colchester, since neither has public buildings beyond those usual in a *colonia*. To judge by its size and buildings, Gloucester was overshadowed economically and by the nearby *civitas* capital at Cirencester, the successor to Bagendon as the capital of the Dobunni. Lincoln was more successful, becoming the geographical centre for the northern sept of the Corieltauvi, whose former focus lay 25 km to the south at Old Sleaford, but was superseded when Leicester developed as the *civitas* centre. The contrast between the two *coloniae* may result from the greater centralization within the

Dobunni, resulting in a more integrated settlement system, of which Gloucester was not a part.

London is a more difficult problem, since it does not fit easily into any defined pattern. Although described as a *polis* of the Cantii (*sic*) by Ptolemy (Rivet and Smith 1979, 396), there is no need to see it as a *civitas* centre. Tacitus (*Annals* 14. 33) describes it as 'not yet a *colonia*' in 60/61. Some form of self-government was presumably achieved through promotion to the rank of *municipium* or *colonia*, but we have no evidence for its status in the early Roman period. Despite recent intensive archaeological work there is no evidence for a fort of the invasion period beneath the later town. Early Roman military evidence is scant and comprises a possible military ditch at St Bride's, Fleet Street (Grimes 1968, 183–4), and a single stretch of fort ditch at Aldgate (Chapman and Johnson 1973, 5–7). Both features are peripheral to the Roman centre, and best interpreted as temporary bases used after the town was founded. The absence of military evidence beneath the city should occasion little surprise, since the road network to the south of London clearly shows that the earliest

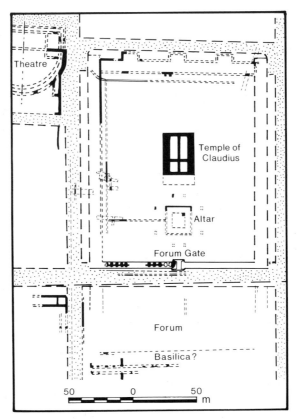

30 The Temple of Claudius at Colchester and the adjacent theatre. The form of the temple and adjacent *forum/basilica* are reminiscent of some continental *fora* (cf. fig. 19). The layout suggests that the whole complex may represent the focus for the new province (after Drury 1984).

river crossing was at Westminster (Marsden 1980, 14). Indeed, this pattern has been taken to suggest that any invasion-period fort should lie in the vicinity of Elephant and Castle (Fuentes 1985). The evidence now available from the extensive excavations both in the City and in Southwark suggests that occupation did not begin much before *c.* 50 and that development was then both rapid and planned (Marsden 1980; Merrifield 1983). The location of the early city was determined by both the solid ground of the river terrace on the northern bank and a series of sand banks forming a causeway above high tide on the southern side of the river (Sheldon 1978, figs. 1–3). The earliest London Bridge joined these two areas and around its northern bridgehead the early Roman harbour was built (Milne 1985, 142), which became important in the first decades after the conquest, since Tacitus in 60/61 describes it as 'an important commercial centre flocking with traders' (*Annals* 14. 33). The recently stated opinion that harbour development was a result, not a cause, of the emergence of London (Milne 1985) is perhaps an over-compensation for the alternative that it was fundamental (Marsden 1980, 25). In this debate it is crucial to distinguish its use as a port from the development of the harbour. The latter was not a necessity, as ships were frequently beached or moored and unloaded with lighters (McGrail 1987, 167ff). Thus the late first-century date (Milne 1985, 27) for the construction of the harbour facilities is of limited importance.

What is significant is the evidence from the north bank, which clearly demonstrates how the core of the pre-Boudiccan city was planned (fig. 31) (Marsden 1987, fig. 16), as such planning is unexpected in the provincial context. The town was not the administrative centre of a *civitas*, and it has already been suggested that Colchester had been selected for development as the provincial capital. One could perhaps argue for the governor having a base separate from the cult centre at Colchester, but there is no obvious reason for it and the absence of colonial status for London at the time of the Boudiccan revolt indicates otherwise. The emergence of London as a focus before 60/61 thus seems to result from trade. The cosmopolitan nature of the city and its early planned core may indicate that foreign traders established the settlement as an organized community at a geographically convenient location for seaborne trade, and at the focus of communications which centred on the bridge over the Thames.

The geographical advantages of the location are not confined to its position at the Thames crossing, but also relate to the political geography of the south-east. Despite Kent's (1978) suggestion that an LPRIA settlement focus existed in west London, there is little to suggest that the Thames valley and London were not peripheral (Merriman 1987). Indeed the concentration of metalwork from the Thames is most consistent with ritual deposition at a boundary (Fitzpatrick 1984). The map of the *civitates* (fig. 16) shows that London also developed at this boundary. Such a location can be seen as politically neutral and this may account for the successful development of a trading community in the early years after the conquest. Lying away from the *civitas* centres, it was outside the control that individual tribal élites may have exercised over economic exchange. Thus foreign traders could establish their own commercial community on neutral ground, establishing a 'Port-of-Trade' (Polanyi 1963). London's early *Romanitas* is evidence for this and reflects an unconstrained development uncharacteristic of the *civitas* centres.

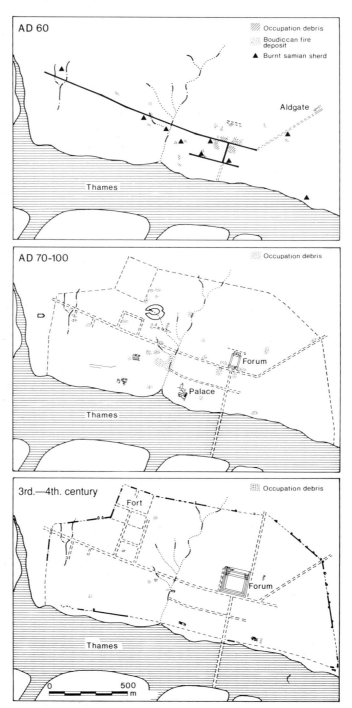

31 The development of Roman London.

After the Boudiccan revolt there is strong evidence that the administration of the province transferred to London. The epigraphic material shows that the Procurator was based there (*RIB* 12; Merrifield 1983) and a structure is plausibly identified as a governor's palace (Marsden 1975), whilst the Cripplegate fort of the early second century seems to have housed a variety of officials seconded to his staff (Hassall 1973). The presence of the provincial administration may also owe its success to the tribally neutral location as well as the communications, and this will have removed any perceived association between Roman power and any particular tribal group. The centralization of power in a successful economic centre encouraged the construction of major public buildings such as the spectacular *forum*, harbour installations and palace which adorned the city by the third decade of the first century (fig. 31). The association of administrative and economic functions does not mean that the two were strongly inter-reliant (below, p. 127), but accounts for the initial success of London. The movement of provincials to and from the city for administrative purposes would have further enhanced its economic success. Thus, whilst traditional power in the tribes remained focused on the *civitas* centres, the new city represented a higher imperial power outside the influence of any pre-existing polity.

A similar pattern can be detected later at York. Here a legionary fortress, latterly of *Legio VI*, has been established during the Flavian period on neutral ground on the boundary between the Brigantes and the Parisi. This location made strategic sense (above, p. 54) as it allowed the Roman army to watch over the Brigantes. The long-term presence of the legion led to the emergence of a dependent settlement across the river. This was promoted to the status of a *colonia* early in the third century (Wacher 1975a, 156), although by this date such promotion was largely a matter of prestige (Salmon 1969, 153). York's success contrasts with the *civitas* centres elsewhere in the north and may result from its boundary location as well as the wealth spent by the military garrison, and the political power it achieved on its promotion to provincial capital on the division of Britain into two provinces (below).

The countryside

It has already been stressed that the essence of the *civitas* was that town and country were encompassed within the same administrative unit derived from the LPRIA tribal group. As there was a predominantly dispersed settlement pattern, the countryside must be considered as fundamental to both the settlement system and the organization of social and political power. Soon after the conquest a series of Romanized buildings, the so-called villas, are added to this pattern.

The term 'villa' is common in archaeological literature (Rivet 1958; Percival 1976), although it presents difficulties and causes confusion. Ambiguities stem from the use of a latin term to describe archaeological sites with which it has no defined or direct relationship. In latin the term means a country house, without necessarily implying a farm. A number of the rural retreats of the Roman élite had farms attached to them but these were not their *raison d'être*. An establishment which existed primarily to exploit the countryside as an economic resource was the farm, *fundus*. As Rivet (1958) has suggested, the essence of the *villa* was that it represented the integration of the town and country as the rural seat of one who needed land to hold power in the *civitas*; as such it was for the display of wealth, not its production. This is most clearly understood when we recall that it was necessary to have wealth to hold power within the Roman political system and that wealth could only legitimately and respectably be held as land. Thus those in power within a municipality generally held estates in its territory and would periodically withdraw to their estates. The embellishment of the houses, *villae*, on these estates was part of the system of expressing and retaining their power and social position. It is thus the rural manifestation of the same phenomenon that led to urban munificence.

The archaeological problem is that we cannot say which site a 'Roman' would have considered to be a *villa* since there are no unambiguous archaeological correlates of the Roman idea. Furthermore, although a *villa* recognized by a Roman generally had lands attached to it, we have absolutely no way of identifying the lands attached to any particular archaeological site, so the widely used term villa-estate has no archaeologically useful function.

In examining the archaeological evidence for the countryside we can identify a series of rural sites which have Romanized houses added to them at different stages. These buildings, characterized by rectangular plans, the use of stone, solid floors (sometimes with mosaics), hypocausts, and baths, are usually referred to as villas. Provided we distinguish this term from the latin (by using the anglicized form), and recognize that they need not have been known as *villae* by a 'Roman' visiting Britain, the usage is acceptable and we can draw inferences from their chronological patterning and spatial distribution.

The evidence for the patterning of the early villas in Britain is shown in figs. 32 and 33, which are largely based on the important study by the late Mark Gregson (1982a; unpublished). These data enable generalizations to be made and demonstrate a series of points which demand explanation. Villas first appear in the south and east, in the *civitates* where there was also a rapid growth of towns. In these areas the earliest villas are on average both large and clustered around the emergent towns. The best known of these are in Sussex (Cunliffe 1973b), but we also see their emergence in Kent (Detsicas 1983), around Verulamium (Neal 1978) and in Essex (Rodwell 1978). All are in the areas where LPRIA centralization was most notable. The development of these sites had often begun by the Flavian period. Their rapid appearance after the conquest demands explanation, as does their size, which is larger on average than the later villas (fig. 33). Todd (1978b) has argued that some of them were constructed by incomers in the wake of the invasion, but most of the evidence shows a continuity of settlement on the sites from the LPRIA to the Roman period. This is more likely to result from a continuity of ownership with a shift towards a more Roman form of status display by the native élite (fig. 34).

This pattern is well illustrated by Park Street (O'Neil 1945), Mileoak (Green and Draper 1978) or Gorhambury (Neal 1978; Selkirk 1983), where villas are constructed directly on sites previously occupied by native settlements. Gorhambury is particularly notable for its location in relation to the LPRIA dyke system which is suggestive of continuity from *oppidum* to villa. This pattern may be compared with that of Fishbourne (fig. 35), where the early villa also lies within the dykes of the *oppidum*

(Haselgrove 1987a, 458). Here Cunliffe (1971) has argued that the large villa was built *de novo* as a palace for the client king Cogidubnus. This is plausible, but two important points should be noted. First, whilst the villa site does not seem to have been founded on that of an LPRIA farmstead it is within the *oppidum* and overlies an invasion-period military base. The chronology proposed by Cunliffe may need revision as the early imported pottery is better explained as LPRIA than invasion-period (Goodburn 1972; Rigby 1978). Furthermore, an analysis of the samian ware shows that there was perhaps a period of abandonment between the brief military phase around 43 and the construction of the first phase of the villa (the 'proto-palace') in the 50s (Millett 1983a, 191–204). This brings into question the hypothesis that the site passed directly from military into civilian hands. We may therefore suggest that the military phase at Fishbourne was transitory and irrelevant to the villa, which was built here because the site lay within the *oppidum*. Such a locational link of villa, *oppidum* and *civitas* capital would directly parallel the Gorhambury–Verulamium pattern, so whilst continuity like this cannot be taken as evidence for the continuance

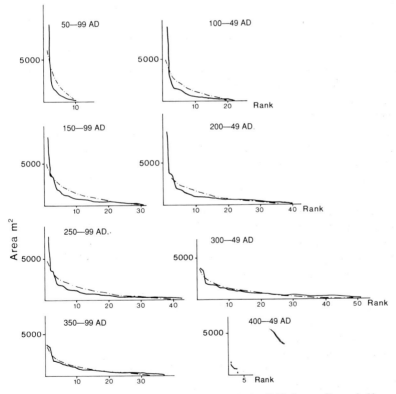

32 Rank-size graphs for villas in Roman Britain, divided according to half-century periods (after Gregson 1982a). (Note: the data on which this illustration, with figs. 33 and 49, are based comprised a full range of excavated sites from which dating evidence was available. Although the information is limited, the patterns shown seem unlikely to be altered radically. The villas are listed in Gregson (unpublished)).

of ownership it would be consistent with the overall model presented. The early villas should thus be seen as a result of the Romanization of the native élite; and the pattern of their distribution and development takes on an added significance by showing how the Roman system of power expressed through property was rapidly adopted in these areas.

It is often taken that the emergence of villas was the result of increased prosperity brought about by the *pax Romana*, which allowed the generation of profits which were spent on villa construction (Applebaum 1972, 223; Frere 1987, 258). The evidence of average villa size (fig. 33) is inconsistent with this hypothesis. The principal problem is that the early villas generally do not grow out of small establishments; instead they appear *de novo* at a substantial size. This implies that existing resources were being spent on their construction, rather than any newly accumulated wealth. This can be illuminated by two further points. First, the construction of a villa is evidence of expenditure, not production. Thus the villa represents the ability and desire of its owner to use resources on a new-style building which need not have been any more comfortable or practicable than the characteristic LPRIA timber house. The motive for the building was thus the desire to appear Romanized.

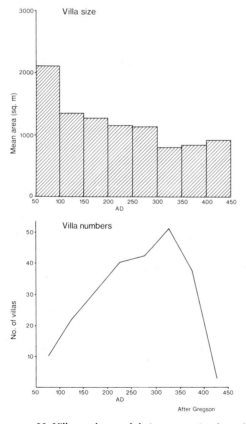

33 Villa numbers and their average size through time (after Gregson 1982a).

94

34 Air photograph of the LPRIA enclosure at The Ditches, Glos, part of the Bagendon *oppidum* complex (shown as 'enclosure' on fig. 7a). This enclosure, which was the focus of the *oppidum*, had a small villa constructed within it (*circled*) during the first century AD. This suggests that here the native élite were adapting to the new style of Roman status display. (*Photograph by courtesy of the Royal Commission on Historical Monuments.*)

Gregson (1982a) has taken this to indicate a change from communal land ownership to private property, since the expenditure represents the conversion of surplus production into a permanent, ultimately disposable form of wealth. Building in stone also changes the house to a durable asset which can be more certainly passed to the next generation. However valuable this insight, it is more likely that effective private control over land had begun to emerge well before the conquest with the division of land by boundaries and the definition of settlements by ditched enclosures. We might agree that villas confirm the emergence of private property, but the nature of the

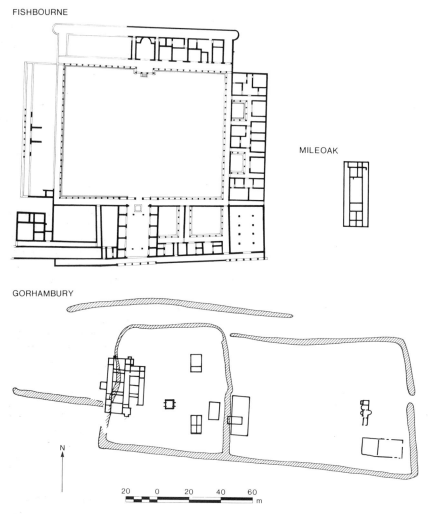

35 Comparative plans of three first-century AD villas in Britain, Fishbourne, Sussex, Mileoak, Northants and Gorhambury, Herts. Fishbourne contrasts with the others both in its scale and its design, which is highly Mediterranean in taste. Nevertheless, all are likely to have been built by members of the native aristocracy. Fishbourne lies within the Chichester Dykes, whilst Gorhambury overlies part of the enclosure system of the Verulamium *oppidum* (see fig. 7a).

system of ownership is open to question in view of J. T. Smith's comments about the dual tenancy of some villas (chapter 8). Villas may not have been possible without the existence of private property, but this probably existed before villas emerged.

Secondly, as villas are evidence of consumption not production, we should not expect a direct correlation between the productivity of the land upon which they are built and the resources expended in their construction. This is clearest on the continent where we know, for instance, of senators and other rich citizens who held land in several places and whose wealth is also likely to have come from sources such as booty from Rome's military conquests, tax farming or even trade (Garnsey and Saller 1987, 64–71). These citizens owned villas through which they expressed their wealth and status, yet an economic analysis of the territory of the attached 'home farms' would produce a wholly misleading indication of the owner's wealth. At the most extreme, Hadrian's villa at Tivoli is an expression of the wealth creamed off from the whole Empire, not its immediate hinterland.

In Britain we can see early villas as a display of wealth that was already in existence, whether collected through social control (tribute and later taxation), the exploitation of resources through agriculture or trade, or even the product of patronage and loans. Against this background we should not be surprised by King's (1978) and M. K. Jones' (1981) studies, which demonstrate a lack of fundamental agricultural change associated with the Roman invasion (fig. 36). Some new exotic crops were consumed, but

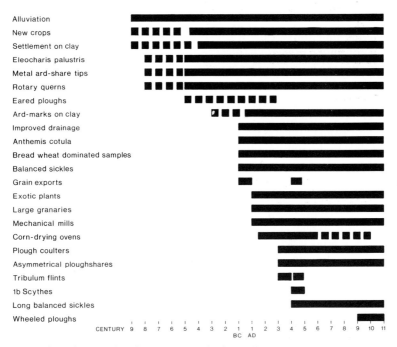

36 Evidence for agricultural innovation in the first millennia BC and AD. Both the major periods of change, in the LPRIA and the later Roman period, seem independent of the Roman invasion (after M. K. Jones 1981).

rural sites were extremely conservative in their production (Jones 1982, 103). The results of the Butser experiments have also demonstrated that LPRIA agriculture was potentially highly productive, so there was no clear requirement for changes to increase productivity following the conquest. Even the stimulus provided by an additional 10 per cent taxation is unlikely as such a burden could probably have been absorbed within existing margins (Millett 1984). Provided sufficient food resources were being produced there was actually a disincentive to change, as it would have been in the interests of those controlling the surplus to ensure first that the production supporting them was not threatened. The conservative farmer's reaction to this may have been to maintain, but perhaps intensify, the known system, rather than attempting something new, entailing possible risk. We should note that any increased requirement for production was often met in the Roman world through buying more land rather than improving what one had (J. Patterson, pers. comm.). The intensification of existing control over production is entirely consistent with the Romans working through the native élite. A comparison with recent episodes in the third world points to the value of this control in protecting farmers from the impact of the market economy. Without such protection the Roman invasion seems more likely to have led to damage to agriculture and not the stimulation so often postulated (Jones 1982; below, chapter 8).

Whilst the towns were beginning to emerge as the Romanized centres of the *civitates*, the élite who controlled them were also Romanizing their holdings in the countryside, exploiting their existing resources and strengthening their power base. Villas are therefore another indication of the transformation of the existing system rather than the superimposition of something new. Alongside the villas many of the farmsteads continued in the LPRIA tradition and seem to have flourished during the early years after the invasion. The majority of sites, indeed, show no sign of physical change so that without artefacts it is impossible to draw any distinction between the pre- and post-conquest periods (e.g. Fasham 1985).

The artefacts arriving on the sites do show a change, with a rapid phase of percolation of Roman objects on to the native sites very soon after the conquest, so that many sites in the south received, for instance, samian ware and brooches in the pre-Flavian period. In Sussex it has been noted that many of these items arrived early, before the towns had developed (Millett 1981). The types of artefact found in early contexts are frequently those, like Roman table wares, which had a high status in the LPRIA. This may suggest rapid commercial exploitation of the conquered territories with traders able to take advantage of the new market (Frere 1987, 281). However, the speed of the process which preceded the development of the towns in some areas suggests that goods were arriving through the existing social network. They thus act as a barium meal in medicine, acting transiently to make visible the normally invisible soft tissues, in this instance giving us a brief glimpse of the social organization of the conquered people. In this model the arrival of samian ware in quantity fulfilled a demand stimulated by the shortage before the conquest. Its previous rarity had made it a prestige good, unavailable down the social hierarchy and so used to define position within society. This demand was sated by increased supplies after the conquest, so it reached more of the population for a short period before its very abundance removed from it any vestige of status value. Thus by the Flavian period it had passed the peak of its popularity on the rural sites of the south-east. During this brief period of abundance it reached many rural sites which never developed into villas (Millett 1981), thus demonstrating that even by this stage they were integrated into a single socio-economic network and so cannot be dismissed as mere subsistence farms. Although less well documented, a similar pattern also seems to have occurred in some areas further north and west after the period of their conquest (cf. Heslop 1987, 73–6).

Synthesis

The evidence discussed in this chapter has been used to suggest that the *civitates* of Roman Britain emerged as an indirect consequence of the impact of Rome, and that they were not due to a set of deliberate acts of policy by the Roman authorities. Instead they developed from the previous framework through the impact of an essentially *laissez-faire* administration on native societies. Those already in power could thus gain or retain more by co-operation than by opposition. Retaining control, even if in a more circumscribed form, was preferable to losing it. The secret of Rome's success was that through devolution she was able to govern with minimal coercion. Difficulties undoubtedly arise in applying this model to areas of the west and particularly the north, where there is less evidence that native civil administration took root. If Romanization does hold the key to understanding the native structure, what differed in the north that led to its failure?

The answer does not simply lie in native organization. The areas with a more developed pre-conquest social hierarchy and a more centralized settlement pattern were assimilated more easily because in these societies power could be exercised through native authority. Nevertheless, in some areas, for instance north-east England and central Scotland, where nascent centralization was present in the LPRIA, Romanization does not succeed. Thus, although centres like Stanwick (Haselgrove and Turnbull 1987) or Traprain Law (Hanson 1987) begin to show characteristics seen in *oppida* further south (above, p. 23), they do not precede *civitas* centres. Groenman-van Waateringe (1980) has pointed to the importance of a strong native infrastructure and economy in areas where Romanization succeeded. Whilst we suspect that the economy of northern areas was weaker than the south, the differential seems insufficient to explain the differences we see.

The key may lie in the other side of the equation: Rome's failure to conquer the whole of Britain, together with the need to keep her army as far from the centre of power as possible (where it would represent a threat to the balance of power) resulted in a substantial force being based in northern England, southern Scotland and Wales when the frontiers were established. The failure of Rome to conquer the whole of Scotland was neither a failure of their military strength nor a defeat by the terrain (Hanson 1987, 151). The nature of the opposition must be the key, for Roman tactics were best adapted to an opposition which had centralized authority and which fought set-piece battles. The problem was that Scotland comprised small-scale societies which could not be defeated in a single battle and, like the Vietcong, chose to melt away to

Table 4.3. *Simplified model of Roman impact on native societies*

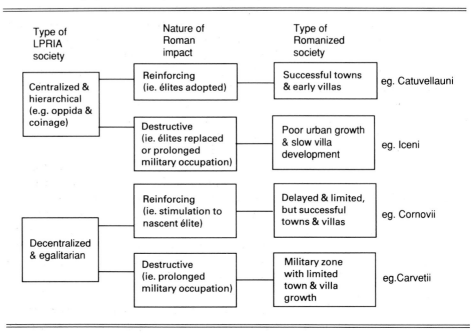

re-emerge elsewhere. This warfare was difficult for Rome as it engaged large numbers of troops and could not readily be brought to a positive conclusion. One may doubt whether, however long the Roman army had remained, a sufficiently centralized authority would have been found to enable a civil administration to take over. Rome had reached the limit of the type of social organization which she could incorporate. We may perhaps wonder whether Domitian was correct in his judgement, whilst Tacitus is misleading us by stating that 'Britain was conquered and then let slip' (*Histories* 1. 2).

The north-east was not exceptionally heavily garrisoned when first conquered, but only after the withdrawal from Scotland, when the frontier began to be developed (Breeze and Dobson 1985, figs. 2–5). Romanization had begun; if it had continued, it may have led to the emergence of a normal pattern of *civitas* administration as seen further south (Heslop 1987; Haselgrove and Turnbull 1987). Instead we suggest that the increase in the army garrison undermined the emergence of civil authority amongst the tribal élite. Careful consideration reveals that such an army of occupation usurped native control and destroyed the very process that Rome relied upon – government by a pro-Roman élite. Accordingly we suggest that it was the rapid move forward of the military in the south and east that led to the success of the later civil province.

Variation in this pattern can be seen in areas where Rome encountered military problems. Thus in the Civitas Icenorum, where revolts occurred in 47 and 60/61, there is little doubt that the Roman military presence subsequently disrupted the native power structure. This pattern of disruption may account for the absence of villas over much of the *civitas* (fig. 48) and for the poorly developed town which emerged as the *civitas* centre (Wacher 1975a, 227). This may equally result from an already decentralized pattern of power which characterized the LPRIA tribe. In contrast the Civitas Cornoviorum was subjected to a fairly long period of military presence before the establishment of the town (Webster 1987). This area has no early villas, but Wroxeter does show a healthy late Roman development. Although there is no evidence of deliberate Romanization of the kind dismissed above, the adaptation of the disused legionary fort as the site for the later town suggests that Rome passively helped in the establishment of that *civitas*. It is significant that the military disposition was designed not to dominate the Cornovii but to oversee either the adjacent Welsh tribes or the district's mineral resources (Hanson 1986). We can thus perhaps see an identity of interest which reinforced rather than undermined native authority in the emergent *civitas*. A similar explanation may be appropriate to the comparable pattern at Exeter. In both these cases we can postulate that the Roman presence was stimulating by passively encouraging the native élite and by vesting in it authority which brought it to a level where civil administration was possible. Throughout Britain there is a series of relationships between civil and military authority which explains some of the variability in the later development of the province (table 4.3).

In summary we can see the successful, Romanized areas as those where the native élite benefited from an alliance with Roman power. In some of these areas Romanization was entirely indigenous, in others it was stimulated by passive encouragement. However, Romanization failed in those areas where, through either warfare or continued military occupation, the Roman presence was socially disruptive.

Table 4.4. *Public towns as centres of administration*

(Names follow Rivet and Smith 1979 unless otherwise stated)

Town name	Modern name	LPRIA centre	Fort	Number of inscriptions showing munificence	Date of *forum*	References/notes
Coloniae, municipia, etc.						
Colonia Claudia Victricensis Camulodunensium (= Camulodunum)	Colchester	yes	yes	10	Unknown	Founded 49 *May* have acted as administrative centre of Civitas Trinovantorum*
Colonia [Domitiana] Lindensium	Lincoln	no	yes	6	Trajanic	Founded 90–96
Colonia Nervia Glevensium	Gloucester	no	yes	2	Trajanic?	Founded 96–98
Colonia Eburacensis (= Eburacum)	York	no	yes	25	Unknown	Promoted in early third century
Londinium	London	no	yes, secondary	10	Boudiccan gravel area; first building c. 80; main structure c. 100	Status uncertain
Verulamium	St Albans	yes	yes, shortlived	9	Dedicated 79	Presumed to have acted as centre of Civitas Catuvellaunorum
Civitas capitals						
Isurium Brigantum	Aldborough	?	yes	2	unknown	
Petuaria [Parisiorum]	Brough-on-Humber	no	yes	1	unknown	Preceded by LPRIA centre at North Ferriby
Venta Silurum	Caerwent	no	yes	4	early 2nd	
Venta Icenorum	Caistor-by-Norwich	?	no	4	early 2nd	Pottery perhaps suggests military phase (Swan 1984, 84)

Durnovernum Cantiacorum	Canterbury	yes	yes	1	unknown	
Luguvalium [Carvetiorum]	Carlisle	no	yes	12	unknown	Status as *civitas* centre uncertain
Moridunum [Demetarum]	Carmarthen	no	yes?	1	unknown	
Noviomagus Reg(i)norum	Chichester	yes	yes	8	unknown	Chichester Dykes are taken as LPRIA centre
Corinium Dobunnorum	Cirencester	no	yes	11	early 2nd (Fulford 1985)	Nearby Bagendon is LPRIA centre
Durnovaria [Durotrigum]	Dorchester (Dorset)	no	no?	—	unknown	Nearby Maiden Castle is LPRIA centre
Isca Dumnoniorum	Exeter	no	yes	—	timber? *c.* 80; stone early 2nd	
Lindinis Durotrigum	Ilchester	yes?	yes	—	unknown	Possible secondary centre promoted later on sub-division of *civitas*
Ratae Corieltauvorum	Leicester	yes	yes	1	Hadrianic-Antonine	For *civitas* name see Tomlin 1983
Calleva Atrebatum	Silchester	yes	yes?	20	first timber *c.* 55/65; second timber *c.* 80/90; stone *c.* 150	Fulford 1986
Venta Belgarum	Winchester	yes	yes	2	late 1st	LPRIA centre dated 1st century BC, so probable gap
Viroconium Cornoviorum	Wroxeter	no	yes	6	129–30	

*This is proposed since the alternative suggestion, that Chelmsford (Caesaromagus) was the centre is supported neither by the nature of its archaeology (Drury 1975) nor the sources (Antonine Itinerary and Ptolemy).

5

THE MATURITY

OF THE 'CIVITATES'

The *civitates* of Roman Britain developed at varying speeds and in different ways according to the impact of the Roman presence on their social systems. Despite these variations in the pattern of development there is a series of characteristics which typifies the British *civitates* to the early third century – through the period often seen as the Golden Age of the Empire. These characteristics define the nature of the whole province, but are most conveniently examined by taking separately the evidence of the towns, the countryside and the flows of goods between them.

The nature of the towns

The *civitas* centres are not generally richly provided with Romanized masonry structures, in particular public buildings, and although they developed as towns within a satisfactorily Roman mould during the second century (table 5.1), they have fewer public buildings than the cities of the Mediterranean. Although our understanding of the British towns is limited by the piecemeal archaeological evidence, which generally does not give a complete picture of any particular town, excavations over the past three decades have, nonetheless, provided evidence from a sufficient variety of sites to draw some sound conclusions. There are three types of evidence, excavated structures, the epigraphic material and, finally, the artistic material found at sites.

The structural evidence from the towns shows that most had been provided with a complete suite of public buildings by the end of the second century (table 5.1). However, the multiplicity of public buildings that has been discovered at some continental cities as a result of competitive munificence is largely absent. The British pattern, with the possible exception of London, probably results from a different social structure common to other of the northern provinces (above, p. 81), which led to an adequate, rather than an excessive, provision of facilities. Experience of the failure to complete over-ambitious building projects in other provinces led governors, including those of Britain, to exercise increasing control over civic extravagance from the late first century onwards (Garnsey and Saller 1987, 37). We should also note (table 4.2) that many British buildings have collective rather than individual dedications (fig. 37), which imply a less competitive society. This in itself limited the sort of munificence which led some towns in other provinces to be over-provided with public monuments. In addition, the size of the public buildings is comparatively modest in contrast with some other provinces, the most obvious explanation being a lack of wealth making extravagance impossible. Whilst this is plausible in part, it is equally likely to result from social organization limiting competitive pressures, since there is otherwise little evidence for poverty in the communities, within the towns themselves or in the investment in their defences.

Rarest in the British *civitas* capitals (table 5.1) are buildings associated with classical religion. Not only were classical temples absent from most *forum-basilica* complexes, but there are few signs of them in most cities (Lewis 1965, 57–72). Theatres, themselves associated with religious practice, are also less common in Britain than we might expect. This pattern contrasts with the ubiquity of the Romano-Celtic temples which do frequently occur in towns (fig. 83); indeed, at Silchester a

37 An inscription (*RIB* 707) which records the presentation of a new stage building for the theatre at Brough-on-Humber in AD 140–4. Such inscriptions recording individual benefactions are comparatively rare in Britain. The text reads
OB HONOR[EM] DOMUS DIVI[NAE] IMP(ERATORIS) CAES(ARIS) T(ITI) AEL(I) H[ADRI]ANI ANTONINI A[UG(USTI) PII] P(ATRIS) P(ATRIAE) CO(N)S(ULIS) I[II] ET NUMINIB(US) A[UG(USTORUM)] M[ARCUS] ULP(IUS) IANUAR[I]U[S] AEDILIS VICI PETU[AR(IENSIS)] PROSCAEN(IUM) [...] DE SUO [DEDIT]
Translated as: 'For the Honour of the Divine House of the Emperor Titus Aelius Hadrianus Antoninus Angustus Pius [i.e. Antoninus Pius], father of his country, three times Consul, and to the Deities of the Emperors, Marcus Ulpius Januarius, magistrate of the community of Petuaria [i.e. Brough], presented this [new] stage building at his own expense.' (*Photograph by courtesy of Hull City Museums.*)

105

Table 5.1. Known public buildings in major towns

Town	Forum/ basilica	Amphitheatre	Theatre	Aqueduct	Baths	Mansio	Sewers	Temples	Triumphal arch	Status
Aldborough					x					Civitas capital
Brough-on-Humber			x							Civitas capital
Caerwent	x	x		x	x	x	x	x		Civitas capital
Caistor-by-Norwich	x			x	x		x	x		Civitas capital
Canterbury	x		x		x		x	x		Civitas capital
Carlisle								x		Civitas capital
Carmarthen		x			x					Civitas capital
Chichester	x	x			x		x	x		Civitas capital
Cirencester	x	x		x	x		x	x		Civitas capital
Colchester	x		x				x	x		Colonia
Dorchester (Dorset)	x	x								Civitas capital
Exeter	x				x					Civitas capital
Gloucester	x			x	x			x		Colonia
Ilchester										Civitas capital
Leicester	x			x	x		x	x		Civitas capital
Lincoln	x			x	x		x	x		Colonia
London	x	x		x	x			x		Uncertain
Silchester	x	x		x	x	x	x	x		Civitas capital
Verulamium	x		x	x	x		x	x	x	Municipium
Winchester	x				x			x		Civitas capital
Wroxeter	x			x	x		x	x		Civitas capital
York	x			x	x		x	x		Colonia

Source: based on Carver 1987 with additions.

cluster inside the East Gate is respected by the street grid (Insula XXX) (Boon 1974, 152ff), so this sanctuary is probably of LPRIA origin. Similar patterns may be postulated for the theatre/temple complexes at Verulamium (fig. 23) (Frere 1983, 73–4), at the Gosbecks site, Colchester (Dunnett 1971, fig. 5; Haselgrove 1987a, 380) and at Canterbury (Bennett 1984, 51ff), although the present evidence is weak. These religious sanctuaries were perhaps originally related to the LPRIA centres of power (especially at Verulamium, where the sanctuary lay beside what may have been an élite compound (above, p. 77). If proven, this pattern emphasizes the distinctive character of some of the British cities and illustrates how the public buildings may be used to understand the social organization of the citizens.

The towns also show a characteristic pattern of housing with substantial, stone-built private houses generally absent until into the second century (Walthew 1975; Perring 1987), well after villas had begun to be built in this style (fig. 33). Instead, most private urban housing comprised rectangular timber and clay buildings, which often combined the functions of house, shop and workshop. These structures are Romanized but appear utilitarian rather than status display oriented (fig. 40). Evidence is limited because few excavations have examined these buildings on a sufficient scale, but examples seen in Verulamium Insula XIV (Frere 1972) and in London (Roskams 1980; Perring 1981) indicate that their town centres were vibrant and dynamic economic entities during the later first and second centuries. More fragmentary evidence from centres like Chichester (Down 1978), Canterbury (Bennett 1984) and Leicester (Clay and Mellor 1985) support this conclusion about the character of the *civitas* centres in the High Empire. The buildings show the commercial character of these towns, with the impression of economic vitality given by their close spacing and in some cases their relatively long plots perpendicular to the street (e.g. Perring 1987, fig. 65), which imply that frontage space was at a premium. This pattern of closely packed unpretentious houses and workshops is essentially what we should expect in economically successful urban communities (cf. Platt 1976).

The problem remains of identifying the housing of the élite who controlled these towns and provided their public buildings. Substantial stone town houses have not been found and only in London have more 'bourgeois' early imperial houses been noted (Perring 1987, 150). Unless we accept that the social stratification was not reflected in housing, we must seek the rich elsewhere. Given the evidence from the villas (fig. 33), we should probably conclude that the curial classes continued to live in the countryside until at least the mid-second century (Walthew 1975, 204). This rural evidence need not have prevented them also playing their leadership rôles in the towns. From the later second century, there is an increase in the number of more substantial town houses which surely signify the residence of an urban élite.

Within the Roman Empire the competitive system in which this élite participated is reflected in the epigraphic record, with those participating advertising their munificence on dedicatory inscriptions both on buildings and items such as statues, which traditionally adorned the public places of Roman towns. Britain is remarkably short of such dedications, but geographical patterning is betrayed by the surviving evidence. Figure 26 maps all urban dedicatory inscriptions which are not demonstrably military, on the assumption that the bulk date to the early Empire. This shows that almost

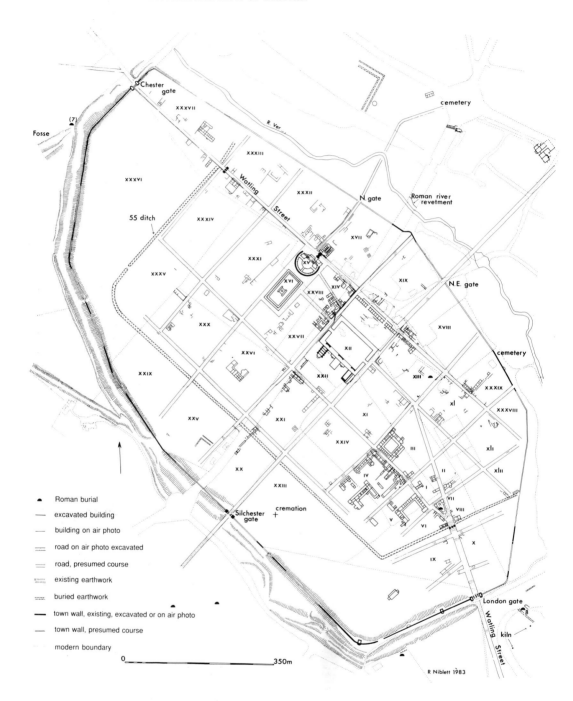

38 Plan of Verulamium based on excavated and air photographic evidence.
Illustration by courtesy of Mrs R. Niblett, Verulamium Museum.)

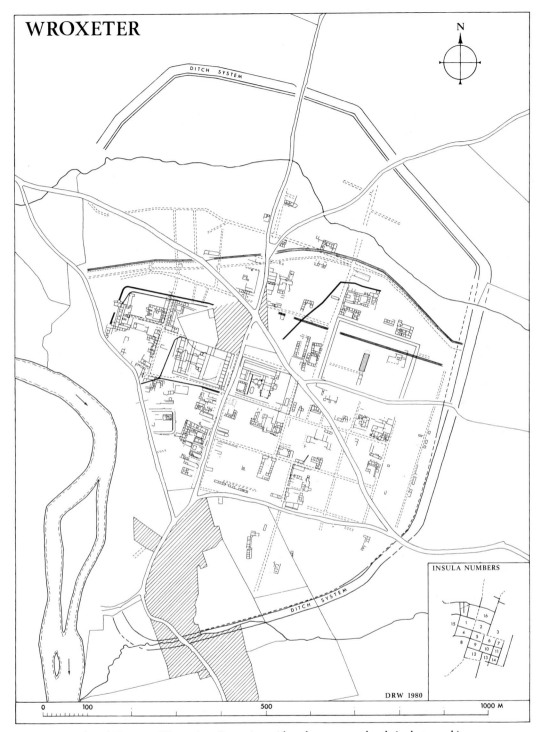

WROXETER

N

DITCH SYSTEM

DITCH SYSTEM

DRW 1980

INSULA NUMBERS

15	1	16		
	4	2	3	
8	5	6	7	
	9	10	11	
	12	13	14	

0   100   500   1000 M

39 Plan of Wroxeter (Viroconium Cornoviorum) based on excavated and air photographic evidence. Some of the air photographic plotting is perhaps subject to distortion, whilst some features can only be interpreted tentatively. (*Illustration by courtesy of D. R. Wilson, Cambridge University Dept. of Aerial Photography.*)

Table 5.2. *Categories/places of origin of people recorded on Bath inscriptions*

	Military	Civilian	Unspecified
	3 × *VI Victrix* (York)	1 × Trier	
	2 × *II Augusta* (Caerleon)	1 × Chartres	
	3 × *XX Valeria Victrix* (Chester)	1 × Gloucester	
	1 × *II Aduitrix* (Chester)	1 × Metz	
	1 × *ala Vettonum* (Binchester)	2 × priests	
	1 × *Centurio Regionarius*	1 × freedwoman	
Total	11 (27.5%)	7 (17.5%)	22 (55%)

all of the Small Towns (below) and most of the *civitas* capitals are poorly represented. Nevertheless, some sites in the north have respectable numbers, although these are convincingly associated with the military, even when this is not explicit (Mann 1985b, 206). London and the *coloniae* have reasonable numbers of inscriptions as do the capitals of some of the more developed *civitates*, together with Bath – really a rural sanctuary rather than a town. Despite intensive archaeological exploration and its wealth of inscriptions nothing supports the identification of a self-governing urban community, so we should thus see the settlement as a spa and religious complex. The associated commercial settlement is small and has no known administrative status (Cunliffe and Davenport 1985, fig. 3; Greene 1975). Furthermore, the inscriptions from the site demonstrate that the springs and temples were largely supported by a metropolitan and military clientele rather than one drawn from the local population (*RIB passim*). Mann (1985b, 206) has however pointed out that most Romano-British dedications which state the donor's origin were gifts by non-locals. In the case of Bath bias is unlikely, given the comparatively large number of dedications and the few anonymous stones which may have been dedicated by locals (table 5.2).

The distribution of inscriptions amongst the *civitas* capitals relates neither very closely to the availability of building stone nor to the apparent distribution of either LPRIA or Roman wealth. We are thus seeing an independent phenomenon, related either to the desire and need of individuals to take part in the system of Romanized status competition or the extent of the 'epigraphic habit' (MacMullen 1982). It is not that the British élites were necessarily less literate than provincials elsewhere in the Empire. There is good evidence of literacy provided by graffiti (Evans 1987), the evidence of spoken latin (Mann 1971, 219) and the presence of writing implements on a wide variety of sites. Furthermore, the absence of monumental inscriptions in a literate province like Britain must be seen as a feature demanding explanation.

We have argued that the dedications provide evidence for the absence of substantial social competition in the British *civitates* as power was concentrated in a limited number of families. Following this argument, the distribution of dedications indicating public munificence (fig. 26) maps the distribution not of wealth but of the more hierarchical social systems in which there was an impetus to compete. In some cases, like the *coloniae* and London, this was probably generated by the presence of those from outside the social system who had a greater need to establish their positions through such competitive processes than did the members of the indigenous élites whose position was embedded in native tradition. This interpretation would be entirely consistent with Mann's observations (1985b, 206) that most dedications giving origins were made by such outsiders.

These factors alone suggest that the character of the towns was not entirely a function of the stamp of imperialism (cf. Reece 1985, 38), but is an expression of different native and Roman aspirations: urban settlements must be seen as active in these social systems, not as a pale reflection of them. Variation is most notable in the differences in the scale of the *civitas* centres as shown by the enclosed areas of the defended towns (fig. 59). Although such circuits do not invariably enclose the whole of the settlement (Esmonde-Cleary 1987) and the density of occupation within them is variable, the size of the enclosures provides a reasonable measure of the wealth, power and aspirations of the communities concerned (Fulford and Startin 1984), whether or not they provide evidence for civic pride (chapter 6). The variation is considerable and demonstrates that, despite the widespread adoption of the urban habit, only in the *civitates* of the midlands and south-east was any level of urbanization reached. In the north, east and south-west its development was very limited. This defines that distribution of social systems in which urban centres were important; those where competition for *Romanitas* was marked and where centralized exchange became important. The pattern which emerges provides an interesting comparison with that of the LPRIA and illustrates the impact of the process of conquest and subsequent change particularly well.

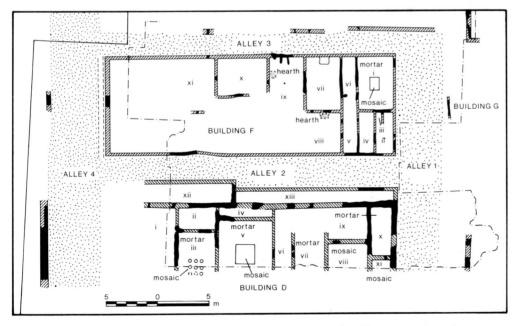

40 Two early Roman urban buildings at Watling Court in London. These structures, used as houses, workshops and shops, although unprepossessing are characteristic of the economically vibrant public towns of the first–second century (after Perring 1987).

Art and Romanization

The urban evidence can be taken to indicate an absence of aspirations towards Romanization in Britain. This conclusion has often been drawn on the basis of the province's art which has been condemned for the poverty of its artistic achievement. R. G. Collingwood (Collingwood and Myres 1937, 247–60), the most eloquent exponent of this view, interpreted it as a result of the Roman suppression of the artistic skills which had been so manifest in the art of the LPRIA (fig. 5) (Fox 1958). The concept of the Celtic character being alien to Roman expression has been developed by Reece (1979b), who has related the flowering of Celtic art of the pre- and post-Roman periods to times of social stress, when ethnic characteristics were accentuated through the process by which competing communities reinforced their identities (Hodder 1982). Such a framework accounts for the excellence of Celtic expression in the LPRIA (figs. 10 and 11) and the early medieval periods, but does little to explain the character of the material from the Roman which lacks the same confidence (figs. 41–7). Collingwood's explanation, involving the encapsulation of Celtic identity (1939, 138–45), in which its expression was driven underground or back into the artists' psyche, is intellectually satisfying but difficult to substantiate archaeologically.

41 Head of a statue of Mercury from the Temple at Uley, Glos. The statue is an acceptable Roman-style carving produced by a competent sculptor. (*Photograph by courtesy of the British Museum.*)

112

The problem common to these approaches is that they fail to distinguish craftsmen from patrons. LPRIA craftsmen produced a series of object types which fulfilled the requirements of their patrons and supported their social rôles (table 2.6). The medium used was thus dictated not by the artists' choice, but by the context within which the objects were to be used. Most of the surviving material is of high social status, the property of a limited section of society. The abstract designs of Celtic art may thus be seen as a system of symbols associated with the status-defining activities, principally warfare and horsemanship, through which the power of the élite was expressed. In the Romanized province traditional patrons (together with incomers) made new types of demand on the artists as the modes of expression of power changed in two major ways. First, the artistic media were altered as Rome forbade the bearing of arms in public (*Lex Julia de vi publica*; *Digest* 48. 6, 1 and 3), so that status competition through the display of arms was impossible: martial equipment had been one of the principal vehicles of LPRIA art. Romanized expressions of social dominance also replaced military display as the social pressures on the élite to appear Roman increased. The new artistic media, including buildings, statuary, small objects and later mosaics thus became vital replacements for the symbols of LPRIA society. As the forms changed so timber buildings, which Glastonbury suggests could have been laden with decorative symbols (Bulleid and Gray 1911), were replaced by more robust

42 Tombstone (*RIB* 200) of M. Favonius Facilis, a centurion of the XXth Legion, found at Colchester, Essex. The stone probably predates the destruction of the site by Boudicca in AD 60/61. It is characteristic of military tombstones, and is executed with competence in a naturalistic style. (*Photograph by courtesy of Colchester and Essex Museum.*)

structures. Stone buildings were constructed and adorned with more permanent decoration. These materials required novel techniques and some artists are known to have arrived from continental provinces bringing with them new styles which altered the British repertoire (Blagg 1980; 1984). The boom in production of small objects which followed the conquest devalued them as status symbols. By the second century the large numbers of small decorative items which survive were available for the first time through a much broader spectrum of site types (cf. Fulford 1982).

The results of the Romanization of art in Britain are not particularly unsatisfactory although they are often unclassical. Although the criteria for establishing such classicism are extremely subjective, Lingren's (1980) study of figurative art from Britain supports this conclusion. *The* characteristic of Roman imperial art is its metropolitan mix (Brendel 1979) and its lack of stylistic unity. Judging Romano-British material by the standards of Graeco-Roman realism (fig. 41) thus fails to take account of this essential point (Phillips 1977), since the objects from Britain need to be compared with those from other peripheral provinces. This would establish not

43 Tombstone found at Chester (*RIB* 491). It is dedicated to M. Aurelius Nepos, a centurion of the XXth Legion *Valeria Victrix*, and his unnamed wife. The stone is in the regular form with the figures in a niche, but the style is distinctly unclassical. The treatment is not naturalistic, but the shapes of the figures and their clothing are used as a medium to develop abstract qualities. (*Photograph by courtesy of the Corinium Museum.*)

44 Relief carving from Cirencester showing three mother goddesses. The stylization of the layout and dress allow the abstract qualities of the presentation to complement the classical, naturalistic idea. (*Photograph by courtesy of the Corinium Museum.*)

45 Relief carving (*CSIR* 1/2, no. 38) from Bath showing three mother goddesses. The highly abstract stylization of this piece completely overshadows its classical form. (*Photograph by courtesy of Bath Museum Service.*)

115

only the artistic canons of the producers and the ways in which they adapted to the new styles but also the cultural aspirations of their patrons.

That many of the artistic achievements of Roman Britain appear poor by any modern aesthetic standard says more about our inability to read their symbols than about their artistic competence or their patrons' taste. It is clear, for instance, that the person commissioning a Roman-style tombstone (figs. 42–3) was betraying his *Romanitas* by that choice rather than by the quality of the end product or its approxi-

46 Relief of Venus and two nymphs from High Rochester, Northumberland (*CSIR* 1/1, no. 218). The subject of this sculpture is classical but the female form betrays a native perception of beauty which contrasts with the classical (cf. fig. 80). (*Photograph by courtesy of the University of Newcastle upon Tyne.*)

47 The mosaic from Room 7 of the villa at Sparsholt, Hants. The design is assigned to the Central Southern School of mosaicists (fig. 72), and its abstract style is characteristic of later Roman mosaics in Britain, showing a confidence of execution absent from most stone sculpture but reminiscent of the designs used in LPRIA metalwork (figs. 5, 10 and 11). (*Photograph by J. Erskine by courtesy of D. E. Johnston.*)

116

Table 5.3. *Figural art in Roman Britain (percentage in brackets)*

Period	Classical style	Fusion of Celtic & classical styles
First century	2 (40)	3 (60)
Second century	22 (54)	19 (46)
Third/fourth century	7 (29)	17 (71)

Source: Lingren 1980.

mation to the Graeco-Roman ideal. Similarly, the consistency in style in some of the Romano-British sculptures (Phillips 1977) – albeit unsatisfactory to our eyes – shows that the product was acceptable to both artist and patron and should be examined on its own terms to obtain an understanding of the canons of Romano-British art (figs. 44–6). In some stone sculpture, for instance, the treatment of clothing tends towards the abstract (Phillips 1977) and is reminiscent of the interest in shape shown in indigenous LPRIA art (Fox 1958). This continuity of abstract expression in the new media later flowers in Romano-British mosaics (fig. 47).

We can therefore discern an important pattern, with classical models used for the art of the province, demonstrating that élite patrons (who held power in the *civitates*) were attempting to express themselves in Roman form during the Early-High Empire. Table 5.3 indeed suggests that the impetus towards the more classical expressions of *Romanitas* was most marked in this period, with a shift back towards the more abstract in the later period. This parallels the rapid Romanization revealed by the villas (fig. 33) and perhaps emphasizes the enhanced status attached to *Romanitas* in the early Empire. In this way Roman style itself came to define prestige in early imperial Britain.

By this measure Romanization had firmly taken root, even if the quality of the art produced in response to patrons' demands was perhaps lacking. This quality illustrates that the models were seen through eyes not attuned to classical thought processes and thus unable to discern the qualities which distinguish classical expression (fig. 46). It is thus unreasonable to condemn the Romanized art of Britain as 'not merely the common vulgar ugliness of the Roman Empire, but a blundering, stupid ugliness that cannot even rise to the level of that vulgarity' (Collingwood and Myres 1937, 250). By analogy with the religious fusion (Henig 1984), we should instead see it as an *interpretatio celtiana*.

The rural patterns

The interrelationships between the towns and the Romanized parts of the countryside have already been stressed. During the second and early third centuries we see this mutual dependency reinforced with a steady increase in the number of villas, at the same time that they spread into areas further from the towns and decrease in average size (figs. 32, 33 and 49). This pattern shows the spread of Romanization down the social hierarchy as more of those with the wealth available chose to express their aspirations through the construction of villa buildings. Even so, the villas remained a numerically minor part of the settlement system, far outnumbered by other types of rural site. The pattern of their distribution is not even, and their spatial dependency on the minor towns remains (chapter 8). This evidence is consistent with the suggestion that the tribal élites who controlled the *civitates* were the owners of these villas, since we have already seen that houses appropriate to their status were not present in the towns until the later second century.

48 Map of Roman Britain showing the distribution of villas in relation to the *civitates*. Filled triangles are certain villas, open symbols probable villas. (*After the Ordnance Survey map of 1978.*)

There are clear variations in the regional pattern with a strong general correlation between the more successful towns and the villas (fig. 48). There are also some contradictions, for instance Dorchester (Dorset) lacks evidence of urban success (Wacher 1975a), but is surrounded by a group of villas. In contrast, there is no significant villa cluster around Exeter despite its similar size and level of urbanization. These variations are potentially informative about the social and economic systems of the different *civitates* (Rivet 1969), although the detailed evidence for villa growth, size and distribution collected by Gregson (1982a; unpublished) is insufficient to sustain detailed comparison between *civitates*. Within the pattern of a regularly increasing number of villas from the first to mid-third centuries, those *civitates* which had witnessed an early growth of substantial villas saw a slowing down in their rate of increase, while others caught up. Thus the distribution pattern in areas where villas were most common was fully established by the middle of the third century (fig. 33).

The significance of this pattern demands careful assessment in relation to the whole population, for although important as élite residences they are limited in number, and numerically far less significant than previous commentators have suggested (chapter 8). The villas that developed are best interpreted as a result of the Roman aspirations of their owners and not agricultural change. Whilst the villas were growing we also see a detectable change in other aspects of rural settlement with LPRIA-style farmsteads in some areas like Surrey and Suffolk showing a decline during the second and third centuries (Applebaum 1953, 124). This may reflect a shift away from enclosed settlements to site types less easily detected by archaeology, although better adapted to the

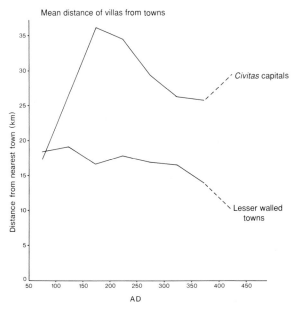

49 Chronological changes in the mean distance of villas from towns in Roman Britain (after Gregson 1982a).

pax Romana. It is also possible that such a change masks the beginning of a shift to the more nucleated pattern discernible later (chapter 8). Without further detailed survey evidence we can substantiate neither hypothesis.

The bulk of the countryside nevertheless still shows a strong continuity from the LPRIA, with even the major planned field-systems of South Yorkshire and Nottinghamshire (fig. 50) now shown to be Iron Age in origin and not the result of significant landscape alterations under Roman influence (Riley 1980; Hayes 1981). Not only is the proportion of the landscape occupied by villas small, but localized variations in density are apparently normal. Thus, the substantial tracts of countryside without known villas should be seen as a result of the normal pattern of landscape variation, the consequence of a continuance of traditional landholding and building patterns; it is the presence rather than the absence of villas which demands explanation.

Land unoccupied by villas has often been identified as part of imperial estates, with the Fenland and Salisbury Plain generally identified as such (Collingwood and Myres 1937, 224; Richmond 1955, 130–1). The arguments upon which these identifications are based are weak as we see if we examine the Fenland example. The proposal that this area represents an imperial estate was put forward by Richmond (1955, 130–1) and developed by Salway (1970), who argued that the large scale of the land reclamation operation with drainage, artificial waterways and roads was indicative of the hand of government. The nature of the settlements, consisting of farmsteads rather than villas, was taken to show that the land was imperially owned and let to tenants. The presence of salt working, assumed to be an imperial monopoly (Salway 1970, 10), and the fact that virgin land automatically belonged to the emperor, supported this hypothesis. Pottery evidence (Hartley and Hartley 1970) showed an expansion of settlement in the first half of the second century, which led to the suggestion that Hadrian was responsible for initiating the reclamation (Potter and Jackson 1982, 118) during his visit to Britain in 122 (Salway 1981, 190). This has been related to his personal interest in land reclamation in other provinces (Frere 1987, 268). On the basis of this interpretation the stone tower at Stonea in the central fens is 'interpreted as an administrative centre for some or all of the region' (Potter and Jackson 1982, 118).

This identification of land as an imperial estate poses several problems beyond those of identifying land ownership already mentioned (chapter 4). First, although such estates were lands held by the emperor, there is no reason to suppose that they are archaeologically distinguishable from land owned by others. Crawford's discussion (1976) of the literary and epigraphic evidence for imperial estates shows a variety of methods of administration with nothing to lend support to the hypothesis that they were devoid of villas (Salway 1970, 10). The only sound evidence for such estates in Britain comprises the inscriptions from the villas at Combe Down, near Bath (*RIB* 179) and Clanville, Hants (*RIB* 98). The interpretation of both is open to doubt as the latter may be a milestone whilst the former could relate to quarrying (Frere 1987, 267). Secondly, if the virgin land was reclaimed for the emperor, we might expect it to have been evenly divided up by centuriation (e.g. Greene 1986, 121). The absence of such regularity and the presence of an essentially organic system of field boundaries (fig. 50) cannot be satisfactorily explained in terms of the topography (cf.

Salway 1981, 189) and is a strong argument against official organization of the reclamation.

There can be little doubt that native social organization was sufficiently developed for the reclamation to have been undertaken by the local community during a period of lowering sea levels. The dislocation of the settlement patterns and the establishment of evenly distributed new sites as the result of imperial activity does not occur. Instead we see organic growth more consistent with a progressive expansion of settlement after the colonization of the newly reclaimed land (fig. 51) (Hodder and Orton 1976, 86–9). Finally, evidence of salt production is now widely known at other coastal locations (de Brisay and Evans 1975), making it inconceivable that its production was an imperial monopoly in Britain.

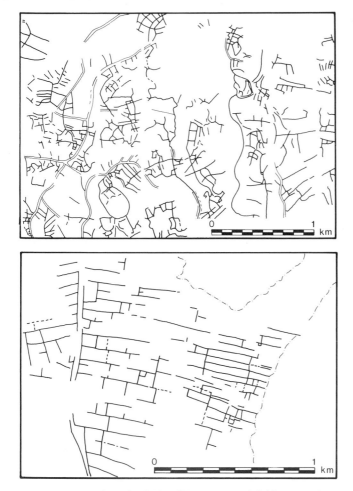

50 Comparative plans of LPRIA and Romano-British field systems. An organic pattern of small early Roman fields and trackways (*upper*) is seen in the Fenland (after Salway 1970). In contrast the layout of rectangular fields in South Yorkshire (*lower*) illustrates a more organized system of land allotment established around the end of the LPRIA (after Riley 1980).

121

Recent studies of the settlement pattern show that landscapes dominated by fields and farmsteads largely without villas are not unusual in areas like Hampshire (Cunliffe 1973a), the Thames valley (Benson and Miles 1974), the north-east (Clack and Haselgrove 1981) and elsewhere (Miles 1982b). The Fenland is only exceptional in the quality of the evidence recorded in that it represents one of the best examples of

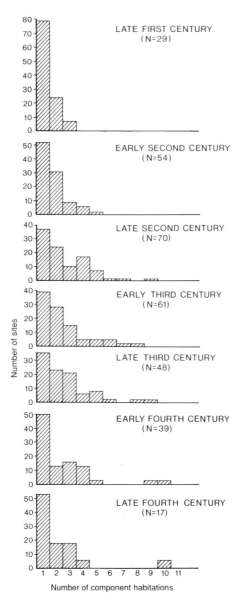

51 The changing size of settlements in the Fenland through the Roman period (data from Salway 1970).

an ordinary Romano-British landscape in an area away from towns of high administrative status (below, p. 190).

Economic interrelationships and control

Our observations of the settlement system suffer from the problem that interrelationships between sites were dynamic, whilst the archaeological data are static. It is only possible to reconstruct anything of the relationships between sites through the distribution of materials which can be related to past economies. Work on these distribution patterns has enabled progress to be made in establishing how settlement sites were serviced by the towns. Most of this work has been concentrated on pottery distributions, and although we must beware of assuming it is a sufficient indicator of these processes, it does provide some useful measure of the areas served by some centres (chapter 7).

Most pottery was a low-value commodity, so it is generally only likely to have travelled over comparatively short distances, as a result of frequent contacts between consumers and the point of supply. Since kiln sites in the Early to High Empire were generally located comparatively close to the towns (fig. 52), we may assume that their products were distributed through them. These pottery distributions may thus represent one level of contact between the towns and their adjacent countryside although this area of contact was generally localized (fig. 53), with few distribution areas covering a radius of more than 15 km (Hodder 1974b) from the towns. It is important to note that the distribution areas are similar in size for the settlements below the rank of the *civitas* centres (the so-called Small Towns). These were beginning to develop as important foci in the second and third centuries (chapter 6), although they only rise to prominence later. Their focal positions in some small-scale distributions illustrate their rôle as economic centres and, as they are indistinguishable from the *civitas* centres in the size of the areas they served, they need to be differentiated from them using other criteria (chapter 6). The network of local distribution is only one of a series of interlocking and overlapping patterns with higher-quality pottery and materials being brought from further afield, either through the same distribution centre, or by occasional visits to larger centres or from itinerant pedlars or periodic fairs. We are unable fully to assess these mechanisms in the absence of sufficient data, but throughout the High Empire the British *civitates* remained heavily dependent on imported goods. This is clearly demonstrated by the ubiquity of samian ware (fig. 54) and the quality of materials which arrived in London (fig. 53) (Green 1980), although as a port it certainly received more of such goods than other centres like Chelmsford (Going 1987). By the middle of the second century this trade was beginning to decline and with this London itself began to change in character.

Larger-scale distributions like that of samian ware were less heavily centred on the towns than might be expected. This indicates an ample sufficiency of supplies and so the demands of any consumer could be filled. Where these objects were not being received the deficiency was of demand, not supply. Thus, in areas like Brigantia, where we have a notable lack of Romanized goods on rural sites, one can postulate a disjunction between the native farmers and the Romanized élite and army. The areas which were reached by items such as samian pottery had Roman aspirations and were integrated within the economic and social system of the province, even though their settlements may not have developed into villas. Such integration need not have been entirely within the sphere of free market forces (cf. Peacock and Williams 1986, 54–66), for we have no reason to believe that economic relationships were free from social controls. In this regard the identity between the *civitas* organization and social groupings is of the utmost importance for two reasons.

First, we may assume that the *civitas* élite exercised close control over marketing and other productive activities. Such economic control is a common feature of pre-industrial societies and is well attested in the Roman world (MacMullen 1970; Mann pers. comm.). Elsewhere in the Empire rights to hold markets were jealously guarded, because of the profits to be gained and power which could be maintained through that control. Written evidence for this economic control is scarce, although we should

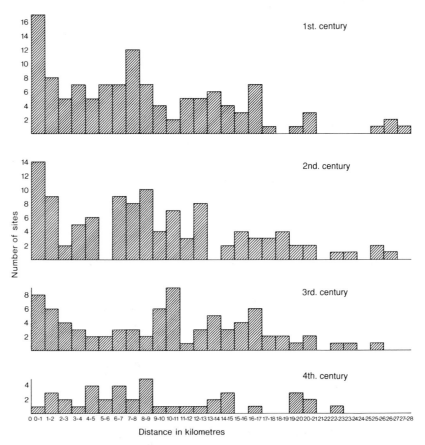

52 The changing pattern of the location of pottery kilns in Roman Britain. The distance of each kiln-site from the nearest Roman town is shown. Whilst there is a reduction in the total number of production sites through time, those furthest from towns are the least affected by the trend. This suggests that industries located away from towns were the more successful (after Saunders 1986; data from Swan 1984).

124

recall the factors which generally constrained Roman writers from discussing economic matters (Finley 1973). The scarcity of evidence should not therefore lead us to underestimate its importance.

Secondly, the centralizing power within the *civitates* in the High Empire seems reinforced by the system of taxation which compelled contact between the citizens of a *civitas* and its centre. Both the land tax (*tributum soli*) and the poll tax (*tributum capitis*) were assessed by census and payable by each *civitas*. The local administration was thus personally responsible for its collection from the citizens and its delivery to the administration (Jones 1974; Mann 1985a). These taxes were due in cash, and presumably collected centrally in the *civitates* in the same way that the census was con-

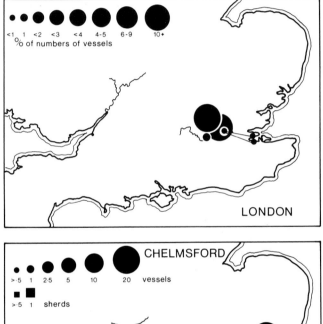

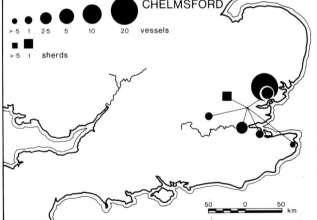

53 The origins of pottery supplied to London and Chelmsford in the later first century AD. In addition to the British products, about 50 per cent of the pottery at London and 10 per cent at Chelmsford came from overseas (after Going 1987 and Green 1980).

125

ducted there. This had two major effects: first, it would have strengthened the power of the magistrates and the corporate identity of the *civitas* by enforcing contact between the centre and its citizens; secondly, it would have enhanced the economic relationships by buttressing the supremacy of the *civitas* centre and encouraging its development as the main economic focus, thereby stimulating its economic growth. This probably accounts for the economic success of these towns. Such a process certainly suggests that the *civitas* centres undertook functions which reinforced their social and legal rôles, and enhanced the power of their ruling élites.

Although subsidiary centres fulfilled a local marketing function (below, p. 153), there is no doubt that the *civitas* capitals were nodal in the High Empire. Their dominance was achieved through a combination of social control, administrative convenience and geographical inertia. These centralizing factors were surely as important in the success of the towns as any postulated act of deliberate policy. Nevertheless we may doubt whether the controls envisaged stimulated new economic development. Successful control of existing wealth seems unlikely to have stimulated innovation or economic change. Thus, whilst these processes allowed the *civitas* capitals their heyday in the Antonine period, there was already a series of new developments beginning which point to emergent contradictions and internal stresses. Thus in the Golden Age the seeds of change within the system had already been sown.

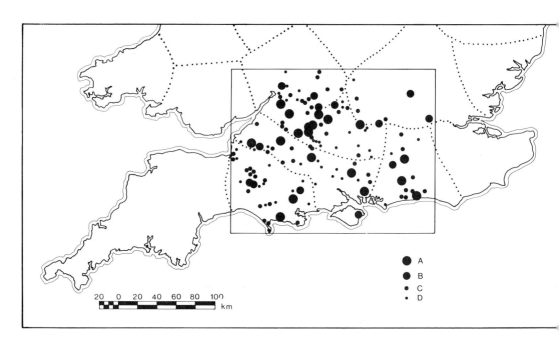

54 The distribution of samian ware in central southern England (based on unpublished data collected by Ian Hodder). The scale is: A = 15%+ of all pottery; B = 9–15%; C = 3–9%; D = less than 3%. Note the widespread and dense distribution, and the failure of major towns to have larger quantities of samian than the other sites. The pattern suggests a saturated distribution system.

6

DEVELOPMENT

AT THE PERIPHERY

The climate of change

By the end of the second century, although a backwater of the Empire, Britain had become a Romanized province. However, the whole Empire had also begun to alter in character and in the following century change accelerated and became more evident to contemporaries. As these processes intensified they were perceived as a crisis: the hitherto stable world was transformed rapidly and unpredictably, as the Golden Age of the second century was replaced by the anarchy of the third (Jones 1973; Brown 1971). The character of much of the archaeological evidence also develops into the pattern characteristic of the later Empire, although it is far from clear precisely how these alterations relate to those referred to in the historical sources. In this chapter the historical processes are outlined first to provide the background. The archaeological evidence is then discussed in relation to the historical changes defined.

When the frontiers of the Empire began to ossify, the structure of the Empire mutated and the internal dynamics of its economy changed radically. The imperial structure had evolved with a reliance on territorial growth, which was fundamental to the social, economic and political system. Territorial expansion fulfilled the aspirations of the élite by providing the military glory on which careers were built; its continuation kept the army active and outward looking, whilst conquest provided a source of wealth through booty (even though this probably did not outweigh the cost of conquest, its impact was tangible for the beneficiaries) (Hopkins 1978).

The end of expansion was not sudden and did not have an immediately catastrophic impact, although it did create a series of stresses which exaggerated the internal contradictions already evident in the structure of the Empire. These form the background to the changes perceived by contemporaries and their resolution results in the emergence of the Late Antique world out of the third-century crisis (Brown 1971).

The economic and social changes may be briefly summarized (table 6.2). First, the distribution of wealth and expenditure had begun to change. In the early Empire, the bulk of taxation was raised from the heartland of the Empire (Hopkins 1980), but since the army, whose pay was the largest single item of imperial expenditure, was located on its fringes, there was a net outflow of wealth from the core to the periphery. This outflow was partially reclaimed, principally by trade in goods from the centre to the frontiers recovering some of the cash (Hopkins 1980). Other returns to the centre comprised interest on loans made to provincials, sometimes at extortionate rates of interest (cf. Badian 1968, 83–4), and perhaps also wealth accumulated by those from the core holding land in the provinces and transferring earnings from it to the centre. The scale of the return flow of wealth to the heartlands is difficult to assess, but in extreme cases (suggested by the Republican analogies) they may have been substantial. Nonetheless, the general effect of the early imperial system was probably to move resources from the centre to the frontier provinces, thereby stimulating economic growth in those areas. Prices became inflated in the outer provinces as a consequence of the inflow of money. Such prices would have increased the profit from production in the frontier areas in comparison with the core provinces, especially when the advantages of local production are contrasted with the high costs of long-distance transport (Jones 1973, 841–2). The result of this is seen in the shift in emphasis from inter-provincial to local trade in Britain (chapter 7). This growth of production at the frontiers must have been detrimental to the core provinces (Reece 1981). The élite families in the central areas may have benefited personally from the control of provincial production and the overall burden of the cost of the Empire may have shifted to fall more heavily on the provinces. However, the drying up of incoming revenues from inter-provincial trade probably meant that the effective burden on the core was not reduced. It is not possible to quantify this redistribution of wealth, although it was probably fundamental to the structure of relationships within the Empire.

A second major trend may be identified. During the Principate there was no progressive taxation system to even out wealth differences in society. Consequently the rich used their wealth to become richer, at the expense of the poor. This increase of the wealth hierarchy seems to have squeezed the ordinary landowners in the central provinces at the time when the inflow of wealth from conquest was first slowing down and then drying up (Hopkins 1978). These processes lie behind the difficulties felt by the decurial classes of the core areas, who relied upon local wealth production more than the imperial élite and so increasingly complain about their burdens during the middle and late Empire. The problem was experienced as a higher level of taxation (Jones 1973, 744), but in reality it need have been no more than a relative rather than absolute change. Thus many at the centre were becoming relatively poorer by accident of movements of wealth within the Empire. As a result they became less and less willing to serve their communities and endow them with gifts and buildings (Walker 1981; Fentress 1981, figs. 13.1–2). The consequent stress led to a destabilization of the system upon which the Empire's government was based: the willingness of the local landowners to govern and bear the burden on Rome's behalf in exchange for local power and a share in the benefits of the Empire. Thus the third century saw both the crisis of the decurions and through them, the cities, as well as the end of a system founded on the economic benefits of continuous territorial expansion.

These alterations coincide with the increased active influence of armies as a social force within the Empire. Gradually from the first century they were no longer always involved in wars of conquest, so that their energies were turned inwards and they became more and more involved in the power politics of the Empire. Throughout the Principate control of the military had been vital to the control of political power, but from the end of the second century the army's rôle shifts from potential to active: from being a power in the background to an active force within politics (cf. Willems 1983, 105–6). The frontier armies thus became increasingly involved in the making and breaking of emperors, whose policies became more and more dictated by their interests. Further, as military threats to the Empire increased from the 230s, the army became more vital to emperors and hence more influential. Anarchy in government, with successive emperors raised and deposed by the army, is a characteristic of the third century and increasing the instability which exacerbated the impact of the other problems facing the Empire.

This increased political power of the military is first clearly seen in the civil wars of the 190s which brought Septimius Severus to the purple. This military power was recognized when he raised army pay by 33 per cent to be followed by Caracalla with another rise of 50 per cent (Birley 1981a, 43). Severus also debased the coinage as the government needed more bullion for minting the extra coinage needed to pay an enlarged army at the higher rates (Jones 1973, 15–16). This metal was easily provided by reducing the bullion content of the coinage, first to 65 per cent and then by 220 to about 45 per cent (Reece 1970, 23). The sudden increase in the face value of the money in circulation sparked off the classic inflationary cycle of too much money chasing too few goods and may thus have been the catalyst for the inflation which subsequently dogged the third century (Reece 1987, 35). Although this inflation was comparatively modest by modern standards, it must be compared with a previously relatively stable currency, and therefore had a disproportionately large psychological effect. The debasement of the coinage and the perceived increase in the burden of taxation on the landowning classes brought about by official requisitions to support the state (Jones 1973, 30) should likewise be measured by their impact on confidence.

One indirect, but important effect of inflation and the failure of government was a reduction in the real value of cash taxes collected through the *civitates* (Mann 1985a; Jones 1974), as rates of tax were not increased in line with inflation or the higher levels of imperial expenditure. Although they continued to be levied for some time, there was first an *ad hoc*, then a more systematic shift towards compulsory requisitions in kind (*annonae*). This burden could be both arbitrary and inconvenient for the citizen, and resulted in discontent (Jones 1973, 30). More important, however, was the structural change brought about by a decline in importance of the *civitas* centres in tax collection, as this may have resulted in a decline in the pivotal rôle of the cities within the settlement system (below, p. 148). These internal problems reduced the total power of the Empire, laying her more open to the barbarians whose invasion attempts might have presented fewer problems under other circumstances. These invasions, which had a devastating physical and psychological impact on the continental provinces, did not directly affect Britain because of the insulation provided by the Channel. Nevertheless the results of the military and political chaos and subsequent reorganization were felt.

The new administrative system was moulded from the old to form a new type of leader, personified by the Emperor Diocletian. He combined absolutism with a rigidly

Table 6.1. *The loss of public buildings in later Roman towns*

Town	Building	Date of loss or change in use
Canterbury	Baths	Re-use in 4th century
Exeter	Baths	2nd century
London	Huggin Hill Baths	Demolished 3rd century
	Cheapside Baths	Disused 3rd century (Marsden 1980)
	Governor's Palace	Demolished 4th century (Marsden 1975)
Silchester	*Forum/basilica*	Change to metalworking in later 3rd century (Fulford 1985)
Wroxeter	*Forum/basilica*	Destroyed by *c*. 330
	Public baths	Destroyed early 4th century

Source: after Brooks 1986, with additions.

bureaucratic and hierarchical state machine, producing a government structure fundamentally different from that of the Principate (Loewenstein 1973). The strength of the new system lay, in part, in the organization which allowed power and prestige to return to the élite who had controlled the cities in the Principate but who now partook of power at the imperial level. The new positions for these people resulted from a vast expansion in the imperial bureaucracy (Jones 1973, 42–52), a consequence of the need for compulsion in collecting taxes, which resulted from the collapse of the curial system of the early Empire, and the emergence of large-scale requisition. Furthermore, this new fiscal system included an annual budget and complex mechanisms of financial control and revenue prediction which themselves demanded a larger civil service (Jones 1973, 448ff). Opportunities were thus given by the new structure of the imperial service which gave tax immunities to state servants. This offered them chances of social advancement by the acquisition of new forms of social status and authority, and by serving in the new bureaucracy (Loewenstein 1973, 438ff). This enlarged Empire-wide government service transferred competition to a plane above that of the individual city and gave those participating more extensive opportunities for progress and prestige than those available in the municipalities. Furthermore, the imperial service gave its servants access to methods of exploiting their positions to make money and thus enhance their personal wealth. Although nominally illegal, the practices compensated for the low salaries provided and the fees paid to obtain the posts.

This structural change fed back both to reinforce the decline of munificence and encourage the selective success of cities like Trier and Milan, which became key in the administrative system as a result of being imperial residences (Wightman 1970; Krautheimer 1983). The bureaucracy thus drained the reservoir of wealthy citizens willing to serve their cities, and this led to the stream of encouragements, inducements and instructions to them to attend to their own communities (Jones 1973, 737ff). The problem, not perceived by contemporaries, was that the power structure no longer offered the motivation for the involvement in the municipalities that had been critical to their flourishing success in the early Empire. The forum of individual power, prestige and advancement had moved from the local city to the imperial service.

130

Consequences for the existing patterns in Britain

The changes within the Empire affected each province in different ways. In Britain, the absence of large-scale barbarian interference, together with the declining military presence (James 1984), perhaps meant that changes were less violent than elsewhere. She was a peripheral province and one where, as already suggested, the ruling élites of the *civitates* were few in number and less involved in status competition through munificence than those in the central provinces. Her peripheral position had been responsible for the presence of the substantial military garrison of just over 50,000 soldiers in *c.* 150, which has been shown to have declined to not more than 33,500 by the fourth century and possibly 15,000 or less (James 1984, 166–9). This fourth-century figure represents a decline from *c.* 12.5 per cent to not more than *c.* 5.5 per cent of the total imperial army. It has been pointed out that this drop to less than half the previous proportion underestimates the effective impact on the nature and cost of the army, since the residue of the British garrison largely comprised poor-quality frontier troops (*limitanei*) rather than members of the crack field army (*comitatenses*) (James 1984). The combined impact of these two factors may have reduced their economic impact to *c.* 20 per cent of its mid-second-century level (James pers. comm.). Together with the likelihood that Britain did not contain a substantial civil service presence, this indicates that the proportion of central imperial expenditure spent in Britain probably declined to a new low in the later Empire. The evidence for the prosperity of the province (chapter 8), which will have been enhanced by the absence of substantial military problems, perhaps means that Britain was an economic asset to Rome and a net contributor to her fiscal revenues. Thus we may perhaps believe Eumenius when he says in 297–8:

> Without doubt Britain . . . was a land that the state could ill afford to lose, so plentiful are its harvests, so numerous are the pasturelands in which it rejoices, so many are the metals of which seams run through it, so much wealth comes from its taxes . . . (*Panegyric to Constantius* 11.1).

We thus see not only the military problems of the third century largely passing Britain by, but also shifts in the balance of the Empire resulting in positive benefits to her economy.

One of the consequences of the third-century crisis which Britain did not avoid was the division of the single early imperial province into smaller units. The first alteration came under Severus in 197 (Herodian 3. 8, 2) with the sub-division into two. The epigraphic evidence (Mann 1961; Frere 1987, 162–3) shows that London became the capital of Britannia Superior, whilst York was the centre of Britannia Inferior. The boundary between the two has been shown to lie to the north of Chester and south of Lincoln, and since we should assume that whole *civitates* were assigned to each province, it seems possible to reconstruct the boundaries (fig. 55). This division by Severus was probably designed to reduce the size of the garrison under one person because the civil wars of the 190s had shown the threat posed by large commands like that of the governor of Britain (Frere 1987, 163). The consequences of these alterations for the settlement archaeology of Britain are unclear, although the advance-

Table 6.2. *Flows of wealth in the Roman Empire*

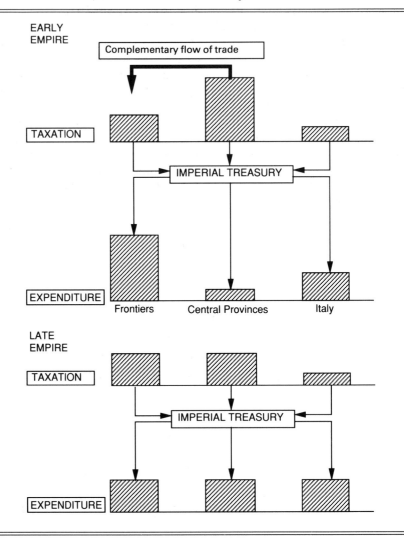

ment of York to the status of *colonia* is perhaps connected, as are the substantial buildings which were constructed there in the third century (Carver *et al.* 1978).

Diocletian's reorganization of the Empire's administration resulted in a further subdivision of the provinces into four, which together formed the Diocese of Britain. This sub-division is one of many in the Empire and need not be a consequence of any desire to reduce the military power of particular governors (Jones 1973, 43). Mann (1961) has identified the capitals of the provinces as London (Maxima Caesariensis), Lincoln (Flavia Caesariensis), York (Britannia Secunda) and Cirencester (Britannia Prima). Secunda and Flavia were carved out of the third-century province of Britannia

Inferior, whilst Superior was divided to form the other two. The logic of administrative organization suggests that the boundaries should be as shown in figure 56. Finally, in 369 a fifth province, Valentia, was created (Ammianus 28. 3, 7), perhaps by the sub-division of Britannia Secunda with a capital at Carlisle (Rivet and Smith 1979, 46). The significance of these divisions for the capitals is unclear, although the defences of York and London may reflect their status. Customs barriers may have existed between the different provinces (Jones 1973, 825), and these perhaps curtailed trade contact (below, p. 165).

There are major developments in the settlement system and economy in Britain which appear to follow from the Empire-wide changes. In outline, there is a relative decline in the vitality of the major administrative centres, at the same time that the countryside shows renewed life, with increased investment in agriculture (chapter 8), a boom in villa building and the development of small towns and rurally located industries (chapter 7).

55 The suggested boundary between the Severan provinces of Britannia Superior and Britannia Inferior.

133

The cities altered significantly, with the differences most obvious in three particulars. First, there was a change in the character of the constituent buildings, with unprepossessing, largely timber artisan houses and workshops gradually being replaced by substantial stone-built houses. For instance, in Verulamium (Frere 1981) the adornment of the city with substantial town houses (figs. 38 and 57) continued to the middle of the third century and their occupation lasted throughout the later Roman period (Frere 1983). A similar picture occurs in other major towns, with the many substantial houses at Silchester probably being later Roman (Boon 1974). Perring (1987) has noted this widespread change in Britain and points towards the opulence of the fourth-century town houses, which contrasts with the working artisan structures which characterize the earlier period. The overall effect of the reduction in the density of occupation and the increased scale of the buildings was to make many of these towns appear as garden cities (cf. Reece 1980). The principal importance of this lies not in the emergence of the more substantial town houses, which might be taken as indicative of increased prosperity, but in the relative reduction in importance

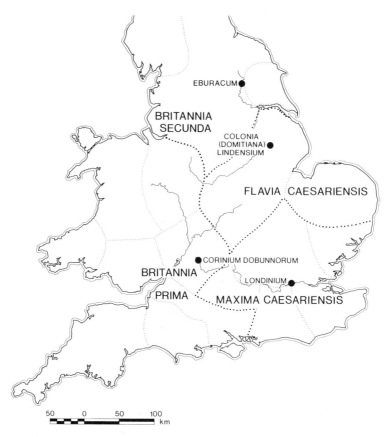

56 The suggested boundaries between the Diocletianic provinces of Maxima Caesariensis, Flavia Caesariensis, Britannia Prima and Britannia Secunda.

134

of the artisan structures, which represents a shift in the productive economic basis that had been present in the Principate. The major towns thus show a population who are spending wealth on themselves and not visibly creating it through trade and manufacture (Perring 1987). This shows a change fundamental to the character of the settlements which was central to society and the system of government during the first and second centuries. The character of the new, large stone-built town houses of the late Roman period suggests a primarily residential function, and there is comparatively little evidence for industry on any scale (Richmond 1966).

As a further contrast, both the character of some of the buildings and the finds from them strongly suggest that agricultural activity was focused in the later towns. This impression is given most strongly by building XII.2 in Cirencester, the plan of which resembles a winged corridor villa (fig. 58; McWhirr 1986). That this building was used as a farm is supported by the finds of a plough coulter and weaving equipment from the outbuildings behind it, although as Rivet (1974) has pointed out, the term 'villa' cannot strictly be used to describe it because the latin word refers exclusively to a country house. This building also interestingly shows the pairing of structures which J. T. Smith (1978a) has noted to be characteristic of British villas (chapter 8). In the Cirencester case, buildings XII.1 and XII.2 are connected by a wall and appear complementary (with XII.2 replacing XII.1 as the high-status building but continuing to rely on it for a bath suite and possibly kitchens). Building XII.2 is also subsequently divided into two units with a second entrance added at the east end (Rooms 15, 19 and 20). This pattern is so similar to that seen in villas that it reinforces the view that the distinction between Public Towns and the countryside was diminishing in the later Roman period (Reece 1980).

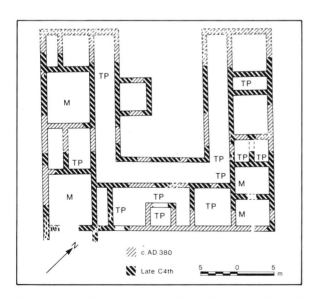

57 A substantial later Roman town house (Verulamium Insula 27, building 2), typical of those which occur in the public towns in the period (after Frere 1983). TP = tessellated pavement; M = mosaic.

135

Evidence for widespread cultivation within these towns is also provided by the black earth which characterizes the archaeological deposits in many of them. We should be wary of assuming that all these deposits are the same, although some have been shown to result from agricultural or horticultural activity (Macphail 1981). This evidence thus points towards the continuance of the major Public Towns, but with a change in them towards a more rustic character. Whilst this trend is perhaps most marked in London (Marsden 1980, 119), which had depended on the inter-provincial trade in decline after the second century (chapter 7), it does occur in most of the centres.

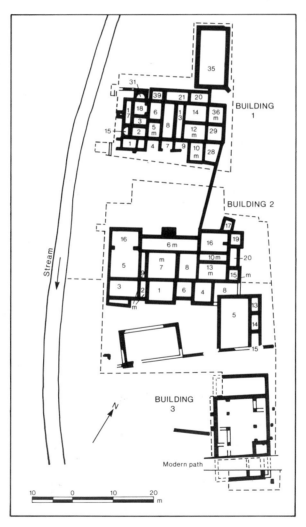

58 The three major houses within the walls of Cirencester (Insula 12). In contrast to that shown in fig. 57, these have a distinctly rural character. Building 2 in particular resembles a winged corridor villa; M = mosaic (after McWhirr 1986).

136

These towns also show an almost complete cessation of the construction of new public buildings after the second century, while some lost through accident or decay were not replaced (Mackreth 1987). Although most of our data is far from perfect, the recent excavations at Silchester have shown that the function of the *basilica* changed during the third century from a public place to somewhere where iron working was undertaken (Fulford 1985, 53–4). This throws into relief the changes noted elsewhere and highlights the probability that, whether or not maintained, public buildings were no longer focal to the principal functions of the settlements (cf. Mackreth 1987). It has already been shown that the British *civitas* capitals were under-provided with public buildings by comparison with the core provinces of the Empire, and it was suggested that this results from the province having a less-developed social hierarchy. It follows that the almost complete halt in construction and repair of public buildings cannot be the result of the towns being already sufficiently provided with facilities, especially in centres like Silchester where major buildings lost their public function (table 6.1). A positive explanation of the phenomenon is surely required, especially in the light of the changes in the character of the towns already described. An explanation may lie in the loss of incentive for the curial classes to remain involved in munificence and status competition within their cities. This may result from the increased burdens on them and the development of the imperial bureaucracy. The consequent shift in power within the Empire-wide administrative hierarchy was itself sparked off by disruption to the old system in the third century. The effect is particularly noticeable in Britain, where the social pyramid was less developed and the towns less elaborate than those in the Mediterranean. Thus the small élite in each *civitas* can have retained its control without the public competition which resulted in wealth being spent on the improvement of their cities, which now lay outside the theatre in which significant power was to be obtained.

In marked contrast to the virtual cessation of other public building, many of the towns were provided with defensive circuits during the later second and third centuries, although a few had already received defences earlier (fig. 59). These defences represent a significant input of labour and resources and thus a major public investment by the communities (Fulford and Startin 1984). The stratigraphic sequences provided by excavation show that the development, starting in the later second century, is often complex, with the separate provision of earthen banks, sometimes with structurally independent but imposing stone gates, then the construction of stone curtain walls mostly in the third century, and finally the addition of external towers during the fourth, thus stretching over a period of up to two hundred years of modification and embellishment (table 6.4; Maloney and Hobley 1983; Crickmore 1984).

Hartley (1983) has demonstrated that the earthen banks which form the primary phases of the majority of the enclosures can be dated to after *c*. 150. He also proposes that they resulted from the initiative of the civic authorities in Britain. In contrast it is often argued that these defences must have been constructed at the initiative of the central authorities of the Empire, either in anticipation of (Wacher 1975a, 75), or in response to, a military emergency (Frere 1984a). Frere has also summarized the complex legal context of the provision of defences, showing that the privilege of being allowed, although not compelled, to defend a city during the first and second centuries was limited to the *coloniae*, *municipia* and perhaps *civitates foederatae*, all of which were technically outside the governor's jurisdiction. This restriction most likely results from the desire to discourage the proliferation of defences in the newly founded province for military reasons. However, we have no evidence that the existing defences of hillforts and *oppida* were systematically slighted. The legal position becomes clearer in the later second century, for the *Digest* shows that after *c.* 170 applications for permission to provide or repair defences had to be referred to the

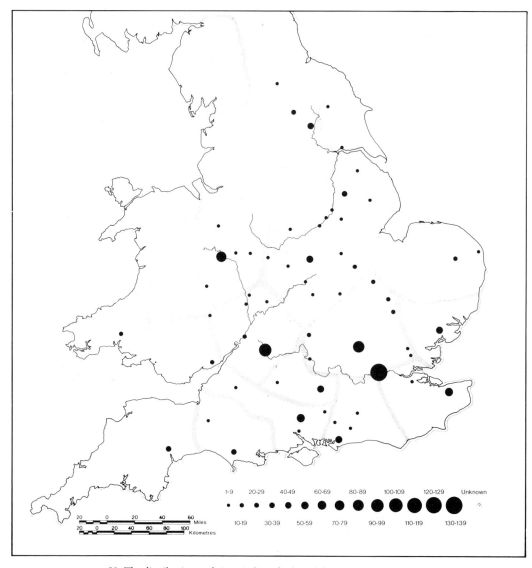

59 The distribution and sizes (in ha) of urban defences in Roman Britain. For data see table 6.4 (p. 152).

emperor and could not be dealt with simply by the governor as they had previously (Frere 1984a, 66–7). This was a result of the general attempt that the central government was making to prevent civic extravagance and its consequences, namely unfinished projects and bankrupt municipalities. There is neither evidence from the sources to show that they were discouraged for strategic reasons nor that they were constructed as a concerted programme at the behest of any central authority. None the less, Frere (1984a, 63) attacks Hartley (1983) for suggesting that defences were the result of civic initiative. He bases this attack on the assumptions, first that earthen defences must result from a concerted programme or chain reaction, and secondly that civic initiative is inappropriate to settlements below the rank of *civitas* capital. Finally, he makes the point that central government attempts to stop feckless municipal extravagance would have applied to Britain as much as to any other province.

However, the suggestion that construction resulted from central initiative seems both unnecessary and implausible, for the known construction dates do not illustrate the clear pattern which would be expected to result from central control (table 6.4). Despite her comparative isolation from barbarian activity, Britain is provided with defences more extensive in area and earlier in date than her directly threatened continental neighbours (Johnson 1983). In the absence of several historically undocumented threats, this suggests that local initiative was responsible. Despite the attempts to relate all defences to the same chronological horizon, the archaeological evidence for their dating is imprecise and an extended sequence is most plausible. Any conclusion based on the premise that all are the consequence of one event should be clearly understood to be the result of assumption, not evidence. Thus the major centres, like London, were not fully defended (Maloney 1983; Sheldon and Tyers 1983) until long after many insignificant roadside settlements (Wacher 1975b); and a town vulnerable to coastal incursions like Canterbury remained undefended until the end of the third century (Frere *et al.* 1982, 17). Where defences are constructed, variability, inconsistent with central control, is the keyword. Furthermore, central initiative of this type is improbable and anachronistic in the second century, for there is little evidence of similar action by the imperial authorities in relation to other municipalities (Garnsey and Saller 1987, 26–40). As central interference was reactive, the construction of defences is most likely to have resulted from the civic authorities asking permission to construct them.

Imperial controls existed to counter potential military threats and to curb munificence which went beyond civic means. Since the British cities can hardly have been seen as a military menace and there is no evidence of civic extravagance in Britain (table 5.1), there is no reason for permission to build walls having been refused. The rather *ad hoc* or random chronological and spatial distribution of defences may thus result from a fashion, stimulated by civic pride and competition between the cities, leading municipalities to seek consent to construct defences around their settlements. This fashion, which occurs earlier in Britain than in other Western provinces, may be the result of a continuation of the prehistoric tradition of defining a settlement's status by the provision of earthen ramparts. This is clearly visible in the LPRIA, where the substantial dykes around first hillforts, then *oppida*, are of such a scale that they must surely have functioned as much for status display as for any purely defensive function.

Furthermore, the area enclosed in *oppida* such as Stanwick or Camulodunum was far in excess of that required for the settlement and so may have been status-defining. This may also explain the extent of the enclosures of Romano-British towns (fig. 59), which in cases like Cirencester (Corinium Dobonnorum) are exceptionally large. Furthermore, the provision of earthen defences around settlements below the rank of *civitas* capital, which Frere (1984a, 68–9) finds difficult to explain as a result of civic pride, may be the result of their being under the control of a local élite at centres of septs of the *civitates* where there was also a wish to define status in the traditional manner (below, p. 149). Finally, in pursuing this argument, we may explain the absence of earthen defences around London, and its walling late in the sequence, as a consequence of the city being a Roman community which had developed separately from the indigenous system. Its very *Romanitas* may thus have removed it from this arena of inter-municipal competition until Roman-style stone defences became the trend in the third century. It may be that the imperial authorities saw no threat in harmless status competition between the British communities and may even have encouraged the provision of civic defences to protect the administrative infrastructure (for instance the installations of the *cursus publicus*). In contrast, the present archaeological information clearly makes the suggestion of any centralized initiative untenable.

On the basis of this view, the distribution of defensive circuits can be seen to show both competition between cities and their ability to build. This may be measured by the size of the defended area, for in contrast to the later circuits on the continent (Johnson 1983), the British towns have large enclosed areas (fig. 59), which even then exclude some of the sprawling suburbs (Esmond-Cleary 1987). As an index of civic pride their distribution is instructive, for the same major towns are represented as had most dedicatory inscriptions in the earlier period (fig. 26). The core of the province in central and southern England is dominated by the largest of the enclosures which, as expected, coincide with the settlements of the most Romanized facilities. The scale of the enclosure at Wroxeter (Viroconium Cornoviorum) is unexpectedly large, perhaps because of the strong continuation of the hillfort tradition thereabouts until the LPRIA. However, Dorchester (Durnovaria [Durotrigum]) in an area with similar late hillforts shows a different pattern. It may also be significant that the cities which become the capitals of the four late Roman provinces are dominant within those areas. The possible exception is Lincoln, whose defences are smaller than those of Leicester, although those at the latter are late (Wacher 1975a, 351), and Lincoln had the superior status of a *colonia*. By this measure the most prestigious and dominant towns were thus chosen to fulfil the new rôle. The scale of the enclosures also demonstrates that any simple functional explanation for their origins as defences for supplies, for tax-gathering facilities or for the mobile field army, is insufficient. Much smaller, simpler circuits like those of the fourth century on the continent would have served these functions as well (Johnson 1983). Nevertheless, once in existence these functions are likely to have been an incentive for the maintenance of existing defences by the hard-pressed administrative and military machine of the late Empire.

Finally, the provision of external towers, sometimes called bastions, also has a symbolic element to it. These towers, which are characteristic of later Roman military fortification, were added to the wall circuits of a number of towns around the middle of the fourth century, necessitating alterations to the ditch systems. Their addition is often claimed to be the result of the restoration of the towns by Count Theodosius in 368 (Frere 1987, 248) on the authority of Ammianus (28. 3, 2), although the text says nothing of town walls (chapter 9). Furthermore, Casey (1983) has shown that a date at or just before the accession of Magnentius in 350 would be more consistent with the coin evidence from several of the towns. Nevertheless, as in the case of the earthen defences, we need not accept the conclusion that all the alterations were part of a concerted programme. We should recognize that such an interpretation is based on an hypothesis of central control. Although this does not seem satisfactory in the third century, the increasing imperial interference in the fourth century makes government pressure more plausible. However, the archaeological evidence provides a variety of dates (table 6.4; Crickmore 1984), and these can be taken at face value to support the interpretation of a comparatively lengthy phase of activity, which results from civic initiative and competition between the municipalities rather than any military directive.

There is little doubt that the towers were tactically important, as they enabled a smaller garrison to defend a city using long-range weapons (bows, slings and catapults) for enfilading fire, although their use for expensive, heavy artillery is extremely doubtful (Baatz 1983). In this way the towns were vital as strong points in the late Roman strategy which Luttwak has called 'defence-in-depth' (1976, 127–90). However, this functional explanation is only partially satisfactory as the defensive mentality represented is analogous to that of the medieval castle, where the presence of an impregnable stronghold was sufficient to deter direct attack. Hence, the walls and towers were symbols of impregnability and as such they were also status indicators; their magnificence can perhaps be seen to result from the rivalry between cities that had partly stimulated public building in the early towns. Support for this interpretation comes from London, where the provision of Roman external towers only on the eastern side (Maloney 1983) implies that they were to impress those approaching by river from the continent. This view is reinforced if the three towers along the riverside at the Tower of London are Roman in origin (Parnell 1985), for while functionally redundant they would provide a distinguished and architecturally embellished corner for the city when approached by river. Such embellishment may have been emulating the fashion set by the Aurelianic walls at Rome (Todd 1978a), later seen in the Constantinian walls at Constantinople (Krautheimer 1983). Similar defensive elaboration occurs on one side of the legionary fortress at York (RCHM 1962, fig. 3; Butler 1971), which like London was the residence of a provincial governor. This indicates that the status of these centres of government was perhaps being signified by their walls and may result from the initiative of the governor rather than the city. Comparable symbolism also applies to the elaborate gates already in existence, and is illustrated by the Arras Medallion (fig. 60) which shows Constantius, 'restorer of eternal light', approaching London by river in 296, with the city shown by the gate towers of its defences.

The large-scale investment in these defences illustrates the continued importance of the administrative towns, and contrasts with their failure to be provided with other urban facilities. Thus we have an image of these towns with magnificent enclosures containing substantial houses and agricultural plots, but few if any new or well-maintained major public buildings. Two complementary interpretations for this pattern may be suggested. In the first the administrative towns of the early Empire are seen to have become irrelevant to the native social and economic needs of the population, and so decline (Reece 1980). They nevertheless remained important to central government, since they lay at critical and defensible strong points on the communications network. They were thus suitable centres for the collecting of taxes in kind (*annonae*) and for the control and distribution of supplies (Biddle 1983, 114–15). In the second model, the towns were less important as places for social display and élite competition but remained focal to the group identity of the *civitas*, as did LPRIA tribal centres (chapter 2). According to this explanation they remain symbolically central, being used as meeting places and for group activities such as periodic markets, while becoming peripheral to the principal economic life of the community. Support for this may be drawn from the fact that substantial cemeteries surround many of the late Roman towns of Britain. These cemeteries vary considerably in character and continue in use throughout the late Roman period. The presence of such cemeteries as those at Cirencester (McWhirr *et al.* 1982), Lankhills, Winchester (Clarke 1979) and Poundbury, Dorchester (Dorset) (Green 1982) is sometimes taken to indicate that the towns remained as major population centres (e.g. Biddle 1983, 112), although this need not be the case as it is not uncommon for the social ceremony of burial to take place away from the place of habitation (as it does today). Thus, burial around the late *civitas* capitals may mean no more than that the *civitas* population still looked to their town as a significant social and religious focus.

This continued focal rôle is also seen in the countryside, for while there is a continuing steady growth in the number of villas (fig. 33), their distribution still shows a strong preference for the areas around the administrative centres, demonstrating their continued potency (chapter 8). The balance of the evidence suggests that, whilst the prime focus of individual élite display had transferred away from the administrative towns, they retained an essential rôle after the third century.

60 Gold medallion found at Arras, northern France. This coin was struck by Constantius I at Trier in *c.* 297–8 to commemorate the restoration of Britain to legitimacy with the defeat of Allectus in 296. The reverse legend reads REDDITOR LUCIS AETERNAE, LONDINIUM – restorer of eternal light. The city gate shown emphasizes the importance of defences as a symbol of urban status. (*Photograph by courtesy of the British Museum.*)

The emergence of the periphery

At the same time that the *civitas* capitals were becoming less economically vibrant, and some of the villas were showing more opulence, the economically essential artisans and traders were not conspicuous at either. They are, however, important in the so-called Minor or Small Towns, which came to prominence in the later Roman period (fig. 61). The terms 'Minor' or 'Small Towns' are really inappropriate, as their

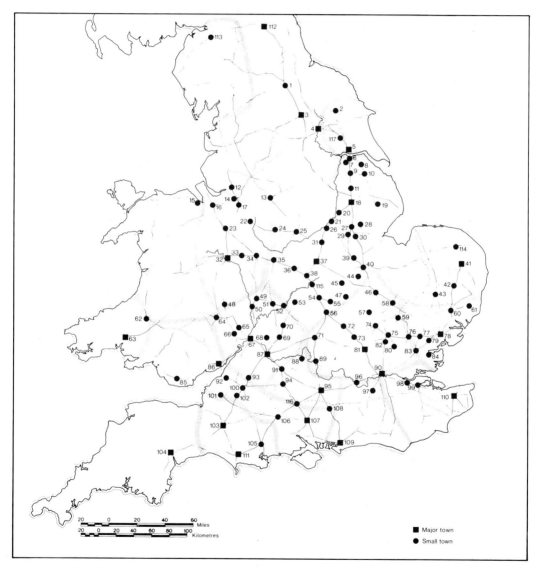

61 The distribution of Major, and Minor or Small Towns in Roman Britain (based on Burnham 1986). For the identification of the sites see table 6.5 (p. 154).

143

size range overlaps with that of the *civitas* capitals (fig. 62). Definition is difficult, because the terms are used for a range of morphologically different types of settlement (Burnham 1987) which are grouped together, because although it is clear that they were concentrations of settlement, they do not have the characteristics of the administrative centres of the early Empire (Wacher 1975a, 20). At the lowest level many of the nucleations may have been only agricultural settlements (chapter 8), but at the other end of the spectrum sites like Water Newton (Durobrivae) are as urban as several of the lesser *civitas* capitals. Many of the sites, especially those on the roads, probably functioned as nodes for marketing and production. Whilst acting as towns in this sense, they lacked the public facilities seen in the administrative centres, so that contemporaries from the Mediterranean would probably not have viewed them as urban (Wacher 1975a, 20). The sites are difficult to assess because of their insubstantial nature and the paucity of large-scale excavation, which results in the available evidence being piecemeal (cf. R. F. Smith 1987).

As far as we can characterize them, they differ from the *civitas* capitals and other Public Towns in two major ways. First, although they were dense concentrations of

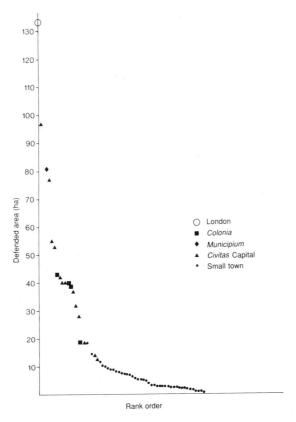

62 Rank-size graph of the defended areas of urban sites in Roman Britain. For data see table 6.4 (p. 152).

settlement, most lack any clear evidence of organized town planning. Burnham (1987) has shown that these sites have a range of different morphological forms (fig. 63), which vary from those which are simply clustered or linear nucleations of settlement to those with some element of organized planning of internal streets, although this almost invariably falls short of the full street grid. We must be wary of equating the absence of Roman-style planning with a lack of settlement organization, for where reasonably extensive excavations have taken place at Neatham in Hampshire it can be shown that the settlement was carefully planned in layout (Millett and Graham 1986; see also R. F. Smith 1987).

Secondly, although some contained major public buildings identified as *mansiones*, or inns run for the imperial post – *cursus publicus* (Burnham 1987, 180), they are generally characterized by the absence of structures indicative of communal display. Even temples are comparatively scarce, and the more Romanized buildings are not invariably found in architecturally dominant positions within the sites. They thus appear as secondary developments, not primary to the rôles of the sites. The streets are instead lined with strip buildings, many of which are best interpreted as small shops and workshops, suggestive of their character as economic centres (figs. 63 and 64). There is a general lack of more than a few peripheral, large private houses, although Todd (1970, 124–8) has noted a recurrent pattern of single extra-mural villas, which may perhaps be the residences of an élite living immediately outside their towns. Examples of this pattern occur, for instance, at Neatham (Millett and Graham 1986), Great Casterton, Margidunum and Ancaster (Todd 1970, fig. 2). In this sense we can see the nucleated centres of the Small Towns as only a part of their settlement systems, apparently representing the residential areas of the craft workers and traders who may well have been under the patronage of the élite living in more sumptuous accommodation just outside the core of the settlements.

There has been a considerable debate about the origins of these sites, which has now been clarified as a result of Burnham's survey of the excavated evidence (1986; cf. R. F. Smith 1987). This shows that just over a third of the sites have good evidence for military origins, a similar proportion having developed from LPRIA predecessors. About half of the remaining sites are located on the road network. However, as Burnham points out, these figures disguise a more complex and informative pattern. In areas most Romanized before the conquest, in the south and east, there is a strongly defined element of site continuity from LPRIA nucleus to Roman Small Town. However, a number of the settlements are bypassed by later development, and their success in the Roman period apparently depended upon how the site fitted into the new provincial framework, especially that of the roads which refocused previous activities (cf. Gaul – Drinkwater 1983, 132–5). In contrast, in the areas of the north and west, the development of the sites was determined much more by the new framework. Through the province the dislocation caused by the roads was reinforced by the development of facilities for the *cursus publicus* (the imperial post). This required *mansiones* (inns) and *mutationes* (roadside stations) to be provided by the local communities at regular intervals along the principal roads. The attachment of such installations to existing settlements or their foundation *de novo* undoubtedly stimulated the growth of some of the Small Towns.

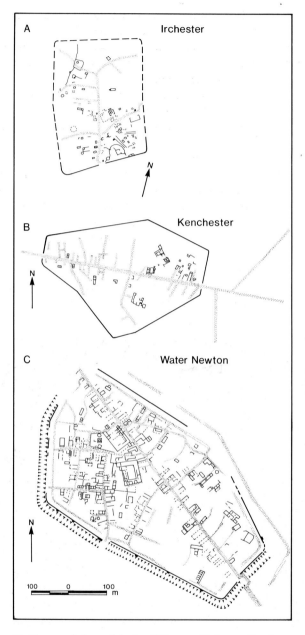

63 The morphology of the Small Towns of Irchester, Kenchester and Water Newton (after Burnham 1987).

Although the evidence collated by Burnham shows that most of the Small Towns had their origins in the earlier Empire, the limited excavation evidence shows that the peak of their prosperity lay in the later Empire. During this period they became prosperous economic centres contrasting with the *civitas* capitals, which are not dominated by the same evidence of vibrant economic activity. A number of the Small Towns are walled (fig. 59) and a few achieve a size comparable with that of the smaller *civitas* capitals (fig. 62) – indeed it is claimed that some were promoted to this status themselves (Wacher 1975a). However, most remained straggling, unpretentious and essentially small in scale but with a range of craft and workshop activities (R. F. Smith 1987, 67–84). The range of building types which characterize these settlements lends support to this hypothesis, for the sites which are well understood are dominated by buildings best seen as artisan houses and workshops, indicative of economically dynamic centres comparable with the Public Towns of the Principate. Their continuance in the Small Towns and their eclipse by more magnificent residences in the Public Towns can thus be taken to indicate a divergence in the economic history of the two urban forms. Thus the economic importance of the Small Towns may belie their size, and contrasts with the fate of the Public Towns.

If we are correct in this interpretation, we need an explanation which accounts for both the rise of the Small Town and the eclipse of the Public Town. Their different

64 Piercebridge, County Durham. Air photograph showing the civil settlement clustered along the road beside the bridgehead on the northern bank of the River Tees. The site, generally seen as a *vicus* attached to a fort, is more probably a Small Town dominated by narrow strip buildings (cf. fig. 63). The later Roman fort lies in a secondary position under the modern village on the right of the photograph, where the defences and internal buildings can be seen under excavation. Across the river in the top left-hand corner is the possible bridge abutment, also under excavation. (*Photograph by courtesy of the Dept of Archaeology, Durham University.*)

Table 6.3. *Taxation and settlement centralization*

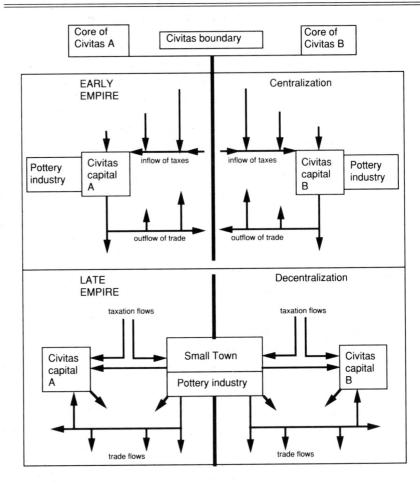

EARLY EMPIRE

Concentration of élite power at *civitas* centre
Villa development near these centres
Social competition at centres
Taxation collected at centres
Production concentrated near centres
Trade concentrated on centres

LATE EMPIRE

Social control continued at centres, stifling economic growth
Competition moved to villas which surround centres
Taxation collected at various places, causing decentralization
Peripheral areas showed economic growth
Producers at boundaries fed goods into several *civitates*

economic histories can perhaps be related directly to changes in the Roman administrative system which resulted from the middle Empire crisis. We have argued that the
tax system helped to focus marketing on *civitas* capitals in the early Empire, as cash
taxes were collected by the *civitates* (table 6.3). Although these taxes continued to be
collected, they were devalued by inflation during the third century (Mann 1985a),
because the administration failed to increase them to compensate for the decline in
value of the currency. These problems led the government to rely increasingly on compulsory requisitions in kind (*annonae*), which were made on the instructions of the
praetorian prefect, who was responsible for the supply of the army (Jones 1973, 411).
The exact organization of the *annona* is difficult to reconstruct, even for the well-
documented central provinces. However, there seems to have been an assumption that
the supplies for the governor, his staff and the imperial post were collected within their
province. In Britain supplies for the frontier troops (*limitanei*) are also likely to have
been requisitioned within the province in which they were stationed (Jones 1973,
458). This may have involved the requisitions being transported over long distances,
since the supplies had to be delivered to the location where they were needed. The size
of the army presence in Britain makes it likely that its inhabitants were often required
to provide requisitions for transport overseas, as Ammianus' reference (18. 2, 3) to
grain being transported from Britain to Gaul in the late 350s illustrates. James (1984)
has made the important point that the small numbers of the field army (*comitatenses*)
in Britain in the later Roman period will have significantly reduced the burden of
arbitrary and localized taxation which they collected for themselves on the authority
of warrants (Jones 1973, 459).

The significant change which perhaps had a major impact on the structure of the
settlement pattern was that the *annonae* were generally collected under the control of
a procurator or susceptor. He was appointed by the local *civitas* from amongst the
decurions who remained responsible for delivery, although officials were used to
collect it at a variety of centres within the territory (Jones 1973, 456–7). We have no
certain indication of the impact of this change, but the decentralization of the collection of taxes through delivery of requisitions to government installations (including
forts and *mansiones*) (Rivet 1975, 112) would have generated new functions for the
Small Towns. This reduced the earlier centralizing tendency of the administrative system which enhanced the pivotal rôle of the *civitas* capitals in the economic system
(table 6.3). In the same way as it had benefited them during the early Empire, so decentralization stimulated the growth of Small Towns.

Whether or not the rôle of the *civitas* centres as tax-gathering points declined as a
result of these alterations (cf. James 1988, 267–8), there is little doubt that the
development of taxation in kind had an economically regressive effect on the collection centres. Any economic multiplier caused by the inflow of tax in money which had
stimulated urban growth in the Principate was lost. This is because the collection of
dues in kind fails to generate secondary economic activity, such as trade to earn
coinage or money-changing to pay taxes. Instead goods are simply delivered to the
state and taken away by it without any by-product for the collection point. The effect
of taxation stimulating the economy was stifled by the new system and would have

had an effect on the *civitas* capitals even if they remained *de facto* focal in tax gathering in the later Roman period.

The other important element in the emergence of the Small Towns as centres of the social and administrative system is perhaps their development as markets. This may have been at the initiative, or under the control, of those individuals whose villas were placed close to them, for there is good evidence that markets were strictly controlled by the imperial administration because of the revenue they could generate (MacMullen 1970, 373). The extent to which this control of markets broke down by the third century is a matter for speculation, as is the extent to which the controls were effective in Britain. It is not easy to provide evidence to support the hypothesis that Small Towns were under élite control. However, in discussing Gaul, Drinkwater (1985, 54) has made the point that these sites provided a forum for a lesser aristocracy to maintain their status at a level below that of the *civitas*. This is perhaps consistent with the idea that such patronage was increasingly important in the late Roman period. The Small Towns thus formed the personal power bases of minor magnates who controlled sub-divisions (*pagi*) of the *civitates* whilst remaining decurions. This pattern may also be applicable to parts of Britain, but we lack the evidence available in Gaul for the organization and importance of the *pagi* (cf. Drinkwater 1979, 93–4). All the epigraphic references in Britain relate to soldiers from other provinces (*RIB* 201, 2107, 2108, 1303). This is not surprising considering the general paucity of the epigraphic record from the smaller sites. Frere has, however, identified five sub-groups of the Brigantes which may have been *pagi* (1987, 46 n. 8), although we know only one of their centres (Corbridge – Coriosopitum). Nonetheless, it is almost certain that many of the British Small Towns, which probably ranked as *vici* (Johnson 1975; Rivet 1975, 122–13), also acted as the centres of *pagi*.

If we compare this organization with that of the LPRIA (chapter 2), a tentative correlation can be made between the Iron Age septs and the *pagi*. This is especially appropriate in the south and east, where Burnham (1986) has shown most continuity of nucleated sites. If we are correct in making this correlation, then the clan leaders of the LPRIA can be seen as the ancestors of the local élite who controlled Small Towns. These sites thus developed as the alternative foci to the *civitas* capitals under their patronage and as their local power bases. Their fluorescence thus results from the patronage transferred to them as the benefits of public display in the *civitas* capital declined and when the decentralization of the tax structure provided a catalyst for the growth of alternative peripheral centres. Thus it is no coincidence that these sites develop at the peripheries of the *civitates*, as far as possible from their social control.

A similar conclusion was arrived at by Hodder (1975), whose classic analysis of the non-random spacing of walled towns (originally published with Hassall in 1971) lends considerable support to the identification of this pattern of development at boundary locations (fig. 61). It is unfortunate that his work was based on only the walled centres, since we have no reason to believe that these were necessarily any more important for marketing than those which remained unenclosed. The strength of Hodder's systematic study is that it pointed towards the administrative, economic and social needs for urban centres which were least fulfilled at the *civitas* margins. These areas are those where the needs were met by the Small Towns. It is probably no coincidence that Hodder was unable to distinguish between the different hypotheses to explain their growth, since all these needs come together to generate the requirement for these towns. They were, however, only fully fulfilled when changing circumstances broke the administrative and economic hold of the *civitas* centres.

If we are correct that the prime elements in society were the élites who maintained a strong control over economic exchange, then the decentralization of the taxation system, the emergence of the Small Towns as *pagus* centres, and the decline of the *civitas* capitals as the principal economic foci are all parts of the same process. Strict conservative control over exchange of *civitas* centres may have inhibited their ability to respond to the new circumstances of society. This would have allowed the economic advantage to pass to the Small Towns, peripheral to the centres of social control. These were either the spontaneous offspring of the economic circumstances or creations of individual magnates, who had distanced themselves from group control. Whichever was the case, they developed to surpass the *civitas* capitals in their economic rôles.

These developments show that the mid-Empire crisis had such a radical impact on the structure of Roman Britain that the late imperial pattern was very different from that of the Principate. The net effect of the changes need not have altered the power structure of society at all, but rather led to a new, more fragmented manifestation. In the early Empire, circumstances conspired to focus the political, social and economic processes on the centres of the *civitates*. The crisis of the third century dismembered this system, leaving the separate elements of production, exchange, administration and social control independent and decentralized within the settlement system, although still articulating as a whole. This represents something of a return to the balance of the LPRIA and led to the peripheries becoming the primary areas of growth. This pattern will be explored more fully in a consideration first of the economy (chapter 7) and then of the countryside (chapter 8).

Table 6.4. Urban defences

Town	Earthwork circuit	Size (ha)	Wall	Size (ha)	External towers	Status
Alcester	2nd+	?[a]	?	?	—[b]	Small Town
Alchester	150–80+	28.0	late 2nd+	10.5		Small Town
Aldborough	?	1.0	193–6+	28.0	early 4th	Civitas capital
Alfoldean	?	?	—	—		Small Town
Ancaster	?	?	250–80	3.6	4th	Small Town
Bannaventa	?	5.0	early 4th	5.0		Small Town
Bath	late 2nd	9.3	?	9.3		Small Town
Bitterne	150+	3.2	364–79+	3.2	?	Small Town
Brampton	?	?	?	?		Small Town
Brough-on-Fosse	?	2.8	?			Small Town
Brough-on-Humber	125+	5.6	270+	2.8	?	Civitas capital
Caerwent	late 2nd–early 3rd+	18.0	330+	5.6	348–9+	Civitas capital
Caistor-by-Norwich	?	14.0	?	18.0	?	Civitas capital
Caistor-by-Yarmouth	Hadrianic	?	early–mid 3rd	14.0		Small Town
Caistor, Lincs.	—	—	?	4.0	?	Small Town
Cambridge	—	—	early 4th+	3.0		Small Town
Canterbury	—	—	270–90+	10.1	?	Civitas capital
Carlisle	?	?	?	53.0	?	Civitas capital
Carmarthen	140–50+	12.5	?	?	?	Civitas capital
Catterick	?	—	early 4th?	12.5		Small Town
Caves Inn	—	1.0	—	6.3		Small Town
Chelmsford	160–75+	6.0	—			Small Town
Chesterton-on-Fosse	?	3.2	first half 4th?			Small Town
Chichester	200+	40.0	late 2nd–early 3rd+	3.2	?	Civitas capital
Cirencester	Antonine+	97.0	early 3rd+	40.0	?	Civitas capital
Colchester	60+	43.0	early 2nd	97.0		Colonia
Corbridge	?	?	?	43.0		Small Town
Dorchester, Dorset	150+	32.0	?	?		Civitas capital
Dorchester, Oxon.	160+	5.5	?	32.0		Small Town
Droitwich	270–90	3.0	—	5.5		Small Town
Exeter	180–210	37.0	late Antonine+			Civitas capital
Fenny Stratford	?	?	—	37.0		Small Town
Gloucester	reused fortress	18.5	3rd			Colonia
Godmanchester	—		270–3+	18.5	?	Small Town
Great Casterton	150–60	7.3	late 2nd+	10.9	337–61+	Small Town
Great Chesterford	—		early 4th+	7.3		Small Town

Hardham	?	1.6	—	—	—	Small Town
Horncastle	—	—	4th	2.4	?	Small Town
Ilchester	mid–late 3rd	8.9	—	8.9	—	*Civitas* capital
Iping	?	1.0	—	—	?	Small Town
Irchester	150–60+	8.0	?	8.0	—	Small Town
Kelvedon	60–225	?	?	—	?	Small Town
Kenchester	140–80+	8.9	?	8.9	?	Small Town
Kirby Thore	?	—	?	?	?	Small Town
Leicester	—	—	late 2nd–early 3rd+	42.0	?	*Civitas* capital
Leintwardine	160–90+	5.6	?	5.6	—	Small Town
Lincoln	reused fortress	16.6	late 1st	39.0	—	*Colonia*
Little Chester	125+	?	mid–2nd+	?	—	Small Town
London	late 2nd–early 3rd	3.2	183–4+	133.5	341–75	Uncertain
Malton	?	?	late 3rd?	3.2	—	Small Town
Mancetter	150–75+	2.1	240–320+	2.1	—	Small Town
Margidunum	?	2.8	?	2.8	—	Small Town
Mildenhall	late 2nd+	6.0	360+	7.7	?	Small Town
Neatham	?	2.5	—	—	—	Small Town
Penkridge	160+	1.7	?	—	—	Small Town
Rocester	170–90+	3.6	270–4+	3.6	—	Small Town
Rochester	160–90	7.5	193–211+	7.5	—	Small Town
Silchester	140–60+	40.0	260–80	40.0	—	*Civitas* capital
Thorpe-by-Newark	early 2nd+	1.8	?	1.8	—	Small Town
Towcester	mid–4th	?	?	?	—	Small Town
Tiddington	?	?	?	?	—	Small Town
Uxacona	?	?	?	0.3	—	Small Town
Verulamium	140–55	81.0	210–70	81.0	—	*Municipium*
Wall	—	—	3rd	2.4	—	Small Town
Wanborough	late 2nd–early 3rd	?	?	?	—	Small Town
Water Newton	—	—	2nd	18.0	?	Small Town
Whitchurch	170+	2.8	?	2.8	—	Small Town
Wickford	late 2nd	1.0	—	—	—	Small Town
Winchester	160+	55.0	early 3rd+	55.0	—	*Civitas* capital
Wixoe	?	?	?	?	?	Small Town
Worcester	late 2nd–3rd	8.1	?	8.1	—	Small Town
Wroxeter	150–95+	76.8	?	76.8	—	*Civitas* capital
Wycomb	?	?	?	?	—	Small Town
York	?	?	?	40.0	—	*Colonia*

[a] ? = uncertain, undated

[b] — = absent

Source: based on Crickmore 1984; Hartley 1983; and Frere 1984a, with additions.

Table 6.5. *Small Towns of Roman Britain shown on fig. 61*

No.	Site name	Roman name	Origin
1	Catterick	Cataractonium	Definite fort
2	Malton	Derventio	Definite fort
3	Aldborough	*Civitas* capital[a]	
4	York	*Colonia*[a]	
5	Brough-on-Humber	*Civitas* capital[a]	
6	Winteringham	—	Probable fort
7	Dragonby	—	Definite LPRIA site
8	Kirmington	—	Dual LPRIA/fort
9	Hibaldstow	—	Communications?
10	Caistor	perhaps Bannovalium	Uncertain
11	Owmby	—	Probable LPRIA site
12	Wilderspool	—	Uncertain
13	Buxton	Aquae Arnemetiae	Dual LPRIA/fort
14	Northwich	Condate	Definite fort
15	Pentre	—	Probable fort
16	Heronbridge	—	Uncertain
17	Middlewich	Salinae	Probable fort
18	Lincoln	*Colonia*[a]	
19	Horncastle	Perhaps Bannovalium	Uncertain
20	Brough-on-Fosse	Crococalana	Communications?
21	Thorpe-by-Newark	Ad Pontem	Definite fort
22	Holditch	—	Definite fort
23	Whitchurch	Mediolanum	Definite fort
24	Rocester	—	Definite fort
25	Littlechester	Derventio	Definite fort
26	East Bridgeford	Margidunum	Probable fort
27	Ancaster	—	Dual LPRIA/fort
28	Sleaford	—	Definite LPRIA site
29	Saltersford	Perhaps Causennis	Communications?
30	Sapperton	Perhaps Causennis	Probable LPRIA site
31	Willoughby	Vernemetum	Communications?
32	Wroxeter	*Civitas* capital[a]	
33	Redhill	Uxacona	Definite fort
34	Penkridge	Pennocrucium	Definite fort
35	Wall	Letocetum	Definite fort
36	Mancetter	Manduessedum	Definite fort
37	Leicester	*Civitas* capital[a]	
38	High Cross	Venonis	Communications?
39	Great Casterton	—	Definite fort
40	Water Newton	Durobrivae	Definite fort
41	Caistor-by-Norwich	*Civitas* capital[a]	
42	Scole	Villa Faustini	Communications?
43	Ixworth	—	Definite fort
44	Ashton	—	Probable LPRIA site
45	Kettering	—	Probable LPRIA site
46	Godmanchester	Durovigutum	Definite fort
47	Irchester	—	Probable LPRIA site
48	Blackwardine	—	Uncertain
49	Droitwich	Salinae	Dual LPRIA/fort
50	Worcester	Perhaps Vertis	Probable LPRIA site
51	Alcester	Alauna	Definite fort
52	Tiddington	—	Uncertain
53	Chesterton-on-Fosse	—	Communications?
54	Whilton Lodge	Bannaventa	Communications?
55	Duston	—	Probable LPRIA site

Table 6.5 (*cont.*)

No.	Site name	Roman name	Origin
56	Towcester	Lactodurum	Communications
57	Sandy	—	Probable LPRIA site
58	Cambridge	Duroliponte	Dual LPRIA/fort
59	Great Chesterford	—	Dual LPRIA/fort
60	Coddenham	Combretovium	Dual LPRIA/fort
61	Hacheston	—	Uncertain
62	Dolaucothi	—	Definite fort
63	Carmarthen	*Civitas* capital[a]	
64	Kenchester	Magnis	Probable fort
65	Dymock	—	Dual LPRIA/fort
66	Weston-under-Penyard	Ariconium	Probable LPRIA site
67	Gloucester	*Colonia*[a]	
68	Wycomb	—	Probable LPRIA site
69	Bourton-on-the-Water	—	Probable LPRIA site
70	Dorn	—	Communications?
71	Alchester	—	Probable fort
72	Dropshot	Magiovinium	Definite fort
73	Dunstable	Durocobrivis	Communications?
74	Baldock	—	Definite LPRIA site
75	Braughing	—	Definite LPRIA site
76	Great Dunmow	—	Uncertain
77	Braintree	—	Definite LPRIA site
78	Colchester	*Colonia*[a]	
79	Kelvedon	Canonium	Dual LPRIA/fort
80	Harlow	—	Definite LPRIA site
81	Verulamium	*Municipium*[a]	
82	Ware	—	Uncertain
83	Chelmsford	Caesaromagus	Definite fort
84	Heybridge	—	Definite LPRIA site
85	Cowbridge	Bovium	Communications?
86	Caerwent	*Civitas* capital[a]	
87	Cirencester	*Civitas* capital[a]	
88	Frilford	—	Definite LPRIA site
89	Dorchester-on-Thames	—	Dual LPRIA/fort
90	London[a]		
91	Wanborough	Durocornovium	Communications?
92	Sea Mills	Abona	Probable fort
93	Nettleton Scrubb	—	Probable fort
94	Mildenhall	Cunetio	Probable fort
95	Silchester	*Civitas* capital[a]	
96	Staines	Pontibus	Probable fort
97	Ewell	—	Probable LPRIA site
98	Springhead	Vagniacis	Definite LPRIA site
99	Rochester	Durobrivae	Definite LPRIA site
100	Bath	Aquae Sulis	Dual LPRIA/fort
101	Charterhouse-on-Mendip	Perhaps Iscalis	Definite fort
102	Camerton	—	Probable LPRIA site
103	Ilchester	*Civitas* capital[a]	
104	Exeter	*Civitas* capital[a]	
105	Badbury	Vindocladia	Probable LPRIA site
106	Old Sarum	Sorviodunum	Probable LPRIA site
107	Winchester	*Civitas* capital[a]	
108	Neatham	Vindonium	Communications?
109	Chichester	*Civitas* capital[a]	
110	Canterbury	*Civitas* capital[a]	

Table 6.5 (*cont.*)

No.	Site name	Roman name	Origin
111	Dorchester	*Civitas* capital[a]	
112	Corbridge	Coriosopitum	Definite fort
113	Carlisle	*Civitas* capital[a]	
114	Brampton	—	Uncertain
115	Cave's Inn	Tripontium	Communications?
116	East Anton	—	Communications?
117	Shiptonthorpe	perhaps Delgovicia	Communications?

[a]See table 4.4.
Source: after Burnham 1986; Rivet and Smith 1979, with additions.

7

THE DEVELOPED ECONOMY

The economy of later Roman Britain, as seen through the archaeological evidence, shows a series of differences from the earlier system. In summary, the pattern shows first an increasing regionalization of exchange at the expense of the inter-provincial trade dominant in the early Empire, and this greater emphasis on trade within Britain is accompanied by a change in industrial location, as rurally located production centres expand at the expense of those productive units near the *civitas* centres which had been most significant in the early Empire.

The archaeological evidence

The bulk of the evidence for exchange comprises non-degradable material. Pottery in particular has been widely studied to produce information about both its production and its distribution patterns, largely as a result of its durability and ubiquity in the archaeological record. Its ease of identification contrasts with most other materials which survive, so that systematic archaeological study has identified the location of much of its production, enabling patterns of distribution to be identified (Fulford 1977a; Peacock 1982). Pottery was, however, a low-value commodity in the ancient world (Pucci 1983, 110), as illustrated by the prices given in Diocletian's Price Edict of 301. These show that ordinary earthenware vessels were cheaper than building bricks (Erim and Reynolds 1973, 108–9) and that manufacturers had a commensurately low social status (cf. Finley 1973, 49; Jones 1973, 862–3). We may therefore doubt whether pottery held the importance then that it now attracts from archaeologists, especially in comparison with other materials which have survived less well, such as the agricultural staples which are certain to have been of greater economic importance (chapter 8).

This is of little importance if pottery can be assumed to be representative of the total pattern of exchange. Fulford has argued this (1977a, 38) on the grounds that most pottery was not transported in its own right in a specialized trade, but was rather carried as part of a mixed cargo with other mainly perishable commodities. Pottery is therefore argued to be a fossilized marker of this more significant trade. The validity of this assumption was questioned by Hopkins (1983b, xxii), who asked: 'would the distribution map for the ancient wool trade look like recent maps for the distribution of ancient pots?' To evaluate this, we must first distinguish pottery vessels, such as table wares, traded for their own value from those used as containers solely for the transport of perishable commodities. The latter, mainly amphorae which were used for the transport of wine, olive oil and fish products, provide direct evidence for the movement of more valuable goods and may therefore reflect the overall pattern of exchange.

However, even the distribution of amphorae cannot be taken to provide an unbiased measure of trade because of the widespread use of other containers like barrels, and the probability that changes occurred in the packaging used (Peacock and Williams 1986, 27). Barrels, for instance, fulfilled the same functions as amphorae but are generally less well preserved in the archaeological record. Those found in Britain were most commonly from the Rhine (Boon 1975, fig. 3; Ellmers 1978) and this introduces the possibility of a regional bias in our data. Thus the absence of amphorae or a decline in their incidence may reflect no more than a change in the direction of trade. This was originally suggested by Richmond (1955, 172), although his assumption that barrels signified a link with Bordeaux was based on a misunderstanding of the wood identifications, which in fact show an Alpine origin for most of the barrels (Peacock 1978, 51). The reliance on amphorae perhaps tends to bias the archaeological evidence in favour of Mediterranean products and against those from northern Europe, which are more likely to have been carried in barrels.

Fine pottery has been shown to have had a greater value to its owners than kitchen wares (Evans 1987) and was thus probably more expensive than the vessels attested in the Price Edict. Although it may therefore have been transported for its own intrinsic worth, it is most unlikely to have been the prime object of the trade between its place of manufacture and Britain. The distribution evidence indicates a very low-volume movement, consistent with the idea that even this pottery was of such a low value that it is unlikely to have generated a profit sufficient to justify its transport as a sole cargo. This conclusion is supported by the evidence from Mediterranean wrecks which never have pottery as either the principal or sole cargo (Fulford 1977a, 38). In the early Empire samian ware may have been the exception, for in this period the flow of wealth to the frontiers had inflated prices in those areas to the extent that profit margins were large enough to make the trading of such low-value goods worthwhile. More generally, the distribution of fine pottery should probably be viewed as a result of it accompanying other goods traded or transported as requisitions in kind (*annonae*) to supply the state. Thus, shippers (*navicularii*) moving foodstuffs or raw materials for themselves or under contract to the state also carried their own cargo with no effective increment to its unit costs. This effectively free transport resulted from the carriage cost being covered by the primary contract. In addition, shippers let spare capacity on their ships for the cargoes of other merchants (Jones 1973, 867). Either of these models may be invoked for cases, like Black Burnished ware, which have a strongly military orientation to their distribution and may result from the regular shipping going to those areas. However, in order for the distribution of such pottery to be taken as a surrogate for other items like wool and grain we know were also moved (Fulford 1977a, 63–5), it must be assumed that there was a regular and

158

structured relationship between them. Although Fulford (1977a; 1978a) has argued that pottery can be used for this purpose, a structured relationship has yet to be established. The pottery distributions must therefore be recognized as having only an inferential rather than a representative value in examining broader patterns of exchange.

In the core areas of a local or regional distribution, pottery may perhaps represent the patterns of contact between producers and consumers with the findspots mapping the pattern (Hodder and Orton 1976, 183ff). Such distribution studies suffer from the problem that they result from the accumulation of evidence over considerable periods, and are thus not susceptible to the identification of changes in patterns over short time spans (Hodder 1974a, 70–5; cf. Pomel 1984). Reliance on them for the identification of general patterns is justified as the pottery findspots provide an index of the frequency of contact between consumers and producers, be they via itinerant traders or at a market. Thus the more frequently a consumer site is in contact with the producer or distribution centre the larger the amount of pottery likely to be represented. Even over the short distances covered by these distributions, we need to be wary of too narrow an interpretation, for it is clear that the range over which different commodities travel varied considerably (Hodder 1974b). The dissimilarity is a result of two factors. The first is the type of exchange, for instance commodities transported for the benefit of the state are likely to travel more freely than those simply serving a local market. In this respect it is important to note that market exchange was only one, and perhaps not the dominant form of exchange in the Roman world (Peacock and Williams 1986, 54–63), so an automatic assumption of the existence of a free and competitive market is unjustified. Secondly, the distance transported depends partly on the commodity's value: fine table wares have been shown to travel further than coarse cooking wares within the same exchange system (Hodder 1974b, fig. 29). The patterns of contact between consumers and producers also differ with the intensity of contact, so that the inhabitants of a rural site might obtain their coarse pottery from c. 10 km distant, whereas the fine wares might be brought from c. 50 km and mosaic designs c. 100 km.

The narrow index of interaction provided by pottery is insufficient, for it is obvious that a site will be served from sources and by contacts which spread over a considerable range of distances. Those further flung and less frequent were often concerned with the higher-value exchanges, which are most difficult to document archaeologically. Thus pottery probably over-emphasizes the local contacts at the expense of those less frequent over long distances. Even with these limitations, pottery is of use for the exploration of economic patterning because of its very ubiquity. We must nevertheless be wary of raising it above the level of an indicator which should be used in conjunction with other evidence.

Interprovincial trade

The most marked alteration in exchange patterns which can be observed in Britain during the later Roman period is a substantial decline in the volume of the pottery traded between Britain and other provinces of the Empire. In the early Empire, large quantities of fine pottery (especially samian ware), together with containers for foods and fluids, flowed into Britain from the western provinces, especially Gaul (table 6.2). A variety of imports is also found in late Roman Britain (fig. 65), and during the third century products from the Rhineland and northern Gaul occur. It has been argued that east Gaulish samian continued to be manufactured and imported until the middle of the third century (King 1981), and to this we may add the Moselkeramik (Rhenish ware) beakers which occur widely but rarely, and often in ritual contexts (Harris 1986). These were perhaps transported with the Cologne beakers which occur in some quantity, coming from the same region and which may also have travelled alongside

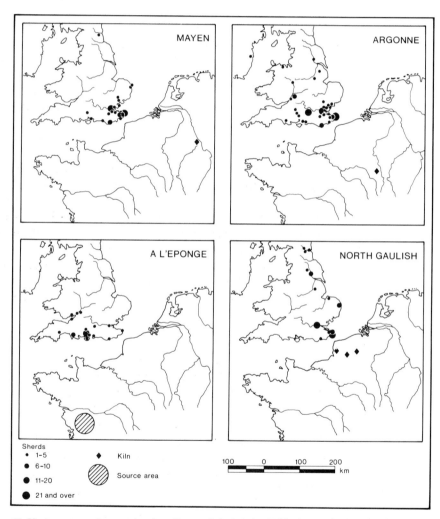

65 Various pottery imports into later Roman Britain (after Fulford 1978a and Richardson and Tyers 1984). These wares are all present only in small quantities, illustrating the self-sufficiency in pottery of Britain in the later Roman period.

samian ware (Anderson *et al.* 1982). In addition, recent excavations in London have identified bowls, jars and flagons which are products of the Somme valley (Richardson 1986, 106–9) and the Atrois/Picardy regions of Gaul (Richardson and Tyers 1984). Although not yet widely recognized, Somme Valley products have also been identified at Faxfleet on the Humber (Sitch 1987) whilst the Atrois/Picardy wares have been found along the East coast as far north as the frontier (Richardson and Tyers 1984, fig. 3). Nonetheless, with the possible exception of London and the continuing imports from eastern Gaul in the first half of the third century, the imports are less numerous and less significant than those of the early Empire. In the fourth century a further range of imports has been identified. These include Eifelkeramik (Mayen ware) (Fulford and Bird 1975) from the Lower Rhineland, Argonne Red Slip wares from eastern Gaul (Fulford 1977a, 76–7) and mottled slip ware referred to as 'ceramique à l'éponge' manufactured somewhere in Aquitania (Galliou *et al.* 1980). In addition to these northern European imports small quantities of African Red Slip wares reached Britain from the central Mediterranean (Bird 1977), together with a limited number of a variety of North African and eastern Mediterranean amphorae (Peacock and Williams 1986, classes 34, 43, 44 and 45). These are found only in small numbers and mostly at times when they were in glut in the Mediterranean.

These fourth-century imports are all represented by a small number of sherds which probably do not represent a substantial ceramic trade. They are more likely to be the by-product of normal movements across the Channel with occasional vessels being brought across the most commonly travelled routes as they had during the LPRIA. Indeed the Mayen vessels are mostly coarse-ware containers, which may have been used for the transport of a perishable commodity (perhaps honey) (Fulford and Bird 1975, 181). It seems improbable that they were transported even in small numbers for any intrinsic value (although cf. Alice Holt ware below). This view would be entirely consistent with the distribution evidence which shows the British findspots of most fourth-century imports to be predominantly coastal. The only exceptions are the red slip wares. Both the African Red Slip ware and Argonne ware are very widely if very thinly distributed (fig. 65), behaving in a similar way to the east Gaulish samian ware with which both are closely related. We may perhaps assume a highly prized status leading to a widespread but thin distribution.

Fulford (1977a; 1978a) has demonstrated that British products also moved in the opposite direction, but in similar small quantities and exclusively from the south-east. These exports comprise entirely the wares most common around southern and eastern England in the later Roman period, namely Black Burnished ware 1 (from Dorset), Alice Holt-Farnham ware from the Surrey/Hampshire borders, New Forest ware and Oxfordshire ware, which, although manufactured in the middle Thames valley, achieved a widespread distribution across southern England. The character of these exports is thus consistent with their distribution being a consequence of normal cross-Channel contact rather than any special trade.

The evidence of the pottery thus demonstrates that, in contrast to the early Empire, the exchange of ceramics was running at a very low level. This compares closely with the LPRIA, when exchange between the two sides of the Channel was perhaps an aspect of kinship links (above, p. 38). The reduction of volume of trade in the late

Empire when compared with the Principate may be a consequence of an equalization of the level of material culture between Britain and the continent caused by Romanization here (Fulford 1978a, 68), but it is more likely to result from an absolute decline in Britain's attractiveness to overseas traders, resulting from the process of economic equalization which was occurring during the third century as a consequence of the changing flows of taxation. Exchange between Britain and the rest of the Empire also declined as the province became more prosperous and self-sufficient with a growing economy (Reece 1981). Fulford has argued against the view that the pottery evidence necessarily shows that inter-provincial trade was declining in the later Roman period (1978a). He bases this on a comparison with the medieval evidence, which suggests that the early Empire pattern was exceptional and later Roman trade was simply reduced to a healthy level. Although it is difficult to disprove this view, serious doubts must be raised over the validity of comparing the later Roman world with High Medieval England, when the rôles of pottery and the nature of the economy cannot be assumed to be the same. Nevertheless, Fulford's fundamental point remains valid, so the absence of ceramic evidence should not lead us to the conclusion that there was limited trade and prosperity in late Roman Britain. Indeed, following the idea of an expansive and more self-sufficient economy, we may even conclude that the absence of imports results from a more prosperous society in this period.

Where we do see a major decline in the evidence by comparison with the Principate is in the incidence of commodities like olive oil, wine and fish sauce which had been traded in amphorae. Although there is some evidence that fish sauce was manufactured in later Roman Britain (Milne 1985, 87–91), the other commodities could not have been replaced by indigenous production even allowing for some viticulture in the province (Frere 1987, 285). As we have noted, the hypothesis that amphora-borne commodities were transported in barrels in the later Roman period is not entirely consistent with the evidence. The bulk of early Roman Spanish amphorae reaching Britain had contained olive oil, and this was not produced in the Rhineland from whence most barrels derive (Boon 1975), whilst most of those from London date to the second century, before the oil apparently ceased to be imported (Wilmott 1982).

The decline in the olive oil trade from Spain (where most of Britain's imports originated) therefore needs further examination and may be accounted for in two ways. First we may note that the dominance of the Baetican oil industries in the Mediterranean was broken during the early third century. Supply thus became more diverse with a wider variety of sources from the western Mediterranean (especially North Africa) supplying needs in that region (Carandini and Panella 1981, fig. 29.1; Keay 1984, 402–5). Whether this was caused by historically attested changes in the ownership of the industry or the mode of transport of the products during the reign of Alexander Severus (222–35), or was a by-product of major shifts in the Mediterranean economy is doubtful, but it seems certain to have interrupted supplies to Britain and the north-west provinces.

Secondly, we have noted that changes took place both in the absolute size and the quality of the British garrison in the third century. Since the supply of the army had probably provided a primary *raison d'être* for overseas traders in the Principate (Middleton 1979), these alterations will have had two major effects which can be related to the decline in the olive oil trade. First, the frontier troops (*limitanei*) would have become almost entirely hereditary, since sons of soldiers were regularly recruited (and from 313 were obliged to serve) (Jones 1973, 615), so the taste for Mediterranean styles of food, including olive oil, may have gradually declined. This loss of Mediterranean tastes is supported by the absence of concentrations of imported pottery on Hadrian's Wall in the fourth century. Secondly, as the army was increasingly paid by requisitions in kind from the locality (Jones 1973, 623), so the availability of cash for them to buy luxuries will have declined, thereby reducing their attractiveness to overseas traders. Combined with these factors was the disruption of the regular military supply networks. This resulted first from the anarchy of the third century and then from Britain's isolation from the Mediterranean during the Gallic Empire and the usurpation of Carausius and Allectus (260–73 and 286–96). We can thus see good reasons why the regular trading contacts supplying Britain may have collapsed through both a decline in demand and interruptions of supply. Combined with the structural changes in the economy already discussed, it is likely that alterations in taste amongst both the civil and military populations then prevented any substantial resurgence of the trade in the fourth century.

The Mediterranean wine trade may have been affected by the same processes. Despite the finds of wine barrels from the Rhineland, their numbers and the intensity of finds of pottery from the same area do not provide support for the idea that there was an increase in that trade to offset the decline in Mediterranean contact. We should nevertheless be wary of placing too much weight on the absence of significant amounts of pottery, since this need not have accompanied any such trade.

In summary we can see that Britain's inter-provincial trade, as seen in the pottery, declined substantially in the later Roman period, although it would be a mistake to assume that this equates with an absolute reduction in the movement in perishable goods. We should, however, see the regular transport of grain attested under Julian (Ammianus 18. 2, 3) as *annona* rather than trade. In the absence of any other evidence, we may thus take the archaeological evidence at face value and conclude that Britain was becoming more self-sufficient; and the inflated prices which had been characteristic of the frontiers in the early imperial period had been equalized by the military and economic changes already outlined. These made it less profitable to supply goods to the frontiers, and had resulted in manufacturing in those provinces becoming fully established and self-sustaining within their own regional economies.

This change in Britain towards self-sufficiency and prosperity is clearly seen in the finds assemblages from all late Roman sites (e.g. fig. 66), but is most visible in London which, it has been argued, originated as a principal trading centre at a neutral location, allowing it to control inter-provincial trade. It is thus significant that London is the centre which shows the earliest and most marked changes in its urban character in the second century, when it begins to lose its vibrancy and fall into a relative economic decline (Marsden 1980, 148; Merrifield 1983, 140ff). It is sometimes argued that this alteration in character is a result of destruction by medieval and modern disturbance, or the misdating of third-century pottery (Morris 1975). However, the change from productive to residential functions is now unquestionable, but simply occurs earlier in London than elsewhere (Perring 1987; Sheldon 1975). The period of apparent economic disruption in London is precisely that at which major new quays and harbours are constructed (fig. 67) at Custom House (Tatton-Brown 1974, 125–6) and St Magnus House (Dyson 1986, 63–4). Whilst it is possible that these were official installations for the provincial government, it seems more probable that their construction was a result of efforts by the citizens to invest in improving its facilities in order to arrest its declining trade. In retrospect, if we accept the argument here that this trade was in decline for more fundamental reasons, we can see that the strategy was futile.

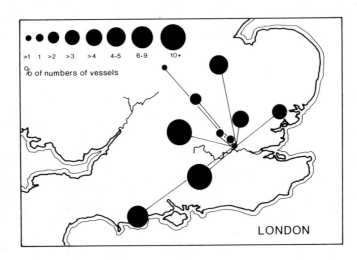

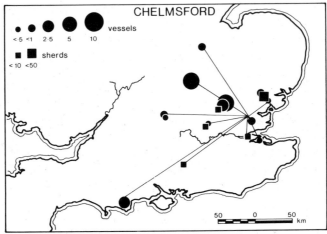

66 The supply of pottery to London and Chelmsford in the fourth century. Imports from overseas additional to the British material represent less than 10 per cent of the pottery at each site (after Going 1987 and Green 1980).

Pottery production and trade within the province

The decline of importation of pottery from the continent coincided with growth in the indigenous pottery production. Unless there was an absolute decline in pottery consumption, British production must have increased. No such decline in pottery use has been documented, but the third- and fourth-century patterns do not simply represent a continuation of the earlier productions and distributions. Two closely related changes can be identified. First, the number of pottery producers gradually declined, with the survivors located in rural rather than urban situations (figs. 52 and 68). Secondly, the average scale of pottery distributions increased, so that they supplied much larger areas and the sources of ordinary pottery for most settlements became further away from them. These developments have been documented in a number of studies and deserve careful examination before their relationship to other alterations is discussed.

67 The substantial timber quay found beneath Cannon Street station in London. The huge horizontal timbers, set on piles, retained a gravel platform upon which the waterfront structures were built. This late-first-century waterfront on the eastern side of the Walbrook stream is part of a larger system which continued eastwards along the Thames frontage to the London Bridge area. Later in the Roman period the waterfronts were extended further along the river towards the Tower of London. Scales each 50 cm long. (*Photograph by courtesy of the Museum of London.*)

165

Characteristic of later Roman Britain were specialist pottery industries comprising clusters of kilns which produced their own distinctive and high-quality products. In addition there were similar kiln groups which manufactured more mundane grey cooking wares, which also had wide distributions. The principal manufacturers are listed in table 7.1. Some of these centres (like those in the New Forest and Oxfordshire) had mixed productions but specialized in high-quality drinking vessels and fine table wares, which replaced the imports of samian ware from the latter part of the third century onwards. They nevertheless also augment the range of those industries as they supplied a series of beakers which did not normally occur in the samian repertoire but had been produced in the Rhineland and at the Nene Valley and Colchester kilns in the early and middle Empire. It is difficult to be certain whether these producers won the markets from the samian producers by competition, or grew up when the imports ceased to be supplied. The redating of late samian production, bringing it well into the third century (King 1981), now makes competition possible and would

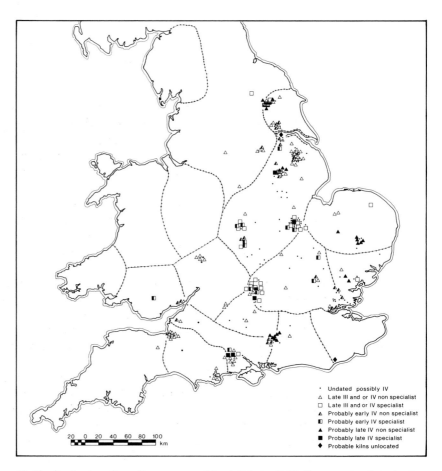

68 The distribution of later Roman pottery kilns in Britain, divided by century and production type (after Swan 1984). Note the clustering of many kilns near *civitas* boundaries.

166

Table 7.1. *Principal late Roman pottery industries in Britain*

Industry	Products	Reference
Crambeck	Coarse and fine wares	Evans 1988
Holme-on-Spalding Moor	Coarse wares	Halkon 1987
Swanpool	Coarse wares	Swan 1984, fiche 451–4
Lower Nene Valley	Principally fine wares	Howe *et al.* n.d.; Hartley 1960
Hartshill/Mancetter	*Mortaria*	Swan 1984, fiche 647–55
Upchurch Marshes	Coarse wares	Monaghan 1987
Oxfordshire	Coarse ware, *mortaria* and principally fine ware	Young 1977
Hadham	Principally fine wares	Roberts 1982; Swan 1984, fiche 356–9
Alice Holt/Farnham	Coarse wares	Lyne and Jefferies 1979; Millett 1979
Dorset Black Burnished	Coarse wares	Swan 1984, fiche 259–64
New Forest	Coarse ware, *mortaria* and principally fine wares	Fulford 1975

explain the imitation of late samian forms by industries like that of Oxford. However, the different range of products supplied by the British manufacturers suggests that they went beyond simply competing with traditional sources.

Most of these major fine ware manufacturers sprang to dominance during the later third century, generally growing out of modest earlier industries or emerging in areas where we have no sure evidence for previous large-scale production. These developments illustrate a centralization of production which outstripped the established fine ware producers like those of the Nene valley, even though some continued to manufacture. Such growth and centralization in production are also seen in some of the industries producing coarse cooking wares. Centres were already in existence either producing coarse wares alone on a large scale (e.g. Dorset, Black Burnished ware or Swanpool, Lincoln) or with specialist production (e.g. Hartshill/Mancetter producing mixing bowls – *mortaria*). These continue to manufacture although none shows the staggering success of some of the other industries. Other kilns, which had very modest early Roman predecessors, do however come to prominence. Notable amongst these is the Alice Holt/Farnham industry which made the grey cooking wares that dominated supply to many sites in the south-east.

If we examine the data from Swan's corpus (1984), we can identify a clear pattern of change taking place through the Roman period (Fulford 1977b; Saunders 1986) (fig. 52). This shows the continuance in production and indeed growth of kiln centres located in rural areas peripheral to the *civitates*, whilst those close to the towns tend to disappear. This pattern may be the natural consequence of competition between producers leading to the survival of those most efficient and best placed. However, any simple interpretation presents difficulties as the successful production centres which emerge are not those one would predict on the basis of a market economy in which the maximization of profit was the principal motive. In such a system the key to productive success would be location within easy reach of the largest and most valuable markets, traditionally seen as the *civitas* capitals. The first- and second-century patterns of kiln location show that positions near these towns were preferred (fig. 52). However, in the later Roman period the producers nearest the *civitas* centres suffer most, with their numbers declining whilst the kilns furthest away survive and indeed thrive. Despite the evidence of the decline of the traditional rôles of the *civitas* capitals, it has been shown that their sites remained major foci and may thus be expected to have been important as markets. The pattern of kiln location is the reverse of that predicted from the simple working of an optimizing marketing strategy. The most successful producers of the later Empire are largely either located rurally (e.g. New Forest, Oxfordshire) or next to Small Towns (e.g. Nene valley or Alice Holt/ Farnham); few lie adjacent to any of the major towns of the early Empire. In short, we have the pattern of successful production in precisely the same areas as we see urban economic growth – on the peripheries of the *civitates*.

The explanation for these areas of growth is not simple, since although some of the kilns do relate directly to the growth of the Small Towns (i.e. Holme-on-Spalding-Moor/Shiptonthorpe; Alice Holt/Neatham), others, especially the major fine ware manufacturers, are located at great distances from even these urban developments (fig. 68). Their growth is not explicable simply in terms of resources, for all pottery producers need raw materials, namely clay, a tempering agent, water and fuel, and all these are widely available in Roman Britain, not being limited to peripheral areas within the *civitates*. Any idea that producers had been reckless enough to have used up fuel supplies (rather than managing and harvesting their woodland) is not credible, whilst Fulford's suggestion (1977b, 307) that coppiced wood is unsuitable for kiln firing is not supported by ethnographic evidence. Increased pressure on land may have put a premium on its value immediately adjacent to the towns and thereby reduced the timber supply (Fulford 1977b, 308), but the poor-quality land needed for coppicing and pottery manufacture is often available immediately beside towns (where indeed pottery had been widely produced in the early Empire). A negative explanation for the success of the rural producers is thus not appropriate, especially as transport costs can be predicted to have put these areas at a disadvantage. We should therefore seek a positive explanation, best related to the broader changes which were occurring in the later Roman period.

Further evidence bearing on the explanation of this is provided by the distribution of the kilns' products, which are generally widely dispersed and in some cases have been subjected to detailed analysis. Although the patterns which emerge from these analyses are not always clear-cut (Pomel 1984), it is plain that the successful industries reached a far wider market than had most of the earlier producers. The products of the British kilns of the Principate in general were limited to the sphere of influence of a single market, whether they were distributed directly from it or via pedlars (above, p. 123; fig. 53). These markets were usually *civitas* capitals or other Public Towns, so the distributions tended to coincide with their spheres of dominance. We have argued that this resulted from the control of marketing by the *civitas* élite, whose centralized power was reinforced by the taxation system (table 6.3), enabling them also to regulate production and the market place thereby reinforcing their wealth and power. The bulk of exchange was thus embedded within social relations and was not solely for profit. The breakdown of this pattern, with an increase in buying and selling outside the sphere of social control in the later Roman period, has been argued to result from a reduction in the effective authority of the centralized élite, with the consequence that exchange was liberated (or became disembedded) from social control so that the economy began to grow. This argument has been developed by Hodder (1979, 194) and reinforced by Reece (1979a, 216–17) on the strength of the coin evidence. It has been shown that there was a massive increase in the numbers of coins lost from the third century onwards and these were of lower denominations than those of the early Roman period (Reece 1972). This evidence is consistent with a pattern of the increased use of coinage for exchange within a marketing system.

Fulford (1981, 196–201) has questioned this interpretation of an increasingly free economy from the third century on several grounds. First, he sees the increase in the scale of pottery distributions adduced by Hodder to support his hypothesis as simply a result of the regionalization of trade as imports declined. He also notes that some of the core areas of these distributions remain limited to the territories they supplied in the Principate. Secondly, he points towards possible disjunctions between LPRIA and Romano-British periods, which he believes betray change towards a different type of economy which resulted from the imposition of taxes. Change in the taxation system is also seen as the cause of the changes in the later Roman period, which Hodder interprets as a result of the reduction of social control over the economy. These criticisms offer valuable insights into the processes at work in Roman Britain, but do not undermine the idea that exchange in the earlier Roman period remained predominantly a part of social interaction. The argument developed earlier (chapter 6) has attempted to show that the changes in taxation are best interpreted as an aspect of that control by the tribal élite. In these circumstances, it is difficult to escape from the conclusion that social organization and aristocratic control were dominant in the processes at play in early Roman Britain.

From this starting point the idea of explaining the changes in pottery and coinage in the late Roman period as a result of the breakdown of an embedded economy is attractive, although a more detailed examination of the evidence shows that the reality is more complex. First, considerable doubts must be expressed over the extent to which the late Roman economy anywhere within the Empire was outside the influence of powerful social groups. Whittaker (1983) has demonstrated that much trade was controlled by the state, church and landowners in the central provinces, so it would require special pleading to see Britain dominated by increasingly free market exchange. Secondly, some of the late Roman pottery distributions remain closely constrained by boundaries already in existence. The East Yorkshire industries, for instance, very clearly reflect the boundaries of the Civitas Parisiorum (Evans 1985; below). Similarly, Fulford (1981, 196) has pointed out that the distributions of the coarse wares from the Oxfordshire and New Forest kilns are the same as those for the earlier products of those industries. This seems to demonstrate the continuity of social groups subsidiary to the *civitates*.

In other areas beneficial locations allowed rural industries to extend their distributions to capture larger markets. Thus, for instance, despite producing only low-value coarse pottery, the Alice Holt/Farnham industry was able to build on its substantial local distribution of the second century to capture a substantial market in southern Britain. This seems to result from its good location on the River Wey. The river system was used to distribute pottery throughout much of the south-east and capture the bulk of the London market, because transport cost advantages were combined with quality and economies of scale achieved through large-scale production (Millett 1979) (fig. 69). This success provides empirical support for the price advantage of water transport adduced from Diocletian's Price Edict (Jones 1973, 841–2). It is likely that once the Farnham industry (fig. 70) had captured these larger markets, it was able to maintain its dominance and there was little opportunity for competitors to gain a foothold, at least until the latter part of the fourth century.

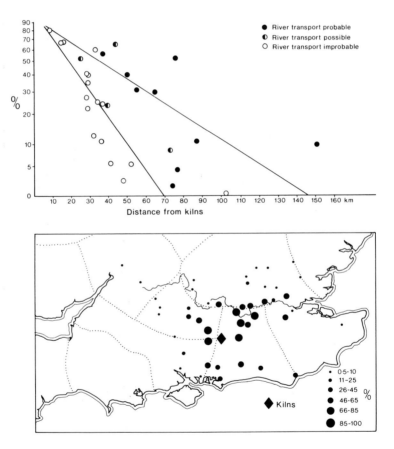

69 The distribution of Alice Holt/Farnham Roman pottery in the fourth century. The lower figure shows the percentage of the ware found on each site, whilst the graph illustrates the importance of water in its transport. The two lines represent the best-fit linear regression lines for pottery from landlocked and water accessible sites respectively. This shows the differential transport costs involved, and the industry's advantage in being located near a navigable river (from Millett 1979, with additional data from Lyne and Jefferies 1979).

170

A similar mechanistic approach has been adopted by Fulford and Hodder (1975) to examine and explain the distribution of Oxfordshire ware. Their analysis of the quantity of Oxfordshire ware in relation to the distance of findspots from the kilns (fig. 71) showed that sites along the Thames and Avon valleys had greater than average quantities of the pottery than expected, purely on the basis of their distance from the kilns. Mapping these deviations from the expected pattern suggested that the distribution was strongly biased by the lower transport costs provided by the use of the Thames and Avon. This led Fulford and Hodder to suggest that the use of water transport had allowed the industry to be especially competitive and consequently

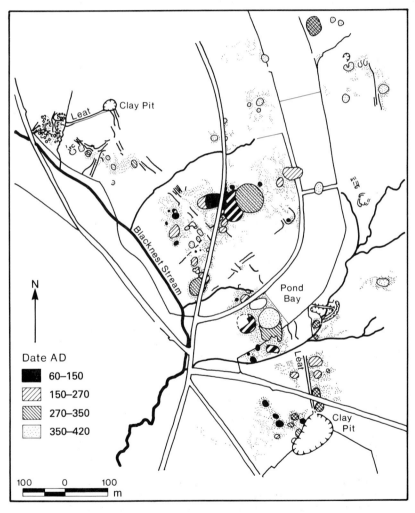

70 The pottery production centre in the Alice Holt Forest, Hampshire. The key shows the dates of the various waster dumps located by fieldwork on either site of the leats which supplied water to the workshops (after Lyne and Jefferies 1979).

171

capture extra markets in these directions. They also observed that to the north and south the distribution was far more limited. An examination of the relative proportions of Oxfordshire and New Forest pottery in the area south of the Oxford kilns led them to the conclusion that the limit to the distribution in that area was a result of competition from the New Forest industry. It is difficult to find an industry to the north to account for the similar pattern. The nearest major producer was Mancetter/Hartshill, which did not produce any widely traded fine pottery, whilst the Hadham and Nene valley industries to the north and east do not penetrate as far west in significant quantities (Pomel 1984, figs. 7, 8, 20 and 21).

The difficulty in explaining the distribution pattern in terms of competition is accentuated when the ceramic assemblages on the distributions margins are examined in detail. Neatham, for instance, lies almost equidistant from the two production centres of Oxfordshire and the New Forest and received pottery from both. However, the pottery supplied by each producer was dominated by the better-quality products of that centre with the result that the two elements in the assemblage are complementary (cf. Hodder 1978, 46). It appears that the Oxford kilns were the dominant suppliers, but where a New Forest product supplemented the Oxfordshire range it was also supplied in quantity (Millett and Graham 1986, 90–1). Thus it is not satisfactory to see the distributions of the two manufacturers as a result of direct competition with the successful industry driving out the unsuccessful. Rather, the two seem to have fulfilled specialist requirements within overlapping markets. In this interpretation, a lack of demand for Oxfordshire-type best explains their scarcity in the midlands.

This hypothesis can be developed further if we examine the unexpectedly large distributions of Oxfordshire ware down the Avon and Thames valleys. The problem with the mechanistic interpretation, which accounts well for the distribution down the Thames, is that it fails to take account of the Cotswolds, which block the route to the west (Young 1977, 7, 234). These hills formed one of the most substantial barriers to water transport in England in the pre-canal era (Hadfield 1966, fig. 2) (fig. 71), so the Severn valley distribution of Oxfordshire ware was possible despite, rather than because of, the natural geography. This strongly implies that the concentration of Oxfordshire ware in the Severn valley was the result of an unusual demand.

When we examine the distribution pattern in relation to human rather than physical geography, we can provide a more satisfactory explanation for the industry's location at the boundary of several *civitates* (fig. 71). This position will have allowed it access to the marketing networks of each of the *civitates*, and seems to have been the key to the success of the Oxfordshire industry. Particularly large quantities of its pottery are found in the Civitas Dobunnorum and the western part of the Civitas Belgarum, perhaps with primary marketing at Ilchester and Cirencester, which lay within easy reach of the kilns by road and possibly river (cf. Young 1977, 7), allowing redistribution to the remainder of the territory. It also achieved success down the Thames (cf. Alice Holt/Farnham), feeding into the *civitates* which border the river. The margins of its distribution were along the south coast (and on the continent) where demand was limited to a narrower range of products. In contrast, it was generally less successful in distributing to the *civitates* of the midlands, where we have suggested that it was positively rejected (above). This explanation suggests that the key to the

Oxfordshire industry's prosperity lay in distribution through markets which, far from being free, remained in the control of the tribal élites who could accept (like the Dobunni) or reject (like the Corieltauvi) a particular product for their network.

An important alternative determinant in these distributions may have been the customs dues (*portoria*) which were levied at provincial boundaries (Jones 1973, 429). Two factors call into question their importance. First, we cannot be certain whether they were applied at boundaries between the provinces in a single diocese, although it is probable that they were. Secondly, the levels which are attested (between 2 and 5 per cent) (Jones 1973, 825) are so low that they seem unlikely to have gener-

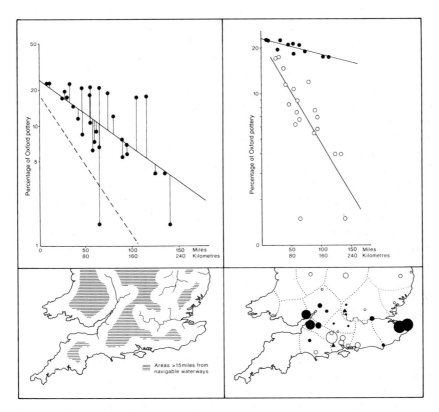

71 The distribution of Oxfordshire Roman pottery. The upper left graph shows how the best-fit regression line fails adequately to summarize variations in the data. The regression residual or deviation of each point from the best-fit line is plotted on the map at the bottom right, with the circle sizes proportional to their distance from the line. Sites which have more pottery than expected (i.e. above the line) are shown in black; those with less are shown as open circles. The graph is replotted (*top right*) with the sites lying on rivers shown in black, and those away from them shown as open circles (cf. fig. 69). This has been taken to indicate the importance of river transport. However, a comparison of the maps shows that although the Cotswolds blocked the riverine route to the west, invalidating the water transport hypothesis, there is a concentration of finds in the lower Severn valley. An examination of the map shows that the pottery may have been distributed via the different *civitas* networks, thus achieving more success in some tribes rather than others.

ated a detectable barrier to trade. Whilst these dues may be reflected in the distributions of artefacts discussed here, the more deeply enduring and embedded influence of the *civitas* boundaries seem more likely to have influenced them.

The third- and fourth-century distributions which have been investigated by Evans (1985, chapters 7–9) provide an important comparison with the Oxfordshire evidence. He has been able to identify a series of changes in supply which demonstrate both the continuation of social constraints on pottery distributions and the effects of transport costs and institutional demands. Evans points out that in the third century the distribution of East Yorkshire products (Knapton, Norton and Holme-on-Spalding Moor wares) are constrained within the Civitas Parisiorum, whilst only specialist products from outside the area are generally found. To the south a similar limitation is found with the distribution of Dalesware mainly limited within the Civitas Corieltauvorum.

This pattern declines somewhat through the fourth century as the Crambeck industry grows. Whilst there is some evidence for the operation of a freer market exchange for some of the minor productions, the major pottery types (Calcite Gritted wares and Crambeck coarse and fine wares) obtain a wide distribution, which shows no discernible effect of transport costs. Thus the quantities of these fabrics are more or less equal over the whole region, and do not show any diminution in quantity within the assemblage with increasing distance from the kilns. This contrasts with the earlier distributions of Black Burnished wares along Hadrian's Wall, which Evans has shown (*contra* Gillam and Greene 1981) to be directly related to the distance of the findspots from the coast via which they were supplied (that is, the west for BB1 and the east for BB2). This distribution, therefore, does not reflect competition between the two types of Black Burnished ware (cf. Oxford/New Forest ware, above). The conclusion arrived at is that after *c.* 370 there was a significant alteration in pottery supply which allowed Crambeck and Calcite Gritted ware to obtain their extraordinary distributions. This is plausibly interpreted as the result of a military contract (Evans 1985, 345–6), and reinforces the view that, as in the south, the exchange of pottery in late Roman north Britain was determined by the social and political structures rather than the operation of a free market.

Thus, far from reflecting a breakdown in the social control of exchange, we can argue that the pottery evidence demonstrates that the late Roman period saw its continued dominance. However, an increased awareness of the social constraints on the economy allowed innovation at the peripheries where such control was at its weakest. Accordingly the location of the successful industries in late Roman Britain seems to represent a successful adaption to the system of embedded exchange rather than indicating its destruction. These developments are probably related to other aspects of rural investment seen in later Roman Britain (chapter 8).

Other economic evidence

Whilst later Roman Britain remained a fundamentally agrarian society, there are further indicators which have considerable potential value in aiding our understanding of the dynamics of the economy. Regrettably, the potential of many of the most ubiquitous materials, especially small metal objects, has yet to be realized. There are nevertheless a few pieces of evidence which have been examined in sufficient detail to supplement the picture provided by the pottery evidence.

The most important additional source of evidence for the spatial organization of later Roman society in Britain is that provided by the distribution of mosaics. In a sequence of important papers D. J. Smith (1969; 1984) has grouped many late Roman mosaics into a series of different artistic schools (fig. 72). Although most of these mosaics (which are fourth century) come from villa sites, they have been shown to form distributions centring on a series of towns. It has thus been realistically argued that the groups represent workshops (*officinae*) based in the major towns from which customers ordered the pavements to be laid in their rural homes. The groups now defined (D. J. Smith 1984) are a Central Southern School (dated 300–25), two successive workshops based on Cirencester (the Corinian Orpheus school of 300–20 and the Corinian Saltire School of 340/50–370+), a Petuarian *officina* (340–50), and finally the Durobrivan group (350/60–370/80). Despite the variation in date, their

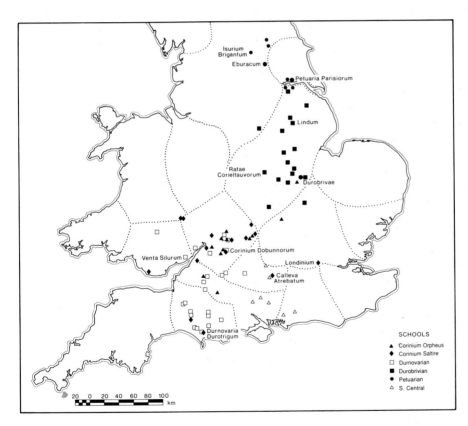

72 The distribution of mosaics from the different schools or workshops in later Roman Britain. There seems a reasonable correlation between the distribution and some of the *civitates* (after D. J. Smith 1984).

175

distributions demonstrate a comparatively tight clustering, consistent with the idea that they were generally commissioned from a single workshop. As these were presumably high-value commodities, they provide a useful contrast with pottery. We should nevertheless beware of over-simplification, since figure 76 shows that the total distribution of mosaics is uneven and partly determined by the social structure of the groups for which they were provided (below, p. 186). Consequently there is an irregular background distribution of mosaic floors against which the schools identified need to be viewed. Despite these problems the distribution map shows that even these high-value commodities had strongly constrained distributions which correlate very closely with the *civitates*. With the exception of the occasional outliers (most of which occur in towns), the schools which D. J. Smith has defined are mainly confined to distribution within a single *civitas*, so the *officinae* could legitimately be renamed after those *civitates* (thus respectively Belgic/Atrebatic, Durotrigian, Parisian and Corieltauvian).

Two significant points emerge from this observation. First, D. J. Smith related all but the Corieltauvian group to a base in one of the *civitas* capitals. In one exceptional case he argued that Durobrivae was the centre, although apparently only on the grounds that tesserae had been manufactured there (1984, 372–3). This does not carry conviction, since one might expect the preparation of tesserae to have taken place at any site where a floor was to be laid, so either Leicester or Lincoln could equally be seen as the centre of this school. On analogy with others the *civitas* capital at Leicester would be most satisfactory. Secondly, the Central Southern group is the only one which is not clearly related to a single *civitas*, although its distribution significantly covers a single LPRIA territory, which may have been divided for the convenience of the Roman administration, although afterwards it perhaps retained some cultural unity, as suggested by this distribution.

The coherence of the spatial groupings of these mosaics is thus significant because their limitation to a single *civitas* or tribal area suggests that these social groupings remained of significance through the fourth century, even where high-value commodities, which might be expected to transcend them are concerned. A potential explanation for this lies in the significance of their use of particular sets of artistic forms as symbols to express membership of a particular tribal group. In this case, the symbolic significance of the patterns as expressions of social identity may have been more important than their monetary or decorative value. The significance may have acted to limit their distribution to the dwellings of those wishing to express that particular group identity, as Hodder (1982) has described in contemporary societies. If this interpretation is correct, it underlies the continuing importance of the ethnic identities in fourth-century Britain. Occasional examples of the styles outside their home territory (especially in towns) may then be interpreted as tribal expatriates expressing their continued allegiance to their home group in a way seen amongst many contemporary Europeans.

One particular example of ceramic tile manufacture also provides a valuable comparison with the pottery evidence. The stamped tiles produced at Minety on the Gloucestershire–Wiltshire border (McWhirr 1979), which largely date to the period before *c.* 250 (Darvill 1979, 312–13), show a surprisingly wide distribution consider-

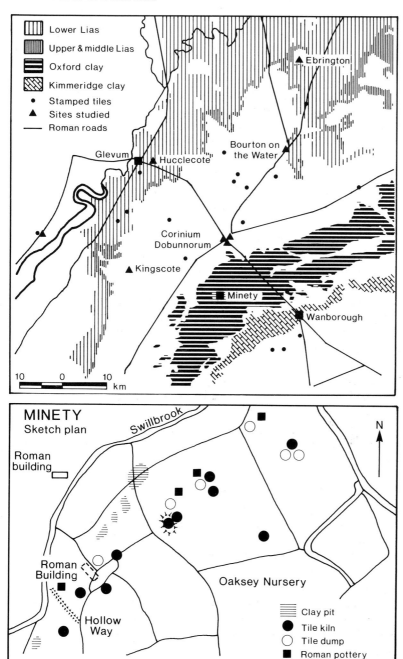

73 The location and layout of the tilery at Minety, Wilts, near the southern boundary of the Civitas Dobunnorum, within which most of the stamped tiles are found. The kilns and waster dumps stretch for approximately 1 km along the bank of the Swillbrook stream (after Darvill 1979).

ing the low value attached to them and their manufacturers according to Diocletian's Price Edict (VII. 2, 14 – Frank 1940, 339; XV. 19–33 – Erim and Reynolds 1973, 101–8). However, like many potteries the Minety kilns are located rurally and near a *civitas* boundary (fig. 73). Aside from this perhaps exceptional case and allowing for the potential problems of itinerant producers, tiles can potentially provide a marker for local distributions from minor market centres, as it seems valid to assume that they were low-value products of high bulk which generally achieved only a local distribution (Hodder 1974b).

The final evidence which requires examination is the low-value bronze coinage found in quantity in later Roman Britain (Reece 1972). Fulford (1978b) has suggested that we can use this to assess the trade connections between Britain and other provinces during the late Empire. This idea originates in the evidence the coins' mint-marks give of their place of manufacture, and thus the potential they provide for measuring their changing levels of contact with Britain. Fulford argued that if coin-ages moved between provinces as a result of trade, then the proportions of the coins from each mint found in Britain should reflect the volume of trade with that area. Fulford (1977a, 65–70) uses this to suggest a shift in the balance of Britain's trade with the continent in the mid-fourth century. Prior to this date he notes that she was closely integrated with Gaul and Germany, but afterwards this link declined, to be supplanted by contact with southern Gaul. This model, however, presupposes a coinage supply pattern which is rational and deliberately facilitated trade. As Reece (1984, 144–6) has pointed out, Roman coinage was primarily produced for the use of the adminis-

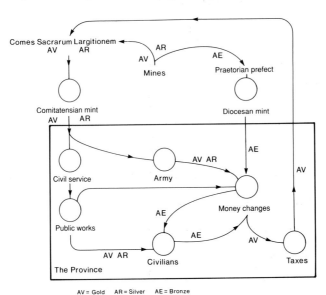

74 Diagram reconstructing the administrative mechanisms involved in the circulation of coinage in the later Roman world. The box represents the individual province. The circulation system is largely determined by taxation and the settlement of state debts, with little apparent way in which market demands could affect supplies of money. Bronze coinage functioned primarily to buy back bullion from circulation (after Reece 1984).

tration. Bullion was produced to service state debts and to pay public servants, while bronze was produced to buy bullion back from circulation and cannot be readily related to a primary function in trading (fig. 74). However, since bronze coinage was not removed from circulation by the state except in unusual circumstances, it will have been used in exchange transactions once in circulation. This supports the literary sources which show that, at least in the Mediterranean, a monetarized market economy existed (Reece 1984, appendix), although the face-value of even the smallest

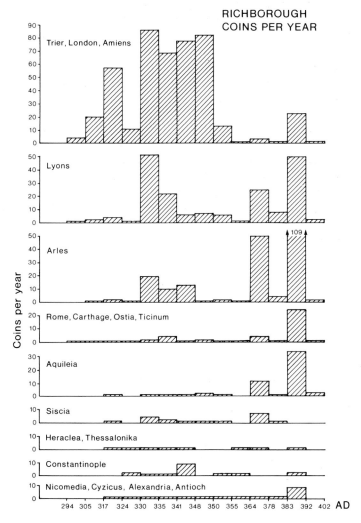

75 The various mints supplying coinage to Richborough in the fourth century illustrate the apparently random changes in the sources of supply. These changes result from the administrative decisions within the system shown in fig. 74, which cannot easily be related to any change in inter-provincial trade (after Reece 1984). The dates along the bottom axis divide the coinage into the principal phases of production within the fourth century.

coin was high by modern standards, limiting the nature of the exchange in which they could be used (Reece 1987, 25–45).

The empirical data support the interpretation that the trading rôle of late Roman coinage was secondary to its official functions, and that supply was liable to arbitrary alteration. First, the patterns of coin supply to late Roman Britain do not show gradual change from one mint to another as would be predicted if supply were reflecting changes in the balance of trade. Instead the overall impression (fig. 75) is of sudden random changes, consistent with apparently arbitrary administrative processes unconnected with trade. Secondly, at several stages during the fourth century bronze coinage failed to reach Britain in quantity, despite having been minted on the continent. In 341–6 and 353–64 the absence of bronze coinage is made up for by copying, which is most satisfactorily explained as the work of the army or civil servants (Reece 1984, 156). Had the main reason for the arrival of bronze coin in Britain been through trading with other provinces, we might reasonably have expected it to continue to arrive during these periods, but its absence supports the model which explains coin supply in terms of the needs of the administration. This unfortunately offers little help in establishing the volume and direction of Britain's late Roman trade, but does reinforce the general view that much exchange in later Roman Britain was still embedded within the social and administrative system rather than being part of a free market. Whilst coinage was almost certainly used for free market exchange it was primarily in circulation for administrative reasons.

Thus all the economic developments in Roman Britain until the later fourth century seem to reflect a broad continuity of the structure of economic and social institutions which we have traced from the LPRIA. Although different areas thrived as the system mutated there is little to show that its fundamentals had changed. This implies a continuance of the power of the traditional élites at their centres, while the newly dominant industries and Small Towns emerged at the tribal boundaries, perhaps under the control of a secondary tier of the aristocracy. The balance of the economy had changed, but the players appear to have remained the same.

8

LATER ROMAN

RURAL DEVELOPMENT

Later Roman Britain saw a series of significant changes in the pattern of settlement which indicate a transfer in the emphasis of activity from the cores of the *civitates* to their peripheries. Whilst these changes affected urban settlements and industrial production, a series of alterations can also be observed in the rural settlement pattern. In the Principate, we saw rural Romanization characterized by the development of villas, and this pattern was shown to be deeply rooted in the existing settlement system. In the later Roman period a series of developments can be observed which reflect a radical deviation from that established in the early Empire. We see an increase in the number of villas, together with alterations in their character, the emergence of nucleated settlements (which may be described loosely as villages), and finally a diversification of production involving innovation in agricultural methods. Taken together with the changes already described in chapters 6 and 7, we may characterize these as representing a flowering of the countryside and the culmination of Roman Britain's achievements. To be understood, they must be examined within the context of the structural alterations we have already described.

The population

Before analysing this changing pattern in detail, we should pause to attempt to evaluate the size of the population of Roman Britain, and the importance of its rural component. The problem of the population size has been tackled by most who have written about the province, although there is no universal view on an acceptable estimate. This is partly because the methods adopted for its estimation have not been uniform (table 8.1), whilst comparison is difficult since the land area considered has rarely been made explicit; and as a number of the current estimates are interdependent, their convergence at around 3 million should be treated with caution. Although this figure is comparable but marginally higher than those suggested for the medieval period, this cannot be used to substantiate the estimate since these too are subject to considerable doubt (Miller and Hatcher 1978, 28–9). A systematic approach to the estimation of the size of the Romano-British population is desirable, even though full evidence is not available. For the purposes of this estimate, I shall consider only those

Table 8.1. *Previous population estimates for Roman Britain*

Authority	Method of estimation/source	Estimate (million)
Collingwood 1929	Towns, villages, villas and army	0.5
Wheeler 1930	Known sites plus food need	1.5
Collingwood & Myres 1937, 180	Settlement pattern	1
Frere 1967 (revised 1987)	Known sites plus food need	2 (3)
Smith, C. 1977	Frere 1967 + new rural density	5–6
Cunliffe 1978b	Frere 1967	2
Fowler 1978	Frere 1967 + new rural density	4
Salway 1981, 544	Extrapolation from survey; Smith 1977	4–6
Fulford 1984, 131	Comparison with medieval figures	max. 2.8

areas which now comprise England and Wales, and will attempt to deal with the optimum period, which I consider to be the first half of the fourth century. Three approaches to this problem are utilized, beginning with the most reliable data. We can reliably estimate the Roman military population of Britain in the fourth century as between 10,000 and 20,000 (James 1984, 169), which with family and dependents might swell to between 50,000 and 200,000 people.

Secondly, we have a reasonable idea of the size of the defended areas of the towns (table 6.4). Esmonde-Cleary (1987) has shown that this size is not the maximum settled area for some of the sites, whilst at others the settlement does not fill the enclosure. Furthermore we know that some of the Small Towns were not defended; however, this figure does provide a working minimum estimate for the urban areas of Roman Britain in the fourth century. We can use this with the multipliers provided by Hassan (1981, 66–7) to generate an urban population estimate for the province. Hassan's figures, suggested as typical in the pre-industrial era, are those for the old quarters of middle-eastern towns (216 people/ha) giving a likely maximum, and for villages in the same areas (137 people/ha) indicating a probable minimum. This gives a range of 183,971 (based on the village densities) to 290,057 (from the urban figure; table 8.2). These densities are above the range suggested by Rivet (1958, 89–90), which converts to 62–185 people/ha (although its basis is not clear) and Boon (1974, 61–2), who proposed a value of 100 people/ha on the basis of the observed density of stone buildings at Silchester. In contrast they are below the estimate derived for Neatham (283 people/ha) based on the density of timber buildings (Millett and Graham 1986, 154). Given these differences, the range can only be taken as a guide, although even a very major change in the assumed density would make a comparatively minor impact on its magnitude relative to the remainder of the population. This is particularly significant in relation to Reece's (1980) points about the low density of settlement within later Roman towns (above, p. 134). In this respect any idea that *civitas* capitals were more densely occupied than the Small Towns cannot be sustained, as the independently derived figures for Neatham and Silchester illustrate. In reality, the average population density within the towns probably lay towards the lower end of the range, since Romano-British towns tend to sprawl rather than being densely packed. Nonetheless, in the absence of more reliable and detailed evidence a range of *c.* 184,000 to 290,000 should stand (table 8.2).

Table 8.2. *Estimated size of the urban population of Roman Britain*

Area of 62 sites whose area is known (table 6.4) = 1,128 ha
These represent 84% of the 74 sites

Population at 137 per ha (Hassan 1981, 66–7) = 154,536 people
Population at 216 per ha (Hassan 1981, 66–7) = 243,648 people

Population range corrected may be corrected to allow for the 16% of sites whose area is not known:

$\dfrac{154,536}{84} \times 100\%$ =183,971 people

$\dfrac{243,648}{84} \times 100\%$ = 290,057 people

Finally we need to estimate the rural population. Here, we can work from two sets of data. First, we must assume that the military and urban peoples were supported by those making a living from the land after allowance is made for farmers within towns and frontier militias who also farmed. This assumption led Frere (1987, 301) to his minimum estimate of 2 million. Secondly, we can take the accumulating data from field surveys which provide evidence for the density of rural settlement. This approach requires a number of assumptions to be made; provided these are explicit the details of the figures can be revised as appropriate at a later date. Although a considerable amount of field survey has been undertaken, those published in detail are limited. The results compiled in table 8.3 cannot pretend to be entirely representative of the variation within England and Wales, but do provide a relatively consistent set of figures for the density of sites discovered in the various surveys. Even in the intensive surveys, it is highly unlikely that all the sites have been discovered and this is likely to compensate for sites not occupied throughout the period. This problem of discontinuity is often overestimated as the settlement pattern in Roman Britain does not seem to have been rapidly shifting. Where detailed figures are available there is a strong pattern of continuity (e.g. Hallam 1970). Accepting the uncertainties we can use the mean figure of 0.8 ± 0.5 sites per hectare as a basic estimate using one standard deviation range. This estimate is based on intensive and non-intensive field surveys alone and excludes figures derived from literature searches or Sites and Monuments Records. Such data consistently provide the lowest estimates, on the bottom limit of the range of the other values (table 8.3). This confirms the likelihood that literature searches and SMRs seriously underestimate the real values.

Though we should be aware of the major problems of differential site visibility which result from different surface conditions and variations in the use of recoverable and datable artefacts (Millett in press (a)), the broad agreement of the present figures makes it unlikely that these factors will significantly alter the present estimated range.

This value of 0.8 ± 0.5 sites per ha could be multiplied by the total area of England and Wales (150,265 km^2), but this would include a significant proportion of land unsuitable for settlement and agriculture. The land area used here has thus been adjusted by the exclusion of the least suitable land. Only the area of grassland, arable and urban areas provided by Edwards and Wibberley (1971) has been included. Since much land which is now rough grazing or woodland was probably occupied in the

Table 8.3. *Rural site densities from surveys*

Area	Type of information	Density	Reference
Bedfordshire	Sites and Monuments Record	0.2 sites/km^2	Simco 1984
Cambridgeshire	Sites and Monuments Record	0.1 sites/km^2	Wilkes and Elrington 1978
Winchester District	Sites and Monuments Record	0.1 sites/km^2	Schadla-Hall 1978
Basingstoke area	Non-intensive survey	0.6 sites/km^2	Millett 1983a, fig. 1
NW Essex	Intensive survey	1.3 sites/km^2	Williamson 1984
Maddle Farm	Intensive survey	0.7 sites/km^2	Gaffney et al. 1985, fig. 8.2
Northamptonshire	Non-intensive survey	0.4 sites/km^2	Taylor 1975, 113
Oxfordshire	Non-intensive survey	1.0 sites/km^2	Miles 1982a, 63
Chalton area	Intensive survey	0.8 sites/km^2	Cunliffe 1973a
Elsted, Sussex	Intensive survey	0.2 sites/km^2	Redknap & Millett 1980
Holme-on-Spalding Moor	Intensive survey	0.8 sites/km^2	Halkon 1987
Tame valley	Non-intensive survey	0.6 sites/km^2	Smith 1977
Fenland	Intensive survey	0.3 sites/km^2	Hallam 1970, 72
Wharram area	Intensive survey	0.5 sites/km^2	Hayfield 1987
West Sussex coastal plain	Non-intensive survey	0.5 sites/km^2	Pitts 1979
Shropshire	Intensive survey	1.7 sites/km^2	Fowler 1972, 119
M5: Somerset– Gloucestershire	Intensive survey (road building)	1.5 sites/km^2	Fowler 1972, 119 (adjusted as Gregson 1982b, 23)
MEAN (all surveys) Standard deviation		0.7 ±0.5 sites/km^2	
MEAN (without SMR) Standard deviation		0.8 ±0.5 sites/km^2	

later Roman period, the figure used (115,938km^2) is almost certainly too low and depresses the population estimate. When multiplied by the density of sites this gives a range of 92,750 ± 57,969 (a range of 34,781 to 150,719) settlement sites within England and Wales in the later Roman period (table 8.4). No distinction is made in this estimate between different types of site, which includes villas, farmsteads and villages. Similarly, the industrial population is here taken to be ordinary members of the rural population. We should perhaps be satisfied with an estimate like this which provides the number of sites in occupation and enables comparison with the analogous figures for England at Domesday, when there were about 275,000 households (Miller and Hatcher 1978, 28), the equivalent of just over two per km^2.

To arrive at a population estimate this range needs to be multiplied by a factor representing the size of the group occupying each site. Collingwood (1929) estimated that villas had an average population of 50, but given the enormous complexes which are now known to surround many (e.g. fig. 93), this may be an underestimate. A much smaller figure is likely for the groups occupying most lesser rural establishments, so 50 is a reasonable ceiling figure. The minimum figure for group size is more difficult, for

Table 8.4. *Estimated rural population of Roman Britain*

Density of sites from surveys (table 8.3; excluding SMR) 0.8 ± 0.5 km^2

Multiply by the available land area (115,938 km^2: grassland, arable and urban area of England and Wales: from Edwards and Wibberley 1971, appendix 8)
$= 92,750 \pm 57,969$ sites
Multiply by possible range of people per site:
@ 20 people per site $= 1,855,000 \pm 1,159,380$
@ 50 people per site $= 4,637,500 \pm 2,898,450$

Mean of two $=$ approximately 3.3 million

Table 8.5. *Estimated population of Roman Britain*

	Mid-range (approximate)	
Range	No.	%
Army 10,000–20,000, plus dependents = 50,000–200,000	125,000	3.4
Urban population = 183,971–290,057	240,000	6.5
Rural population = 1.8 ± 1.2 to 4.6 ± 2.9 million	3,300,000	90
Total	3,665,000	

we have no informed idea about the type of family organization in Roman Britain, and we may reasonably assume that this varied from area to area. The evidence from the core provinces suggests that the norm was a nuclear rather than an extended family (Saller and Shaw 1984) and this would suggest a size of perhaps 4–5 people – the figure used by Hallam and supported by medieval sources (1970, 71–2). However, Stevens has argued that kinship groups may have lived in extended families as happened in early medieval Wales (Stevens 1966). This would produce a larger group size of up to 30 or so. Most excavated settlements do not seem to have been occupied by a small nuclear group of 4–5, so the two extremes (4/5–50) may be unimportant, especially since nuclear families can have lived in adjacent houses on the same site (Hallam 1970, table E). This would suggest a reasonable minimal estimate for the number of people within each site as 20. Taking the multipliers of 20 and 50 to provide a range, we obtain estimates for the rural population of 1.8 ± 1.2 to 4.6 ± 2.9 million (table 8.4). The uncertainties make the range very large, although we can be reasonably certain that the real value lies somewhere within it. Taking the middle point of the estimates we arrive at a rough estimate of *c.* 3.7 million (table 8.5). Although imprecise, this is sufficient to show that the population is unlikely to have been either as high as 5 to 6 million (C. Smith 1977) or lower than the Domesday figure (Fulford 1984, 131).

The estimated range is unlikely to be much broadened by future work and it is equally certain that new work will not reduce the predominance of the rural element. The urban population is only about 6.5 per cent of the total on the present evidence.

This reinforces both the view that Roman Britain was a fundamentally agrarian society, and that any postulated shift of population from the towns to the countryside in the late Roman period, although representing a major change for the towns, would have had only a very marginal effect in increasing the total rural population, thereby having only a minor effect on pressure on land. This pressure would also have been minimal as the élite already owned rural estates. Thus, although the importance of any numerical change in balance of the population between town and country was insignificant, residence and investment by the élite may have had an important impact. A shift of their attention to the countryside is suggested by the changes in the nature of villas, and the innovations seen in agriculture.

The villas

The later Roman period witnessed differences in the characteristics of the villas (fig. 33). On average they were smaller in area than those of the earlier Empire in Britain, although this characteristic masks two contrasting trends. First there are a larger number of villas until the first half of the fourth century, after which the number of dated villas begins to decline, and at the same time the trend of decreased average size established in the second century continues. These smaller villas include a number of the cottage-type villas such as Barton Court Farm (fig. 77) which emerge during the third century, and may be taken to represent the popularization of the villa idea leading to its devaluation: taste for rural *Romanitas* had moved down the social and economic scale so that more modest members of the community, hitherto presumably satisfied with a traditional timber dwelling, began to construct villas for themselves. Whilst this shows a continuing process of Romanization through to the first half of the fourth century, the number of villas remained a small proportion of the total number of settlements. If we assume that about 500 of the known villas were occupied during the fourth century, this comprises less than 1 per cent of the estimated number of rural settlement sites and probably a similar percentage of the population (table 8.4). Thus even the modest villas were probably high-status accommodation for the lesser aristocracy (fig. 76), and despite their modest scale and pretensions, they should not be taken as insignificant.

The pattern of the declining villa numbers in the later fourth century (fig. 33) is significant since the reduction in their numbers corresponds with a continued decline in average size. This pattern is not consistent with the commonly held idea that some villas grew as estates were consolidated into larger holdings, for this would surely have led to the larger continuing at the expense of the smaller. Even an increase in absentee landlords overseas should have been marked by a maintenance of the existing pattern of size rather than a decline. Instead, the observed decline of villa numbers affected the large slightly more than the small, causing a minor reduction in average villa size. It may be that the economies of the owners of the smaller villas were the more robust, although we should not lose sight of the fact that villa buildings represent capital expenditure rather than agricultural production.

Whilst of considerable significance, the predominance of the smaller sites masks a second contrasting trend, as there is a wide range of villa sizes, including a number of

186

palatial residences which are themselves a characteristic of later Roman Britain. Some were planned unitary structures like Woodchester (fig. 78) (Clarke 1982), while the fourth-century buildings at others like Bignor (Frere 1982), Chedworth (Goodburn 1979) and Rockbourne represent the culmination of a gradual aggrandizement from the early Empire onwards (fig. 79). The largest villas were far from modest in their pretensions, with fine mosaics (figs. 80 and 81) and internal decorations, together

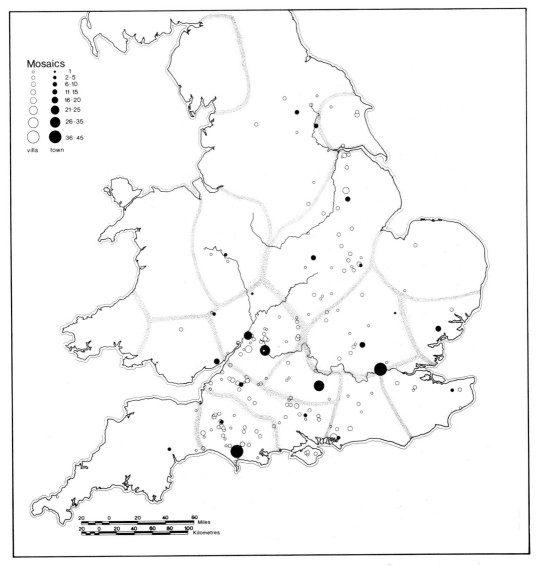

76 The distribution of mosaics in Roman Britain (data from Rainey 1973). Open symbols are rural settlement, filled circles towns.

with an architectural unity provided by the addition of features such as porticoed façades (see Gibson's reconstruction of Chedworth in Goodburn 1979).

These larger villas show that there was considerable investment in private rural building in the fourth century. D. J. Smith (1969) and Branigan (1972; 1973) have suggested that some of this was a consequence of an influx of capital from Gaul resulting from barbarian disruptions there. Although it is difficult to see how estates in Gaul could have been sold in order to transfer resources to Britain, given the barbarian invasions which were the cause of the proposed move, such an influx of capital and immigrants has been proposed as the explanation for the supposed similarities in plan between some British and continental villas (Branigan 1972; 1973). J. T. Smith has comprehensively reviewed these claims and the evidence on which they were based,

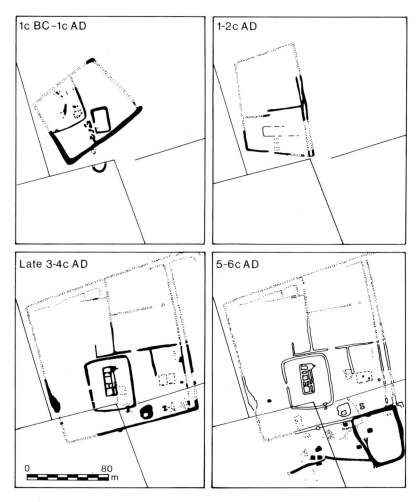

77 The development and decline of the Iron Age farmstead and Roman villa at Barton Court Farm, Oxon (after Miles 1984).

showing them to be entirely without foundation (1978b; 1983). He concludes that the flowering of villas in fourth-century Britain must be related to more general causes (below, p. 195). This is not to deny that foreign capital may have come into Britain; indeed as Britain seems to have been prosperous and secure in the late Roman period (especially in comparison with the continental provinces), the rich from overseas may have seen it as a secure place to buy land. There is nevertheless no evidence to support this, and it is difficult to see what evidence could be found. Finally, since villa building represents expenditure on display rather than investment in production, the idea of relating it to an inflow of capital investment is fundamentally misguided.

In the absence of epigraphic evidence we cannot know which individuals lived in these villas, although the archaeological evidence does enable some more general inferences to be drawn about the occupants. It is sometimes suggested that changes in the buildings at particular sites result from the absence of landlords and the residence of bailiffs and tenants who were left to run the estates (e.g. Frere 1987, 259). Although we cannot be certain about their application to later Roman Britain, the classical sources make it seem unlikely that bailiffs' residences would have been any less opulent than those occupied by landowners themselves (Rivet 1969, 179; Liversidge 1969, 157–8). We know of one absentee landowner overseas (Melania, c. 383–439; Jones 1973, 782), but there is no possibility of identifying the estates of such owners or even the particular lands attached to any individual villa.

Although specific evidence about landownership cannot be provided archaeologi-

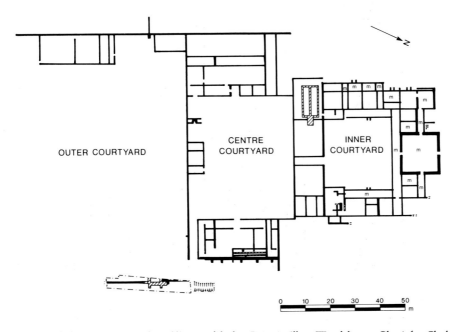

78 The monumental and axial layout of the late Roman villa at Woodchester, Glos (after Clarke 1982). Although this villa has earlier phases, the planned late Roman form has a unified design; m = mosaic.

cally, the pattern of villa distribution has been shown to provide valuable data about
the general relationship between villas and the remainder of the settlement pattern
(Rivet 1969). The clear spatial clustering of villas around towns was originally noted
by Rivet (1955), who emphasized the interrelationships between villa occupiers and
those inhabiting the towns. These connections are both economic and social, for those
in the administration of the towns were landowners, and the surplus production from
rural estates was presumably largely consumed by urban dwellers not engaged in
agriculture. Clearly the greater attraction of a town and the larger a market it provided, the more likely it is to have a large cluster of villas around it.

The distributions upon which Rivet's general observations were based have been
more systematically studied in an attempt to understand the processes at work more
closely. The density of distribution of villas around the towns in Roman Britain was
examined by Hodder and Millett in an attempt to draw conclusions about the shape

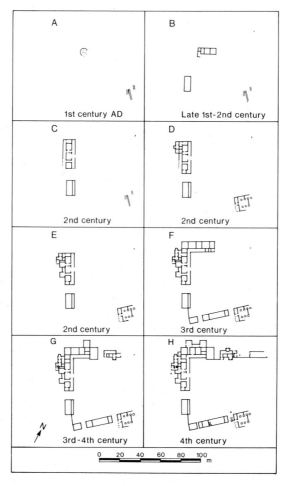

79 The development of the courtyard villa at Rockbourne, Hants (after R.C.H.M. 1983).

of such distributions. This analysis had the advantage that it did not rely on the absolute numbers of villas in a particular locality but rather looked at the change in their density (numbers per km^2) with distance away from each town. Only towns with villas in more than five 2 km-wide bands around them could be subjected to this analysis but even so some thirty-one distributions were compared (Hodder and Millett 1980, 72).

This method of analysis overcomes most of the problems of sample bias, although as in any such analysis the complex decisions which led to the location of particular sites are ignored in favour of an attempt to make generalized statements (Gregson 1982a, 158–9). The analysis demonstrated first that the density declined more gradually away from some towns than others. The more gradual the decline, presumably the more worthwhile it was to locate one's villa near that town. One of the statistics calculated (the *beta*-value; table 8.6) measured the steepness of the decline in density away from the towns (fig. 82, inset). The higher its value the more steeply the density of the villas declines as one moves away from the town in question. The second statistic (the *alpha*-value; table 8.6) measures the shape of the decline in density with distance from the town (fig. 82, inset). The higher its value, the more convex the distribution curve away from the town; the lower its value, the more concave. The greater the concavity of the curve, the more worthwhile it was to live close to the town.

80 The central panel of the mid-fourth-century Venus mosaic from the villa at Rudston, East Yorks. The form of the figure betrays a native perception of female beauty (cf. fig. 46) and the workmanship is rather crude but the design is classical in intent. (*Photograph by courtesy of Hull City Museum.*)

Table 8.6. *Results of analysis of villa distributions around Romano-British towns*

The towns are ordered in ascending order of *beta*-value, that is, in descending order of attraction to villas.

Town	Status	Defended area (ha)	alpha-value	beta-value
Silchester	*Civitas* capital	40	2.5	−0.003
Verulamium	*Municipium*	81	2.5	−0.004
Colchester	*Colonia*	43	2.5	−0.005
Dorchester (Dorset)	*Civitas* capital	32	1.8	−0.005
Mildenhall	Small Town	7.7	2.5	−0.006
Winchester	*Civitas* capital	55	2.5	−0.006
Dorchester (Oxon.)	Small Town	5.5	2.5	−0.007
Ewell	Small Town	undefended	1.9	−0.007
Ilchester	*Civitas* capital	8.9	2.5	−0.008
Chichester	*Civitas* capital	40	1.4	−0.008
Gloucester	*Colonia*	18.5	2.4	−0.009
Cirencester	*Civitas* capital	97	0.5	−0.009
Cambridge	Small Town	10.1	0.9	−0.009
Great Dunmow	Small Town	undefended	0.9	−0.009
Wanborough	Small Town	unknown	1.4	−0.010
Bath	Small Town	9.3	1.5	−0.011
Water Newton	Small Town	18	0.7	−0.012
Speen	Small Town	undefended	0.1	−0.014
Harlow	Small Town	undefended	0.6	−0.014
Bourton-on-the-Water	Small Town	undefended	0.8	−0.014
Sandy Lane	Small Town	undefended	0.8	−0.014
Great Chesterford	Small Town	14.5	0.8	−0.015
Springhead	Small Town	undefended	0.9	−0.016
Alchester	Small Town	10.5	0.4	−0.018
Rochester	Small Town	7.5	0.6	−0.018
Maidstone	Small Town	undefended	0.5	−0.019
Neatham	Small Town	2.5	0.7	−0.020
Sansom's Platt	Small Town	undefended	0.6	−0.022
Great Casterton	Small Town	7.3	0.7	−0.022

Source: Hodder & Millett 1980.

In general the results show that the major towns (*civitas* capitals, *municipia* and *coloniae*) had the most shallow and convex curves, showing that they had a greater attraction to villas than the small towns, which generally had steep and concave curves. This indicates that the attraction to villas of the major towns declined more slowly with distance than was the case with Small Towns and demonstrates that the administrative centres were the most important in influencing villa distributions.

At first sight this analysis simply confirms the observations made by Rivet (1955) about the clustering of villas around the most Romanized centres. However, the analysis contains more valuable information as a comparison with other data shows. The idea that the villa concentrations reflect the importance of the towns as markets is widespread (e.g. Frere 1987, 258), but has not previously been tested. If the economic pull of the towns was responsible for the concentration of villas around them, then one would expect the largest towns to have the biggest markets, and therefore the greatest concentrations of villas. It is immediately clear that this is not the case, even allowing for biases in the evidence, as Britain's largest town, London, has far too few villas in its vicinity (Merrifield 1983, 134–5, fig. 20). This cannot be dismissed on the grounds that the modern urban sprawl has destroyed them, for villas are amongst the most visible and commonly reported sites. Furthermore, the relationship between the values produced by the distribution analysis do not show the clear relationship between villa distribution and town size that might be expected (fig. 82), even if we allow for the fact that the defended area (which is all that can be conveniently plotted) does not provide the best measure of town size. This is particularly true when we look at the steepness of the decline in density of villas with distance from the towns, where it is notable that the Small Towns have a full range of values irrespective of their size, while the major towns generally have shallow gradients, indicative of their strong attraction to villas.

This makes little sense in relation to the simple hypothesis of marketing pull, but the pattern does show a clear relationship between a town's administrative status and its attraction to villas. This supports the social interpretation, which sees the villas as the residences of the tribal élite who preferred to be near the centres in whose administration they were involved, and raises two fundamental points. First, it explains the

81 The Charioteer mosaic from the villa at Rudston, East Yorks, probably of the early fourth century AD. The central panel shows a highly Roman scene, with the corners of the pavements containing the heads of the four seasons, a characteristic Romano-British theme. The whole scheme defines the aspirations of the patron. (*Photograph by courtesy of Hull City Museums.*)

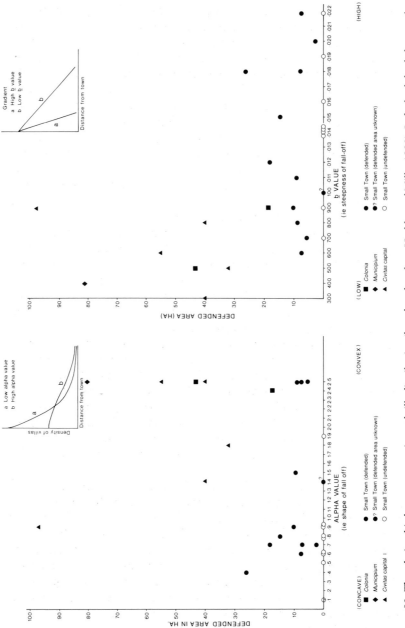

82   The relationship between town size and villa distribution (based on data from Hodder and Millet 1980). *Left:* the defended areas of the towns compared with the shape of the fall-off in density of villas with distance from them. A convex shape indicates a high attraction to villas, a concave one a more limited spatial influence. Note how the Public Towns with a demonstrable administrative rôle tend to have more convex curves than those of the Small Towns. *Right:* the defended areas of the towns are compared with the steepness of the fall-off in villa density away from them. The steeper the fall-off (i.e. the higher the *beta*-value) the less attractive the town was to villas. This graph shows clearly that towns with an administrative rôle were more attractive to villas than the Small Towns.

absence of villas around London, for, although that city had a high status as a provincial capital, it never seems to have fulfilled a rôle in the local administration and so did not attract the same group of landowning decurions. Second and more importantly, as Reece has pointed out (in Hodder and Millett 1980, 72), the spatial relationship is between essentially second-century towns and fourth-century villas, since the floruit of the villas comes later than that of the towns. By the fourth century the Public Towns at the *civitas* centres had been equalled as economic centres by the Small Towns. This is not reflected in the villa distributions, despite the fourth-century date for their maximum extent. Thus, although the villas and public towns are connected this is not simply a function of a marketing relationship. We can explain the attraction of villas to these centres as a result of the continuing focal functions of the cantonal centres (above, p. 142), but we must not forget that the later villas are centres of élite display. It is suggested that the élite, who had controlled and endowed the Public Towns in the early Empire, were increasingly resident at its rural estates in the late Empire. They thus endowed these structures more richly than previously while maintaining an interest in the towns which remained the foci for the *civitates*. This is entirely consistent with the changing patterns in the Empire at large, where the curial classes were taking less interest in display in their local municipalities (chapter 6). The comparatively slighter attraction of the villas to the Small Towns can be related both to the continuing rôles of the traditional centres and the probability that they themselves were under the patronage of a lesser aristocracy.

The villas are numerous (fig. 48), often opulent, with a significant number containing fine mosaics (fig. 76), wall decorations and hypocaust systems. As such they represent an important index of Romanization. Their distributions, although undifferentiated by date, nevertheless provide useful information about its pattern. The mosaic distribution provides a useful index of private patronage and demonstrates clearly how this is both regionally differentiated and predominantly rural. A comparison of this with that of the villas shows that rural mosaics tend to be contained within the core areas covered by the villas, although East Anglia has fewer than expected given the number of villas found.

If we look at the patterns as indices of Romanization in relation to the *civitates* (cf. Rivet 1969, 209–14), we can see that the areas of the central-south and south-west were those most developed. This compares fairly closely with the distributions of urban walled areas (fig. 59) and dedicatory inscriptions (fig. 26), with a few exceptions. Most notable amongst these are the gap around London and the strength of the rural pattern in the territory of the Durotriges, which contrasts with its weakness in the earlier urban evidence. The balance of the evidence (table 8.6) supports the proposition of a strong continuity from the early towns to late countryside, supporting the view that members of the social élites were now competing with each other through this new form of personal status display in the countryside.

This switch of patronage to rural locations is also seen in the distribution of temples (fig. 83) as analysed by Horne (1981, 21–6). Although the number of pagan temples used in the towns declines in the later period, the reverse is seen in the countryside, where the peak is contemporary with that of the villas in the middle of the fourth century. Since the distribution of the rural temples closely mirrors that of the villas (fig. 33), their construction must be as much a function of élite display as of religious practice. The function of religion and the priesthoods in the Roman world was closely tied to the political and social power of the aristocracy, so their transfer should be seen in relation to the other shifts towards the countryside (Horne 1981, 21–3) rather than as a result of supposed Christian persecution.

Even when compared with the larger houses which are characteristic of the Public Towns during the fourth century, it is clear that the villas represent the prime places for status display and were thus the principal residences of the élite, the heirs of earlier decurions, now exercising their power from their rural seats. Taken with the evidence of the relative decline in public building in the towns, we may conclude that a fundamental change had taken place. Since the distributions of late Roman rural display can be closely related to the earlier pattern, we cannot reasonably argue for a total disjunction. However, in considering the earlier pattern, we concluded that power in the British *civitates* was usually personal to a small élite, whose social competition was circumscribed. The removal of the incentive for involvement in even this public display at the towns resulted from the relative decline in the importance of municipal government in the later Empire, although the tribal aristocrats will not have lost their power and influence in society. However, no longer impelled to flaunt it in the towns they instead moved to their rural estates, where they indulged their wealth in personal display with the embellishment of their villas and the temples. In this sense we see a return to the LPRIA pattern. This does not imply that they were no longer controlling

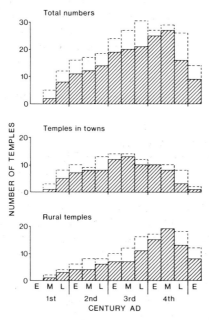

83 The numbers of Romano-Celtic temples in use in Roman Britain through the Roman period. The solid line shows the probable cases, the dotted line the possible (after Horne 1981). The general pattern shows a difference between town and country which reflects the general shift in the pattern of Romanization in the later Empire.

social power or that they had withdrawn from public life. We can see that in the Roman world power remained essentially personal, from the emperor downwards (Millar 1977, 203–59), so we must think of power acting through central persons rather than central places. Those clients and others who sought action from the powerful would come to them for an audience, at their rural residence if appropriate. This practice is seen at work at the provincial level in the life of Sidonius Apollinaris (Stevens 1933) in fifth-century Gaul. Given the expanding opportunities for the social élite in the later Empire, the increased emphasis on personal display at rural centres should occasion no surprise. Thus the later Roman villas of Britain should be seen as a new manifestation of the traditional power structure, which now directed the surpluses of society towards personalized rather than communal display.

Villas and social organization

Despite the amount that has been written about villas, comparatively little analysis of their plans has been undertaken beyond simple classification (Collingwood and Richmond 1969, chapter 7). This is unfortunate, for despite the poor quality of much of the information about their dating, their plans are well known and provide a considerable resource for the understanding of the social organization of the people who inhabited them. Pioneering work in this field has been undertaken by Gregson (1982a) and in particular in a series of important papers by J. T. Smith (1964; 1978a; 1984; 1985; 1987), which recognize and exploit the potential of their plans. Smith starts from the position that all villa plans are fundamentally expressions of classical architectural pretension. This being so, any deviation from the classical canons of symmetry in elevation and plan, the use of axial emphasis and regular geometric configurations, are potentially significant. Because of the importance laid upon the classical façade, it is crucial to distinguish between the outward appearance which expresses the classical aspirations and the plan of the house which is more informative of the organization of those using the building.

A close examination of villa buildings in Britain and continental Europe north of the Alps has enabled J. T. Smith to identify two different architectural forms which are recurrent and demand explanation in relation to social structure. The first group of villas conforms to what has been called the unit system (J. T. Smith 1978a; Hemp and Gresham 1943). Instead of a single dwelling house, these villas comprise two or more individual occupation units which are self-contained (for example, Beadlam, Yorks) (fig. 84). A significant number of these sites has been identified (fig. 85) and their regularity makes it impossible to dismiss them simply as one building succeeding the other. J. T. Smith has identified a number of recurrent elements, including the use of a water tank, plausibly a shrine at the boundary between the adjacent units. This is consistent with the common idea of a shrine being placed on a boundary to give protection to contacts across it. These sites appear to indicate multiple residences with the relationships between the units defined by the layout of the plan. Thus there is evidence in some instances for the subservience of one unit to another whilst others show careful equality. In some instances, like Marshfield (J. T. Smith 1987), it is possible to trace the dual division back into the LPRIA, although it is emphasized that the change to a Romanized architectural form has the utmost symbolic significance. J. T. Smith finally detects some move away from the unit system in the later Roman period towards more unified landholdings, although the evidence for this is difficult to sustain until we can be certain that the rate of decrease in this form is significantly greater than the overall rate of villa disappearance.

Identification of this pattern is certainly more easily achieved than a satisfactory explanation for it. Whilst there can be no real doubt that we are seeing a system of multiple occupancy which was sufficiently important for it to overcome the canons of classical architecture, it is difficult to follow J. T. Smith in seeing this as a result of a Celtic rather than Roman legal system being in operation in Britain (1978a, 170). The logic of such a system, as described by Stevens (1947), is clear and could have allowed two different proprietors to arrive at an equal right to a property, but it must be doubted that it would have led to dual residence occurring as widely as the evidence of the unit villas shows. Stevens' interpretation of the Theodosian Code (XI. 7, 2) supports the suggestion that the reclaiming of an estate which had passed like this into the hands of others was the exception rather than the rule. Furthermore, although we must follow Stevens (1947; 1966) in his assertion that Rome did not force her law onto provincial communities, it seems unlikely that local laws would have remained as widespread as he implies after the grant of universal citizenship in 212 (Rivet 1969, 184–5), especially amongst those in the villa-dominated areas which were consistently the most Romanized. Furthermore, the single land sale document we have from Britain, found at Chew Stoke in Somerset, certainly attests the use of Roman civil law (Turner 1956, 117–18). Similarly, any suggestion that the unit system resulted from partible inheritance as practised both in Celtic society (where it was known as *tir gwelyawg* – Stevens 1966) and in Roman law seems unlikely, since this would pre-

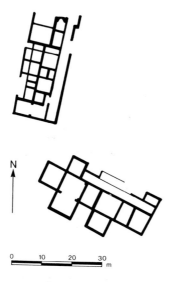

84 Beadlam, Yorks, a Roman villa of the unit-type (after J. T. Smith 1978a). The impression is that the villa comprises two houses rather than one.

198

sumably have led to the successive division of houses into smaller and more numerous units unless very successful systems of population control were maintained (cf. Hopkins 1983a). As it is we see the general continuation of the dual pattern.

We have thus identified a particular form of élite residence pattern, one interpretation of which is that the proprietor and heir maintained the estate jointly, whilst living with their nuclear families in separate adjacent dwellings. A second alternative explanation for this widespread and influential residence rule was that it represents a dual holding of power in a family. This would echo the dual magistracies through which power had been held in some LPRIA tribes like the Corieltauvi (above, table 2.3). Finally, it could result from the landowner's periodic absence to fulfil a political rôle in the municipality or the imperial bureaucracy, necessitating leaving the running of the estate in the hands of another, be it an heir, tenant, relative or bailiff, for whom a second dwelling was provided. This explanation suffers from the same weakness as an appeal to Stevens' conflict of laws as it seems likely to have been the exception rather than the rule, and the information collected by J. T. Smith demonstrates that we are dealing with a more widespread residential rule.

The second villa plan that has been identified as relatively common in Britain is the hall-type which is far more widespread in Germany (J. T. Smith 1978a; 1978b). In this form of house, for instance, King's Weston, Avon (fig. 86), the hall dominates the

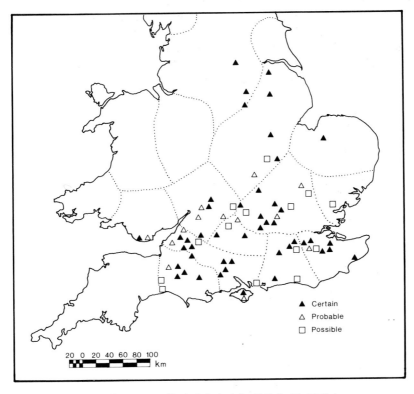

85 The distribution of unit-type villas in Britain (after J. T. Smith 1978a).

building and is often central. Although the British examples give less importance to the hall than is seen on the continent, an emphasis remains (fig. 86). The implication to be drawn is clear. The halls imply use by a single group, in contrast to most British villas which have a multitude of small rooms or sets of rooms more appropriate to occupation by several. The size of the hall-type villas has been taken by J. T. Smith to support hypotheses of occupancy by an extended family larger than the three-generation nuclear family. This residence pattern has a strong parallel with the aisled houses which are also common in Roman Britain, and which were generally for habitation rather than agricultural use (J. T. Smith 1963; Hadman 1978).

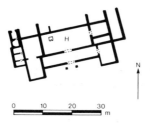

86 King's Weston, Avon, a Roman villa of the hall-type (after J. T. Smith 1978b). H = hall.

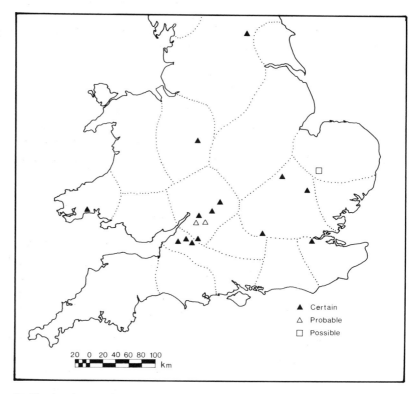

87 The distribution of hall-type villas in Britain (after J. T. Smith 1978a).

200

Aisled houses were less structurally complex than the hall-type villas but commonly show the same development pattern, with an increasing partitioning of the open area into private spaces. The origin of these structures has been sought on the continent in the long halls of the Low Countries (J. T. Smith 1963). The form could alternatively be seen as a Romanized, rectangular expression of the Iron Age round house with which it shares the large common central area and the more private quarters behind the roof supports around the perimeter, which could suitably be partitioned off for privacy (fig. 88). The tendency for aisled buildings to have more permanently partitioned rooms might then be seen as the later stage in the evolution of the same type. Like the hall-type villas, these structures would be sitable for a single extended family group living in a tradition which continued directly from that of the LPRIA (fig. 89).

The differences in the social structure of the groups inhabiting these various forms of house seem evident, but there is no clear differentiation in their distributions (figs. 85, 87 and 89) and no particular clustering differentiates them from the total pattern of villa distribution (fig. 48). The only exception is the apparent group of aisled buildings in Corieltauvian territory, although this may simply result from the sample bias since the latest study (Hadman 1978) was based in that locality. We must bear in mind that this form also occurs in timber but that distribution is less reliably mapped than that of stone villas. Aside from this possible clustering, the evidence strongly demonstrates that Roman Britain contained a mixed variety of social forms even at the level of detail we can observe. The complexities of organization of the majority of the population who did not live in villas remains unknown.

The agricultural economy

The display of wealth exhibited by the villas supports the suggestion that even the most modest represent a transfer of activity by decurions to the countryside. It is notable that this movement in emphasis takes place around the time we see the first major agricultural innovations since the LPRIA (fig. 36). The innovations observed by King (1978; 1984) and M. K. Jones (1981, fig. 6.4) comprise both changes in arable

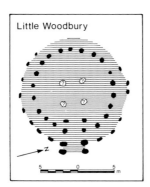
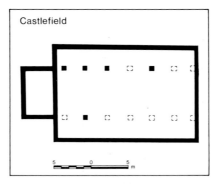

88 Comparative plans of an Iron Age round house at Little Woodbury, Wilts and a Romano-British aisled building at Castlefield, Hants.

agriculture and animal husbandry. Late Roman animal-bone assemblages show an overall decrease in the dominance of sheep and an increase in the exploitation of woodland for pannage and hunting (King 1978). In arable agriculture there were changes in ploughs, with the first use of asymmetrical shares and coulters, both of which suggest the use of the mould-board (Rees 1979, 65). These are clearly aimed at the more efficient utilization of deep heavy loams. Secondly, there is strong evidence from southern Britain of a full crop rotation in the later Roman period (M. K. Jones 1981, 113) and there are also signs of innovation in harvesting and processing activities. This is shown by the first known use of the *tribulum* or threshing sledge (Rees 1979, 486), together with the introduction of the long balanced sickle and the scythe (which was almost certainly for cutting hay). Finally, the so-called corn-drying ovens become a common characteristic of third- and fourth-century sites (Morris 1979, table 1) and whatever their use, it certainly relates to crop processing (see below).

All these arable changes represent an increased investment in rural production and, when taken with the development of rural industry (chapter 7), they appear consistent with diversification. Such a pattern of change is important, not least because agricultural communities are often inherently conservative in their production methods

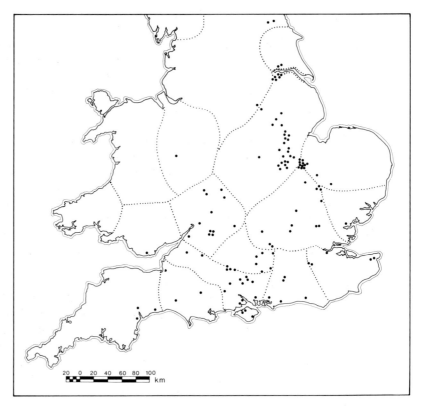

89 The distribution of aisled buildings in Britain (after Hadman 1978).

(M. K. Jones 1982), because innovation might upset productivity and this could threaten their livelihood. This must be especially true in an agricultural economy like that of early Roman Britain which was already productive. Since innovation had not taken place at the time of the conquest, the motivation for it should not be seen as either straightforward or simply the result of experimentation resulting from any increasing demand on the system. Since we can be certain that the observed changes in techniques required investment, it may be no coincidence that these developments are contemporary with the floruit of the villas which required similar expenditure. The development of their rural dwellings has been related to the increased presence of the élite in the countryside. This may also be the cause of the increase in the hunting of wild animals (King 1978, 216), often an élite rather than a subsistence activity. We suggest that such rich landowners were more willing to invest and experiment with new methods than their less wealthy neighbours who had more to lose, and are also likely to have had the spare capacity on their estates and thus the resources with which to innovate without such a serious risk as would have faced a smaller landowner working nearer the subsistence margin. Furthermore, the presence of rich landowners with leisure time may itself have stimulated agricultural experimentation, since they had the time available to think without the preoccupation with production of those who relied for their food on manual labour.

Alongside this, the scale of the change in agriculture suggests that external factors were also exerting pressures on production, thereby encouraging innovation. Three such stimuli can be isolated. First, the increased size of estates, secondly the effects of possible changes in the exchange system and finally the impact of changes in the nature and burden of taxation. An increase in the size of landholdings is suggested by the historical sources from elsewhere in the Empire (Jones 1973, 769ff). Indeed, this is an expected byproduct of the concentration of resources in the hands of the rich which resulted from the Roman taxation system. This concentration of land led to the development of the colonate system, whereby a landowner (dominus) whose estate was sufficiently large to need cultivation by others used tenants rather than slaves as labourers. These tenants (coloni) became tied to the land, and even to particular estates, both by custom and by the law, which required them to remain on the land for taxation purposes. The system developed into a form of hereditary service which became de facto feudal, at least in provinces where, unlike Britain, there were severe pressures on agricultural production (Jones 1973, 795–808). The conditions of the coloni are far from clear, even in the literary sources, and it would be a mistake simply to equate this class with poverty.

We cannot relate villa buildings directly to this process, because the buildings do not mirror productive output, and there is insufficient literary evidence from Roman Britain to establish a system of tenure here. However, one reference in the Theodosian Code (XI. 7, 2 of 20 November 319) makes it clear that the colonate system did exist in Britain (Haverfield 1912, 45) but, given the uncertainties, it is impossible to assess its importance in Britain or evaluate its possible effects. At a minimal level we may see the system as simply a regularization or development from the obligations of the peasantry to the aristocracy, the roots of which lay in tribal organization and the social ties entailed. Thus the system of the colonate may simply reflect existing social relations through the late Roman tax structure. Equally, the effect of the increased legal emphasis on the status of *coloni* may have been to reinforce social links which were strained by the polarization of wealth. As an explanation for agricultural change it has some small value, providing implicit evidence for the concentration of wealth in the hands of the few, who we suggest invested more actively in agriculture.

The second factor, change in the economic system, has already been discussed, and it has been noted that there may be a case for identifying a weakening of the bonds in later Roman-period society, especially at the peripheries, with a resultant crumbling of the socially embedded economy (Hodder 1979; Reece 1979b). The development of a more rigid system of obligation between tenants and landowners may be a side effect of this weakening and its translation into more purely economic obligations. If this process can be identified as important in late Roman Britain, it may be of particular significance to agriculture, since M. K. Jones (1982) has noted that systems of embedded exchange protect crop producers, as disposal of their surplus through the social network is guaranteed and their income protected. In contrast, a competitive, market-based system suffers from the difficulty that the same crops arrive on the market at the same time, and as prices are fixed by demand, they are depressed when the producer is most in need of income. Furthermore, any increase in productivity without an increase in demand has no advantage to the producer, who is even worse off. Any increase in production is counter-productive, although the freeing of exchange from social obligations may have stimulated diversification in order to break out of the trap (below). Thus any evidence for a weakening or breakdown in the socially embedded economy provides some explanation for innovation in the country-side coming from peasants as well as landowners. This model supplements that already presented, although the doubts about the breakdown in social control over production question its applicability to later Roman Britain.

Finally, the later Roman taxation system may be identified as having a major indirect effect on the countryside. First, we know that the perceived burden of taxation was increasing as a result of the increased size of the imperial bureaucracy and the more even distribution of the load, at least under Diocletian (Jones 1973, 67). Thus those paying taxes believed them to be more costly, although this may result from a decline in their willingness to shoulder the burden rather than from any real increase in tax levels (cf. Goffart 1974, 91–4). Nevertheless, the changes in the tax structure led to a series of additional pressures. To begin with, tax was collected on the basis of both a poll tax (*capitatio*) and a land tax (*iugatio*). For the latter the land was divided by census into taxable units (*iuga*) which were sometimes of estimated equal productivity, but elsewhere of equal size (Jones 1973, 62–3). The land tax was collected at a rate adjusted according to the varying annual needs of the state, and was assessed irrespective of the actual productivity of the land (Jones 1973, 449). The failure to revise the census at regular intervals and the practice of levying tax on land no longer in production (Jones 1973, 454) would have combined to provide a strong incentive to use all land to its utmost, especially as the commuting of taxation in kind to gold (in the second half of the fourth century) led to the need to generate more cash. This will have provided an incentive for agricultural innovation as well as the use of agricultural land for industries like pottery production which could generate ready money. The pressure is likely to have been greatest on those who had not become beneficiaries of the tax system by being able to acquire exemptions through imperial service or simple bribery.

Both changes in exchange and taxation can be seen as incentives towards a diversification in production in order to overcome the impossibility of increasing income through additional arable production. This is seen very clearly in the development of pottery or quarrying, which we consider industrial but which were based on the resources of the land and would have been considered a normal part of estate production in the classical world. A similar diversification may be suggested to explain the appearance of so-called corn driers. These structures (Morris 1979, 5–22) comprise subterranean flues in a variety of forms, which were first identified as ovens for the drying of corn prior to storage (Cocks 1921). His interpretation has been widely supported because many of them have produced deposits of carbonized grain. Recent experimental work at Butser has demonstrated that one of the forms of drier did not function to remove moisture unless the grain was spread unrealistically thinly on the floor (Reynolds and Langley 1979, 38–9). This, combined with an analysis of the barley found in one such drier at Barton Court Farm, has led to the suggestion that these ovens were used for malting as part of the process of producing ale (Reynolds and Langley 1979, 40–1). Not all recent botanical evidence supports this conclusion (van der Veen pers. comm.), although there seems no doubt that some were used for this purpose.

M. K. Jones (1981, 115–18) points to the production of beer as a strategy which helps arable farmers to circumvent their seasonal cash-flow problem, since it enables surplus arable products to be converted into a product which can be sold at different times of the year when its value will be maintained. In this way it is possible to see another of the innovations observed in later Roman agriculture as directly connected with the increased need to raise cash, and thus to the structural changes which have been outlined. It is probable that these interrelationships between production, innovation and social change could be further elucidated by continued systematic work.

The emergence of the village

The final sphere where we see a remarkable change in the settlement pattern in the later Roman period is in the more widespread occurrence of small nucleated agricultural settlements (which may perhaps be called villages, but without the medieval tenurial implications being assumed). These settlements are presently almost impossible to distinguish from the less-developed Small Towns, and almost certainly overlap with them in function, although many are not located on the major roads. Some undoubtedly existed in the early Roman period, but they appear far more characteristic of the later period. Our knowledge of them is limited since they have failed to attract widespread attention from excavators. The elucidation of their character and chronological development is thus extremely difficult.

These sites were seen by Collingwood and Myres (1937, 209ff) as the backbone of peasant settlement in Roman Britain. Since then the recognition of individual farmsteads has resulted in their being all but ignored in many interpretations of the Romano-British countryside. Nevertheless, Hallam (1964; 1970) stressed that they were an important element in the landscape of the Fens from the late second century, becoming increasingly distinct in size from the remainder of the settlements (fig. 51). One of these villages, at Grandford (Cambs), has been excavated and shown to be a small agricultural centre with timber buildings and a little industrial activity (Potter 1981; Potter and Potter 1982). Similarly the Chalton survey (Cunliffe 1973a) located three ridge-top villages, which were integrated with the field and track systems and existed alongside the individual farmsteads (fig. 90). One of these was subjected to limited excavation (Cunliffe 1977) and proved to have developed from an early Roman origin to achieve a village layout with cultivation plots by the end of the second century (fig. 91). Again the buildings were timber and rectangular, although poorly understood.

Elsewhere in southern England similar sites with timber buildings have been examined at a number of locations (Cunliffe 1977, 66; Bowen and Fowler 1966; Branigan 1985, 138–40). Comparabale sites from the stone-using areas of the Cotswolds are better known (Leech 1976) with several having been excavated on a

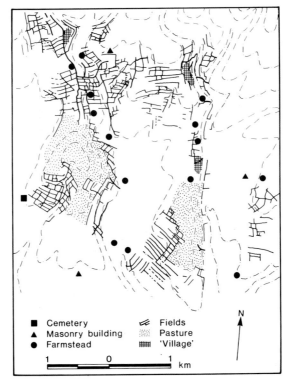

90 Map of the Chalton, Hants survey showing the mixture of fields, individual farmsteads and villages in the Roman period. The blank areas are those from which evidence does not survive (after Cunliffe 1973a).

reasonable scale: for example, Camerton (Wedlake 1958) and Nettleton Scrubb (Wedlake 1982), the best known being Catsgore (Leech 1982a; Ellis 1984). This last settlement comprised a series of farms, undifferentiated by size but grouped together as a village (fig. 92), with the faunal and finds evidence pointing towards a comparatively poor community engaged primarily in agriculture. Although a variety of minor

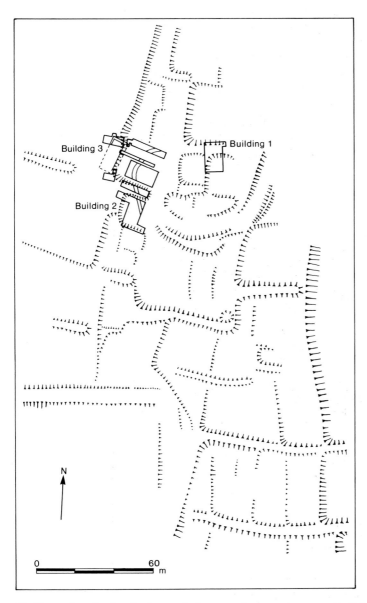

91 The earthworks, showing house platforms, trackways and excavated buildings, at one of the Romano-British villages at Chalton, Hants (after Cunliffe 1977).

craft and industrial activities are associated, none is inappropriate to an agricultural village and a similar conclusion can be drawn even for the pewter production at Camerton. Catsgore originates in the second century, but reaches its peak in the third and fourth centuries when it comprised a series of twelve farms each in its own enclosure. It is suggested that these were subject to a villa which lay some way from the village (Leech 1982a, 38–9).

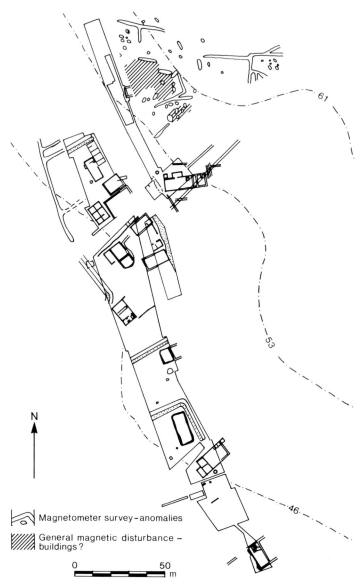

N

Magnetometer survey–anomalies

General magnetic disturbance – buildings?

0   50
            m

92 The Romano-British village at Catsgore, Glos, showing the buildings located by excavated and survey together with their individual enclosures (after Leech 1982a and Ellis 1984).

A clearer example of the close relationship of villas and villages is seen at Kingscote in Gloucestershire (Selkirk 1979, 294–9) (fig. 93) and perhaps at Stanwick in Northamptonshire (Neal 1987), where in both instances comparatively modest villas are closely associated with villages which appear to comprise farmsteads like those at Catsgore. In spite of the fine wall painting from Kingscote (Swain and Ling 1981), neither villa seems of sufficient size or pretension to be the dominant dwelling on a major landowner's estate. A similar settlement existed at Gatcombe where the villa – even if it existed – was small, and the whole village was surrounded by an enormous defensive wall (Branigan 1977). The site at Nettleton Scrubb in Wiltshire is similar (Wedlake 1982), although its excavator saw it as dependent upon the Temple of Apollo. This is difficult to substantiate, for the temple lies on the edge of the settlement and away from the Fosse Way around which the village is built, so the temple is probably better interpreted as a secondary feature. This being so these sites can be best interpreted as members of the same class as the other villages.

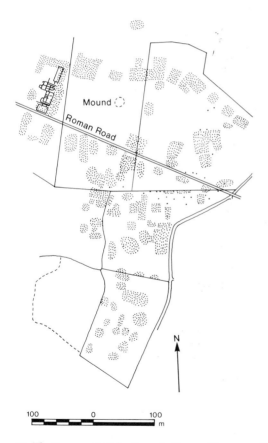

93 The Romano-British villa and village at Kingscote, Glos. The villa is shown in outline. The stipple shows the concentration of surface debris indicative of other buildings (after Selkirk 1979).

Although not numerous, they clearly form an extremely important part of the rural settlement system. However, besides being primarily agricultural, it is difficult to see how they fit into the pattern. Similar villages are common in other provinces in the later Roman period. In Africa, Garnsey (1978, 225) suggests that they were integrated with, or closely related to the villa-based estates, and Middleton has drawn the same conclusion about the villa and village at Chatalka in Bulgaria (1977, 229). Salway (1970, 12) has suggested that this relationship occurred also in Britain, so we are encouraged to see the villages as the residences for a peasantry working the estates of the owners of nearby villas. In northern Gaul, Agache (1970, 207ff) has suggested that these villages outlive the villas and provide a link to the middle ages (see below, p. 223).

The British evidence does not seem wholly consistent with the hypothesis of the dependence of villages on villas. First, the association between the two types of settlement has not been frequently demonstrated, although we must note that spatial proximity is not a necessary precondition of such a tenurial relationship. When it has been noted, there is little to suggest any major status differentiation. Thus the villas at Kingscote and Stanwick are neither particularly substantial nor well differentiated from the other structures which surround them, and as such they could perhaps be the houses of a village leader or bailiff, but hardly the principal residence of a great landowner. The possibility that the site at Kingscote housed workers on an imperial estate is raised by the discovery of an apparently official seal of late third-century date on the site (Henig 1978, 17–18). These villages could thus represent the workforce for the estate of any major absentee landlord, although this is beyond proof in the absence of epigraphic evidence.

Secondly, the organization of most of the settlements which lack villas suggests a broadly egalitarian system, with small peasant farmers grouped together in communities. These people may have been subservient to absentee landowners, but the settlements may equally have been occupied by an independent peasantry. This hypothesis of independent peasants cannot be proven, but we should recall that the Gallic Praefecture (which included Britain) is known to have had *coloni* who were registered for tax in their own villages rather than on the estates of other landowners. Jones (1973, 797) takes this to indicate that these *coloni* remained free and were not tied to any landowner. This provides an alternative explanation to that proposed by Stevens (1947) for the entry in the Theodosian Code (XI. 7, 2) which defines the tax liability of a British landowner. This tenurial system, with independent villagers cultivating their own plots while perhaps also working for wages or providing customary (perhaps tribal) service on the estates, may provide an adequate explanation for the majority of villages within Roman Britain. Elsewhere, as at Nettleton Scrubb, settlements may have housed the tenants working on estates owned by temples (Casey pers. comm.), although the archaeological evidence alone makes it difficult to identify these.

What remains important in this visible shift in settlement emphasis is a major social change which was perhaps stimulated by the concentration of wealth and land in fewer and fewer hands, leaving a peasant underclass to develop their new social and settlement forms away from the centres of political authority. Unlike the early Empire, where élite display resulted in public munificence to the benefit of the whole *civitas*, the later Empire saw the same wealth indulged on individual private consumption, which may ultimately have been socially divisive.

9

EPILOGUE: DECLINE AND FALL?

In the previous chapters I have reviewed the archaeological evidence for the Romaniz-ation of Britain within its historical context and in relation to the social organization of the population. This exercise has inevitably ranged widely and raised a series of sometimes contentious interpretations, but it has shown that there is a set of coherent strands which allows a reasonably consistent interpretation of the archaeology as a reflection of the competition between and within the societies in the province. Roman-ization has thus been seen not as a passive reflection of change, but rather as an active ingredient used by people to assert, project and maintain their social status. Further-more, Romanization has been seen as largely indigenous in its motivation, with emulation of Roman ways and styles being first a means of obtaining or retaining social dominance, then being used to express and define it while its manifestations evolved.

I have traced the development of Romanization in terms of the aspirations of the tribal élites first becoming Roman and distinguishing themselves from their peoples. Then, as *Romanitas* permeated the whole of society, its different forms and expressions become key to an understanding of the power structures within the province as the aristocracy indulged in various forms of display through their art, buildings and manners. Finally, as Roman Britain matured in the fourth century, although its power structures mutated and there is a reversion to a rural rather than an urban context, the impetus to display wealth and power through Roman styles remained, whilst at the peripheries the economy seems to have been developing in new directions. Thus during the third quarter of the fourth century Britain was utterly Roman. Legally and culturally there was little to distinguish her inhabitants from those of any other province, except perhaps for some Celtic rather than Hellenistic or Italic undertones. Given this successful integration into the Roman world, how was it that by the first quarter of the sixth century virtually nothing of this *Romanitas* remained, and why was its disappearance so much more thorough in Britain than else-where in the western Empire? There are serious problems in obtaining a clear picture from the evidence so it is impossible to arrive at any complete explanation. The aim here is to provide separate outlines of the historical and archaeological evidence, before presenting an hypothesis which appears to integrate them into an explanation which is consistent with the remainder of my account.

The historical context

The outline of events which affected the western provinces in the later fourth and fifth centuries is clear, although the details are open to considerable dispute. The Empire had reached a temporary stability under Constantine and his immediate successors, but the internal stresses re-emerged under the sequence of rather weaker rulers of both halves of the empire under the house of Valentinian (364–78). Despite the period in power of Theodosius the Great (379–95), that of his successors was unimpressive.

The internal weakness of administration need not have presented a major problem to successful government were it not for the increasing pressures on the Empire. These comprised first the internal stresses brought about by the fundamental shortage of resources in relation to state expenditure, with a consequent heavy burden on a small number of taxpayers. Second were the external problems resulting from barbarian groups increasingly seeking land within the Empire, both because of the pressures on their territories from further east and the attractiveness of the various areas of under-used land within the Empire (Halphen 1939). Contact between the Empire and the barbarian peoples was not one of simple opposition, for the peoples beyond the frontier had increasingly been brought into the imperial military service through the fourth century as manpower shortages had forced the Empire to look beyond its borders to recruit soldiers. This provided a route to power and wealth for some of the Germans who became extremely important in the Empire. Some individuals became highly Romanized and rose to the highest office, with Stilicho, for instance, being the effective ruler of the West as Honorius' *Magister Militum* (chief of staff) from 395 to 408 (Bury 1923, 106–73).

Increasing pressure from these barbarians was exacerbated by the division of the Empire into two halves, which reduced the power and resources of each part and encouraged the rivalries which continually emerged between their ruling élites, distracting attention from possible external threats. The split also effectively reduced the taxation base available to pay for the military defence of the West, which suffered most from barbarian incursions. Although the West accounted for only 41 per cent of the total army (Jones 1973, 1449) there seems little doubt that this was a proportionally heavier burden than on the East for two reasons. First, the proportion of higher-paid comitatensian troops was greater in the West – 45 per cent, compared with 29 per cent of the total army list (Jones 1973, 1449). Secondly, there is little doubt that its cost represented a heavier load on the West, as it was less wealthy than the East and thus had a smaller taxation base. This itself seems likely to have exaggerated the stresses within our half of the Empire.

The military inabilities of the West to remain impregnable to the barbarians led to a progressive ceding of territories to federate Germans, who took the land in exchange for their services in defending the Empire. The breakdown of these arrangements, with the rebellion of some groups together with the arrival of others, increased the pressures and was met with successive attempts to buy off the threats. Such bribery involved the payment of substantial subsidies, removing more wealth from the West and reducing further the ability of the taxpayers to raise money for the payment of their troops, and thus seems likely to have forced an increase in the scale of tax demands. In this process, the circumstances deteriorated (Bury 1923) into a spiral whereby failure fuelled insecurity, presenting further opportunities for the barbarians and culminating in the total loss of the Western Empire by 476. In a paradoxical sense, this spiral represents the reverse of that by which Rome had first acquired these territories (Millett in press (b)).

Within Britain, the history of the period in relation to the events in the rest of the West is less clear. Whereas the previous barbarian incursions into the Empire during the third century had little or no direct effect on Britain, save for a reduction in the size of the garrison, the events of the later fourth and fifth centuries had a much more direct impact. Britain had remained a comparatively peaceful and certainly prosperous province until the third quarter of the fourth century, for although there had been periodic problems to the north of Hadrian's Wall it seems certain that these had little impact on the south. The northern defences of Britain thus appear to have been successful despite the reductions in troop levels (James 1984), while the sea insulated the island from the large-scale invasions which affected Gaul. The troops remaining on Hadrian's Wall and its region were not top-rate soldiers of the field army (the *comitatenses*), but rather frontier soldiers (*limitanei*), perhaps best characterized as a frontier militia whose rôle was confined to the defence of their frontier. The perception of a barbarian threat to the coasts of the south and east had led to the progressive provision of a network of forts known as the Forts of the Saxon Shore from the third century onwards (Johnson 1976; Johnston 1977). Although these forts were substantially defended by huge and impressive stone walls, they show few signs of any massive or permanent military occupation, and we may legitimately infer that the presence of the forts alone had been sufficient to deter barbarian attack if this had been contemplated. The peace of fourth-century Britain accounts in part for both its prosperity and the low level of its military defence, which in turn created a vulnerability to attack.

The attack came in 367, when we are told by Ammianus Marcellinus (27. 8, 1):

> Valentinian therefore was marching quickly from Amiens to Trier when serious and alarming news reached him to the effect that a conspiracy of the barbarians had brought Britain to her knees; Count Nectaridus, officer responsible for coastal defences, had been killed, and the general Fullofaudes had been circumvented by the enemy.

Ammianus (27. 8; 28. 3) goes on to describe how Count Theodosius was sent to deal with the situation by the emperor, first recapturing London, and then in the subsequent year reconquering the remainder of the island before restoring the forts, towns and administration. Whether these events took place in 367–8 (Tomlin 1974) or 368–9 (Blockley 1980) is of little consequence, for the source makes clear that the emergency was serious. We must, however, be cautious about our interpretation of these events for two reasons. First, Ammianus was writing at the court of Theodosius I, son of Count Theodosius (Morris 1973, 15–16; Jones *et al.* 1971, 902–4), so the information recorded about the general has a panegyric quality such that it 'results more from the elevation to the throne of his son Theodosius I, emperor from 379 to

395 and the founder of the dynasty which lasted until the mid-fifth century than from the importance of the crisis of 367 and the significance of Theodosius' measures' (Birley 1981b, 336). Secondly, the archaeological evidence for the impact of these events is slight if at all detectable. Morris (1973, 15–16) showed that there was little evidence from southern Britain, whilst Evans (1984, 44–6) has shown that none of the claimed destruction deposits on the northern frontier sustain critical scrutiny. Evans concludes that the circumventing of the *Dux*, Fullofaudes, implies that the barbarians by-passed the northern frontier and made their attack further south.

In addition to the absence of evidence supporting widespread destruction, the assumption that the restoration of the cities (Ammianus 28. 3, 2) can be equated with the construction of external towers on town walls (Frere 1987, 248) is highly questionable. This reference is unspecific, and should not be used to support such a precise archaeological interpretation given both the limitations of the text and especially the evidence that several of these towers are earlier (above, p. 141). The only archaeological evidence which is apparently consistent with Ammianus' account is the construction of the signal stations on the Yorkshire coast (Evans 1984, 45), although even these may plausibly have been a little later (Casey 1979, 75–6). We may thus conclude that the disruption caused by barbarians in 367–9 has been exaggerated, giving the events, which were part of a series of minor disruptions through the 360s (Frere 1987, 339), an unjustified importance. Nevertheless, they have come to symbolize the beginning of the end of Roman Britain.

Britain's place in the history of the Empire in the later fourth century is assured next by the usurpation of Magnus Maximus (383) and his campaigns to attain the purple up to his death in 388 (Casey 1979). These events have sometimes been associated with the permanent withdrawal of troops from the province, but Casey's reinterpretation has shown that this need not be the case. Indeed the fourth-century garrison was anyway already small at *c.* 10,000–20,000 (James 1984, 164–70) and included only a small number of the *comitatenses*, who need not have been formally based here until perhaps the 390s (James pers. comm.). The only firm evidence for troop withdrawals comes in 401/2. Claudian (*De Bello Gothico*, 416–18) states that Stilicho removed a British legion then to help in the defence of Italy against Alaric's invasion (Bury 1923, 160–2), but even this reference has been dismissed as 'a poet's fantasy' (Birley 1981b, 375). Given the panegyric quality of the text we cannot assess the size of the pull-out even if we accept its veracity. The withdrawal of these troops shows the prime importance of the defence of Italy, and illustrates the fact that despite any perceived threat to Britain she remained unimportant compared with Rome.

The *Notitia Dignitatum* is the only documentary source which has a bearing on the problems of the size and nature of the British garrison at this date (Goodburn and Bartholomew 1976; Rivet and Smith 1979, 216–25). It lists the chief civil and military dignitaries of the Empire together with their insignia. The copy which has come down to us was probably compiled in its present form at Ravenna around 425. This document is unfortunately a composite and contains some information which is obsolete by the date of its compilation. Mann (1976) considers that the British section was collated after 395, and haphazardly amended up to 408, when Britain moved outside the orbit of Ravenna. The difficulties with the list (Frere 1987, 218ff) are such that it is impossible to use it as unequivocal evidence to support the presence of an official military presence in Britain down to 423 as A. H. M. Jones attempted (1973, 191), although it does provide information about the units that were and were not present around the beginning of the fifth century. Despite the small size of the British garrison there is no evidence that the province was reinforced by Germanic units, whether within the army (*laeti*) or under their own leaders (*foederati*). Such units are found reinforcing the army elsewhere, presumably a result of external threats, so their absence implies that Britain was perceived as secure as she had remained during the third century.

The often repeated suggestion that some types of military metalwork represent such Germanic units sometimes referred to as mercenaries (Hawkes and Dunning 1961; cf. Hawkes 1974) is totally without foundation (Simpson 1976; Clarke 1979, 264–91). These items of metalwork were in fact from the regular uniforms of the late Roman army and civil service (Tomlin 1976) which sometimes occur in graves outside the Empire in Free Germany. This emphasizes the point made by Brown (1974) that allied Germanic peoples were themselves becoming Romanized because of their desire to be part of the Empire. Individual barbarians were undoubtedly present in the army of Britain (thus Nectaridus and Fullofaudes mentioned by Ammianus), but they are likely to be archaeologically indistinguishable from their contemporaries. Similarly, other foreign units, like the Vandals and Burgundians sent to Britain in 277–8, were regularized into the army (Frere 1987, 209). In general their use of objects and dress during life is likely to have been Romanized, although we should note that Frisian-type pottery is associated with units of the same origin on Hadrian's Wall (Jobey 1979). This is exceptional, and religious practice together with burial customs generally seem more likely to betray their presence, as these are less susceptible to rapid change. These considerations add weight to the method used for the identification of such individuals in the Lankhills cemetery at Winchester, even if the conclusions Clarke (1979) reached are suspect (Baldwin 1985).

The impression of all being well in Britain while the core of the Empire suffered is reinforced by the events which occurred at the beginning of the fifth century. These events are clouded by uncertainty because our sources are difficult to interpret. To continental writers Britain was of marginal interest, given the momentous events with which they were concerned, and the increasing isolation which the continental barbarian incursions caused. The insular sources, upon which we are thus increasingly reliant (e.g. Gildas), are 'made up of half-truths, for they are abstracts derived from lost originals, distorted by the ignorance of their compilers' (Morris 1973, xiv). Despite these difficulties, the last decade has seen considerable work which now makes the events recorded in these sources much clearer (see especially Thompson 1977; 1983; 1984; Dumville 1977; 1984; Wood 1984; 1987). An attempt has been made to summarize this information together with the references in table 9.2, which is presented in lieu of an extended discussion. Despite considerable remaining uncertainties, the general pattern of events now seems certain.

In 406–7, while Gaul was overrun by the barbarians, Britain renounced the authority of Honorius. First Marcus then Gratian were raised to the purple before one Constantine was selected to replace him. He crossed to Gaul where the military situation was now serious, taking with him an army to attack the barbarians. Bury (1923, 189) points out how unlikely it is that Constantine III would have removed the bulk of the troops from Britain, as it was his aim to retain Britain whilst gaining territory on the continent, and this makes sense of Zosimus' statement that he left Justinian and Neviogastes in command of the army in Britain. He was initially successful in defeating or coming to terms with the invaders in Gaul and Spain, thus gaining control of a substantial territory. However, his gains were lost as a result of further incursions and a resurgence of Honorius' fortunes, which eventually led to the usurper's death after his defeat at the siege of Arles in 411.

The usurpations of 406 onwards effectively took Britain outside the authority of the legitimate emperor in Ravenna, but nevertheless emphasize the desire of the Britons to remain Roman. However, the peace of Britain was broken in 408–9 when barbarians invaded. The people took up arms to free their cities first from the barbarians and then from the Roman government. This revolt, with its rejection of the emperor's power, continued until at least 411, and there is no evidence that imperial control was ever re-established. The reference to Honorius writing to the cities of Britain in 410 telling them to look to their own defence legitimates this revolt, but may be irrelevant since some believe that it refers to Bruttium in southern Italy rather than Britain (Mann and Penman 1978, 61). This view may be seriously doubted as there is also a reference to the same imperial rescript in Gildas (E. A. Thompson 1983, 272–4). Our broad conclusion is unaffected, for we know anyway that Britain had broken from the central authority of the West and hence remained *de facto* isolated from the central authority of Italy.

Britain subsequently remained distant from our historical sources, with the exception of a few incidents. First, Constantius' Life of St Germanus shows that when he visited Britain to deal with the Pelagian heresy in 429 and subsequently in 435 (Wood 1987, 251–3), the province was still effectively Roman in character whatever its *de jure* status. A further important insight into the period is given by the Life of St Patrick (Thomas 1981, 307–46), who was the son of a British decurion captured by Irish raiders at his father's villa at the age of about sixteen and taken to Ireland. He subsequently escaped but returned to Ireland as a missionary. The villa from where he was taken lay near a place referred to as *vicus bannavem taburniae*. It is argued that this was somewhere in the west, although its precise location is uncertain, and there are serious doubts about the form of the name (Rivet and Smith 1979, 511–12). However, Thomas (1981, 312–13) favours an identification with the Birdoswald area of Cumbria. Wherever the place was located, its importance lies in the essential *Romanitas* of Patrick's background, as there is no doubt that his ministry took place in the fifth century. If we accept Thomas' proposed chronology (1981, 319–27), he was born around 415 (rather than 389) and thus brought up and educated in an independent but very Romanized Britain before being carried off around 430. The Lives of Germanus and Patrick provide valuable information about the Romanized community in Britain after the revolt of 409.

The first part of the fifth century is thus marked by a continuation of some form of *Romanitas*, the character of which remains obscure. Despite the barbarian raids of 408–9 and what features as a battle in Germanus' visit of 429, little leads us to conclude that they led to any substantial loss of territory. There is a change from raiding to settlement in the 440s when the sources combine to suggest that a considerable amount of territory was lost to the Saxons (table 9.2). The key to its understanding seems to be the fragmentation of the Romanized area into a series of different territories no longer knitted together into the single whole which had existed before the expulsion of the imperial administration in 409. As such their defence was potentially weakened. Military power now lay in the hands of individuals (referred to as tyrants) whose power was personal, continuing the trend of the fourth century. One of the favoured ways of organizing this defence was through the invitation of barbarian federates who were paid with a grant of territory. This had been used on the continent and saved the Romanized groups from the necessity of expending cash on defence. It also had the disadvantage of giving barbarians a foothold should they no longer remain loyal.

The description of Vortigern's invitation to Hengist and Horsa well illustrates this process, whether or not we should rely on these accounts (Thompson 1984, 95), and irrespective of the date being 428 or 449. Hengist and Horsa are said to have arrived as federates together with three shiploads of followers and were granted the Island of Thanet, but they subsequently revolted and invited their compatriots to settle in Kent. Such piecemeal privations, which seem to have culminated in the massive loss of territory in the south and east in the 440s, were clearly seen as of major importance in the following centuries.

The selectivity of the information about Britain in the Roman sources is determined by events on the continent. Comments in them about the 440s and their silence about the later events results from the chaos on the continent which followed the death of Aetius (454) and Valentinian III (455) and should not be taken as the foundation for conclusions about the total loss of Britain (Wood 1987). The insular sources report events from the standpoint of either the loss of much of Britain to the barbarians, resulting from divine punishment (Gildas), or as foundation myths for the new medieval élite (*Anglo-Saxon Chronicle*; Bede). Although these sources contain much valuable material (Harrison 1976; Dumville 1984) which can be related to the continental evidence, they present major difficulties. The general impression is that the Saxon take-over in the 440s was not total, but affected the hitherto most Romanized areas of the south and east, leaving *Romanitas* surviving only on the peripheries of the west and north in the second half of the fifth century. The invasion pressures around 480–90 (Dumville 1984, 83) led to the re-establishment of some more centralized control amongst the Romanized groups under a war leader (*superbus tyrannus*). He had to deal with Pictish and Scottish raids which led him to invite Saxons to help defend the north-east. This was followed by their revolt, which led the Britons to the appointment of Ambrosius Aurelianus to lead them. The Saxon revolt was only finally put down at the battle of Mons Badonicus in about 500, allowing the areas remaining within the Romanized sphere to continue their lifestyle into the sixth century. We do not know what territory the Britons retained, but Saxon settlement was already well established in the hitherto most Romanized areas which have been the subject of this study.

The historical evidence, although based on inadequate sources, therefore provides

218

a story of the decline of *Romanitas* in fits and starts as barbarian pressures developed. We see a series of minor setbacks and resurgences, but the move was constantly in favour of the Germanic ascendancy. With the breakdown of the Roman administration power was retained by sub-Roman élites, although now acting as tyrants. The evidence thus shows some continuity of personal rather than institutional power, continuing the trend towards the increased importance of personal power which we have noted in the fourth century.

The archaeological evidence

The archaeological evidence for the period from the end of the fourth century to the final demise of Romanized settlement is fraught with difficulties, most of which originate from the problem of dating. There are two reasons for this: first, most fourth-century dating ultimately relies on bronze coins found in association with other materials, which can thus be dated. Whilst the varied patterns of intensity of fourth-century coin-loss present some interpretative problems (Reece 1987), it is generally possible to use them to provide adequate dates for other categories of finds, notably pottery, and thus establish reasonably reliable site chronologies. The last bulk consignments of Roman bronze coinage which came to Britain were minted in 395–402 (Kent 1979, 21–2), so the dating of subsequent deposits is extremely difficult. Although occasional later finds of silver and gold do occur, they are extremely rare as site finds (below, p. 226) and so provide little opportunity for the dating of other archaeological finds or deposits. This problem is exacerbated by the relative scarcity of coins of 378 onwards, which means that it is frequently only possible to date a deposit to after 378, or at best post-402. This fundamental problem makes it difficult to chart the history of sites at the end of Roman Britain.

Secondly, the historical evidence does not provide any fixed points which can be related to the archaeological evidence to provide a firm chronology. Even where we have a positive association between the sources and the archaeology (as in the case of St Germanus' visit to Verulamium in 429), it has no substance as a fixed point in the relation to the archaeology of particular sites. Even general conclusions about its implications for the status of the settlement at the time are difficult to substantiate. When we deal with the more generalized 'events' like areas passing under Saxon control, there is no sound basis for arriving at conclusions about the implications for specific sites.

The result of these difficulties is that, from the final quarter of the fourth century, the archaeological evidence must be treated as essentially prehistoric, since there can be no reliance on direct correlations between the historical and archaeological sources (cf. S. Haselgrove 1979). This is equally the case for material from Anglo-Saxon contexts, the chronology of which is unfortunately heavily reliant on extremely simplistic historical models for the chronology of the migrations. Thus pottery dating is founded on the scheme developed by Plettke which, although supported by other methods, is based on the historical dates of the migrations; hence 'types found in both Britain and Germany are in principle 5th-century; those found in Germany alone are 4th-century or earlier, and those in Britain alone are 6th-century or later' (Morris 1974, 227).

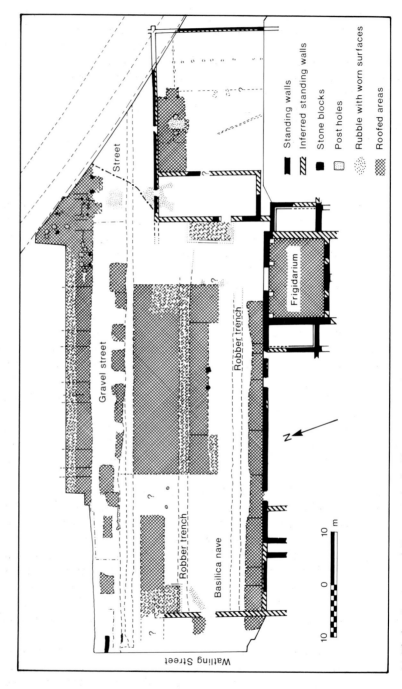

94 The late Roman or sub-Roman timber buildings constructed amongst the ruins of the Baths Basilica at Wroxeter. The central structure, reminiscent of a winged-corridor villa, was monumental in scale despite its timber construction (after Barker 1981).

Using this chronology it is therefore logically impossible to date an Anglo-Saxon burial urn in Britain to before the historically attested date for the migrations. This completely undermines the case that has been made for the presence of fourth-century *laeti* in Norfolk (Myres and Green 1973) and now accepted by Frere (1987, 266 n. 5). Given these difficulties and the dangers of moulding the evidence to suit a particular historical hypothesis, it seems inappropriate to attempt a detailed archaeological survey of the collapse of Romanization. Instead I shall follow the themes of urban settlement, the countryside and trade, trying to define the limits within which any interpretation should lie, before presenting an outline model to account for the pattern.

The towns

We have already seen (chapter 6) that the urban pattern had changed during the later Roman period, so that whilst the administrative centres of the Principate still existed, they were no longer principally economic foci but rather defended centres for their districts, which contained large private houses but comparatively little productive capacity. This contrasts with some of the Small Towns which seem to have developed an economic vibrancy which was retained throughout the later Empire.

The number of sites where we have anything like a clear picture of what was happening in the latest Roman levels is very limited. This is significant in itself, for although these layers are the most susceptible to later disturbance, the paucity of information indicates that structures were less substantial than we would expect had the towns continued to thrive. A recent survey of the evidence summarizes the data (Brooks 1986), showing that there was a lower level of urban activity in the Public Towns in the late fourth century and positive evidence for the loss or decline of public buildings before the fifth century (for instance the *fora* at Leicester, Silchester and Exeter or the theatre at Verulamium). Brooks secondly demonstrates that whilst some sites show clear evidence for the continuance of individual buildings in use into the fifth century, it is extremely difficult to push the chronology of many as far as 450. There are a few exceptions to this pattern. First, we know of a structure at Verulamium Insula XXVII constructed around 430–50 which was cut by a water pipe perhaps twenty years later. This has been taken to bolster the idea of a continuity of urban functions into the later fifth century (Frere 1983, 225). Secondly, we know of several large masonry structures which lasted well beyond the Roman period. Most notably the *principia* in the fortress at York remained in a usable form well into the early medieval period (Brooks 1986, 85; Selkirk 1969). Finally there is an impressive complex of monumental timber structures in Roman style built on top of the Baths Basilica at Wroxeter, which had been demolished after 330. This sequence seems certain to continue well into the fifth century, although we cannot yet be certain for how long (Barker 1981).

The longevity of individual structures need occasion no surprise given what is known of the history of the period, but none of the evidence we have supports the hypothesis of continuity of urban functions (even to the extent that these existed in the fourth century) much beyond the first decades of the fifth. The splendid sequence of timber buildings at Wroxeter (fig. 94) perhaps illustrates this best, with the structures

Table 9.1. *Transmission of major Roman town names to the present*

Roman name	Intermediate form	Modern name
Colonia Claudia Victricensis Camulodunensium	‹Colonia Castrum›	Colchester
Colonia [Domitiana] Lindensium	‹Lindum Colonia›	Lincoln
Colonia Nervia Glevensium	‹Glevum Castrum›	Gloucester
Colonia Eburacensis	¦[1]	York
Londinium	Londinium	London
Verulamium	¦[2]	St Albans
Isurium Brigantum	‹Vetus Burgus›[3]	Aldborough
Petuaria Parisiorum	‹Burg›	Brough-on-Humber
Venta Silurum	‹Caer Venta›	Caerwent
Venta Icenorum	‹Castrum›	Caistor-by-Norwich
Durnovernum Cantiacorum	‹Cantiaci Burgh›	Canterbury
Luguvalium Carvetiorum	‹Caer Luguvalium›[4]	Carlisle
Moridunum Demetarum	‹Caer Moridunum›	Carmarthen
Noviomagus Reg(i)norum	‹Cissi Castrum›[5]	Chichester
Corinium Dobunnorum	‹Corinium Castrum›	Cirencester
Durnovaria Durotrigum	‹Durnovaria Castrum›	Dorchester
Isca Dumnoniorum	‹Isca Castrum›[6]	Exeter
Lindinis Durotrigum	‹Iuel Castrum›[7]	Ilchester
Ratae Corieltauvorum	‹? Castrum›	Leicester
Calleva Atrebatum	‹Calleva Castrum›[8]	Silchester
Venta Belgarum	‹Venta Castrum›	Winchester
Viroconium Cornoviorum	‹Viroconium Castrum›[9]	Wroxeter

Notes: The three most common forms (Castrum, Caer and Burg) with their various derived forms all mean 'fortified enclosure'. The derivation is clear except in the following cases:
[1] The modern name is the direct successor to the Anglo-Scandinavian, Jorvik.
[2] The modern name is taken from the matyrium of the Roman, Saint Alban.
[3] Vetus Burgus, old fort, perhaps implies discontinuity.
[4] Caer Luguvalium – Caer Liwelyd.
[5] Cissa was son of Aelli, late-fifth-century king of the South Saxons.
[6] Isca – Esca – Esce – Esk – Axe – Exe.
[7] Iuel Castrum, fort on the River Yeo.
[8] Calleva – Cill – Sil . . .
[9] The etymology is obscure but appears to derive from Viroconium.
Source: all interpretations are based on Ekwall 1960.

uncovered by Barker probably most satisfactorily interpreted as a magnate's residence rather than a town. This supports the hypothesis of a continuity of central persons, even after the economic functions of the central places had gone. The basic evidence currently available thus suggests a rapid disappearance of the urban functions which had characterized the Roman towns, although the defensive networks that they provided remained available for use when needed.

At some sites, notably Canterbury, there is strong evidence from both structures and finds for the occupation of the town site early in the Anglo-Saxon period (Frere 1966). However, it has recently been argued that there is a gap in occupation even in this town (Brooks 1988). When reoccupation began in the mid- to late fifth century it is difficult to see it as different in character from contemporary rural sites. The same is true of the similar early material from other sites, for example Neatham (Millett and Graham 1986, 160), so we may conclude that even where there is resumed occupation a functional continuity is not indicated.

The evidence for a break in occupation and legal tradition (below) is supported by the place-name evidence. In Britain only the modern name of Canterbury continues the use of the Romano-British tribal suffix. The other towns have had their names transmitted to the later period, using the town name alone (table 9.1). This is in marked contrast to Gaul (Rivet 1966, 107–8), where the tribal names almost universally survive. The importance of this lies in part in demonstrating a different pattern of transfer to barbarian control in Britain. In much of Gaul the direct legal transfer of territories to barbarian control encouraged the legal institutions to be passed on, while in Britain a less-ordered process excluded this possibility. The place-names also indicate a different perception of what the later Roman town represented. In Gaul, it is clear that the idea of the urban centre encapsulating the people and its land (the *civitas*) remained important, for it would not otherwise have been transmitted to the medieval period. In Britain, the names almost universally ignore this concept, but instead convey the idea of a defended enceinte by including terms like *castrum* (table 9.1). This word clearly derives from late Roman use as it does not occur in other Germanic languages (Jackson 1953, 252). It thus appears that the concept of the *civitas* of the early Empire had disappeared to be replaced by that of the defended place, be it a former military or civilian site. This reinforces the idea that political power had become personalized and now existed at the place where the leader lived rather than at any particular centre.

The archaeological evidence thus suggests a pattern of disappearance of urban functions from the major towns, which now remained as only defended foci. A similar picture may be posited for the Small Towns, although the evidence for these is poorer and has yet to be fully collated. It cannot therefore be relied upon beyond the notable absence of any sustained claims for continuity, except perhaps at Dorchester-on-Thames (Rowley 1974), where a gap also seems likely (Brooks 1986).

Rural settlement

The evidence from villas and other rural settlements is if anything more difficult to assess than that of the towns because of the few that have both been adequately excavated and produced evidence of occupation after the fourth century. Gregson's evidence (fig. 33) clearly shows a marked decline in the number of villas dated after 350, although we should be acutely aware of the dating problems which may account for this (above, p. 219). The majority of villas seem to have gone out of use gradually during the later fourth century (Arnold 1984, 48–83), and amongst those where continued occupation is demonstrated there is a handful where continued occupation may be indicated by the structural or finds evidence. Most notable amongst these are the sites at Orton Hall Farm, Peterborough (Mackreth 1978), Barton Court Farm, Abingdon (Miles 1984), Shakenoak, Oxfordshire (Brodribb *et al.* 1978, 205–10) and Rivenhall, Essex (Rodwell and Rodwell 1986). The demonstration of any settlement continuity requires an extremely high quality of evidence, which has been shown to be lacking in the case of Rivenhall (Millett 1987b). In all cases we can see a sequence which continues to the period around 400, to be succeeded by Saxon material, generally comprising timber buildings and rubbish deposits. Because of the chronological problems already described, the evidence is ambiguous and we cannot be certain whether the juxtaposition of Romano-British and Anglo-Saxon material results from a continuity of ownership, contemporaneous occupation by two groups, a transfer of the settlement to Germanic ownership or reoccupation at a good location following a gap (e.g. Miles 1984, 49–54). The present evidence is generally not of sufficient quality to enable us to distinguish between these different explanations, and it is indeed difficult to see how archaeological evidence could be used to assess this satisfactorily even in ideal circumstances.

We can be certain that the peoples of the fifth century and after required food to eat and, once Germanic settlers arrived, we can assume that they cultivated the land. Similarly, the population surviving from Roman Britain will have continued to exploit the land, so some very basic level of continuity of exploitation is to be expected. Given these fundamental assumptions, the lack of evidence from most villa sites suggests a basic tenurial discontinuity amongst the landowning élites who had occupied villas. Exactly when this break took place is uncertain, but a broadly similar chronology to that of the towns is probable, given the interrelationship between villas and towns.

Given this pattern of discontinuity (cf. Percival 1976), the paucity of archaeological evidence from the nucleated rural sites which appear important in the fourth century is unfortunate. The evidence of the timber buildings of the sixth–seventh centuries strongly suggests that the early medieval architectural tradition is a hybrid of the Romano-British and continental Iron Age traditions (James *et al.* 1985), and it is surely at the level of the peasant settlements of the late Roman period where we might expect to find the connections. At this level of society, as one élite was replaced by another, it is probable that many Romano-British peasants remained to become Anglo-Saxon peasants.

Trade and industry

One of the clearest signs of the collapse of Roman Britain is seen in the sudden disappearance of pottery production around the beginning of the fifth century. These changes have been examined by Fulford (1979) and Evans (1985), with the details of the evidence of the south-east examined by Pomel (1984). There is some regional variation evident. Thus the stagnation and decline of the major industries of the south originates during the later fourth century (Fulford 1979). It is seen particularly in the New Forest industry (Fulford 1975), which gradually declines from about 350. Similar typological stagnation, with the production of fewer new types, has been suggested for other major producers, although despite this the Farnham industry remained strong into the early fifth century (Millett 1979). The pattern in the south and east does not show a complete breakdown and innovations do occur. We see the emergence of a series of new smaller manufacturers during the fourth century, producing low technology, often hand-made products which came to supply significant regions (fig. 95) (Pomel 1984). Indeed, the Shell Tempered wares studied by Sanders (1973) obtained an enormous distribution in the midlands and south. The explanation of this pattern of production is difficult, but may lie in small low-cost producers filling the gaps left by the failure of supplies from the larger manufacturers. These may

224

have resulted from disruptions in communications (Fulford 1979, 126) and other difficulties associated with the gradual decline of *Romanitas* seen in the pattern of the towns and villas. We also see the emergence of new styles of decoration, including the use of stamps and bosses (previously erroneously known as 'Romano-Saxon') (Gillam 1979; Roberts 1982), which became widespread in the later fourth century. These innovations coincide with the success of the Oxford (Young 1977) and Farnham industries (Lyne and Jefferies 1979), together with the continuation of importation of small quantities of continental pottery from northern Gaul and the Rhineland (Fulford 1979, 126).

This evidence perhaps amends Fulford's view of a gradual decline of the production centres all over the south from about 350, but there is no doubt that soon after 400 large-scale pottery production came to an end. The chronological difficulties make the charting of this difficult, but the impression created by the present evidence suggests that its termination was abrupt.

In the north, the large-scale pottery production seems to continue longer. Evans (1985) has demonstrated that there was a continuation of many of the industries at strength down to the end of the fourth century, and the boom in Crambeck production is known to follow *c.* 370. Even in these areas, the pattern is not uniform, with the

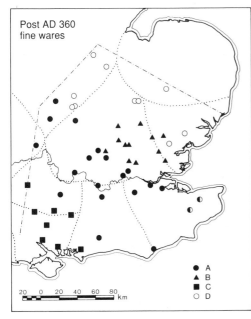
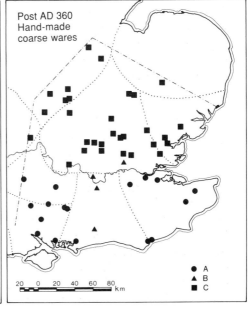

A   Oxfordshire ware
B   Much Hadham ware
C   New Forest ware
D   Nene Valley ware

A   Late Roman Grog tempered ware
B   Tilford ware
C   Late Roman Shell tempered ware

95 The distribution of the dominant fabrics in late-fourth-century pottery assemblages in S.E. England. At each site only the most frequently occurring fabric is shown (based on Pomel 1984).

Holme-on-Spalding Moor industry, for instance, apparently declining rapidly in the later fourth century at about the time Black Burnished wares almost entirely disappear from the region. Evans also makes two important observations about the end of production, which seems sudden as in the south. First came some resurgence in the production of hand-made pottery towards the end of the sequence, using forms reminiscent of LPRIA types. Secondly, he notes that there is a greater volume of late material from a number of sites than expected, given the quantities from previous periods. This may simply result from a breakdown of rubbish disposal habits (Evans 1985, 390), but perhaps indicates that supplies continued to arrive for a longer period than in the south. This underlines the contrast that Evans draws between the gradual running down of pottery production suggested by Fulford, and the sudden cessation he identifies in the north.

What is most remarkable about all the currently available pottery data is the sharpness of the break in production and distribution. Around 390 all appears well; by c. 410 all appears to have gone and there is no attempt to develop or expand low-technology manufacture, although it had existed right across the country in the later fourth century. This strongly suggests a break in demand rather than an interruption in supply. Although some industries apparently did better than others, none survived significantly longer. Thus sites which continued to be occupied struggle on with a late fourth-century assemblage until this is replaced by non-ceramic and consequently archaeologically undetectable materials (Burrows 1979).

The last vestiges of continental trade emerge in Wales and western England during the decades 475–550 (Fulford 1979, 127–8), when Mediterranean fine wares and amphorae appear for a short period. The confinement of these to the 'Celtic West' demonstrates that the south-east was now outside the Roman orbit. However, the arrival of these goods probably has more to do with the temporary resurgence of Roman fortunes in the western Mediterranean than with Gildas' Golden Age.

A similar sudden break in the pattern applies to the coin evidence, for, when supplies of bronze coinage ended after 395–402 (Kent 1979) there was no minting of copies to ensure that supplies continued to be available, as had occurred earlier in the fourth century, with for instance the copies of the FEL TEMP REPARATIO issues in 353–64 (Brickstock 1987). Such copies would appear to have been produced by state servants in the province when official coinage failed to arrive (Reece 1984, 156). The absence of regular bronze coinage after 402 is a result of the disruptions on the continent and also affects most of the western provinces (Reece 1984, figs. 2–4). Kent (1979) suggests that sufficient stockpiles of coinage were available in Britain for the short-term needs of the administration, allowing the fiscal system to continue for a few years. Gold and silver coins of Constantine III are found in Britain, as are those minted up to c. 420 (Archer 1979), but the end of large-scale coin use seems to be abrupt.

Since we know that bullion coinage was principally for the payment of state debts and the bronze was minted and supplied to claw bullion back from circulation (fig. 74), we must assume that the final end of bronze coinage and the failure to produce copies indicates the end of this system. Reece (1984) associates this breakdown with the removal of troops, and this may be so in 401–2, but it cannot be the full explanation because the state would have required coinage up to 409 as Constantine III had an army which we may assume needed payment by the traditional means. A more reasonable context would seem to be the revolt of 409 (table 9.2), when the Britons 'freed themselves, expelling their Roman governors and setting up their own administration as best they could' (Zosimus 6. 5, 2).

That the end of large-scale coin use had an effect on the economy is certain, although the nature of this remains uncertain, since much exchange probably took place within a social rather than a purely economic context, and there is some suggestion that changes in the economy originated before the cessation of regular coin supplies (above, p. 224).

A model for decline and fall

What follows is a *possible* explanation for the end of Roman Britain. It is tentatively offered as consistent with both the present evidence and the argument of the rest of this book.

The archaeological and historical evidence provide two rather different although complementary views of the end of Roman Britain. The archaeology indicated a pattern of abrupt change in the decade or two following 400, whilst the historical sources illustrate a longer drawn-out process emphasizing the survival of *Romanitas*, while Germanic groups arrived, settled and took over most of the country. These two views are not incompatible, provided we remember that the two types of evidence portray different aspects of reality. On the one hand the surviving vestiges of Romanized society continued, leaving some records of their history (although not necessarily any tangible archaeological trace). On the other, the economic superstructure and the bulk of the social organization which had brought with them the material manifestations of *Romanitas* had gone. Whether or not there was a great loss of life or a vast migration of Germanic peoples to Britain in the fifth century (Thompson 1984), the archaeology shows that most material symbols of *Romanitas* had gone by about 420, so such a catastrophe cannot be invoked as the cause of this change. The speed of the alteration in the archaeological record may be compared with the systems collapse model discussed by Renfrew (1979) and embraced by Arnold (1984), although it contrasts with the longevity of *Romanitas* indicated by the historical sources. However, since the archaeological material was generated by the socio-economic system it cannot be taken to contradict the historical evidence, which is a product of another element of the system.

The economy of the Roman province has been shown throughout this study to result from the interaction of the state system with the ruling élite. Taking this as the basis for our explanation, we can characterize the fourth century as a period of prosperity during which there was increasing social and economic differentiation accompanied by a greater separation of the rich aristocracy from the remainder of society. The province remained largely insulated from the military incursions suffered by the rest of the West (despite the problems of the 360s), and she thus had a comparatively small military garrison. As a result prosperity continued into the second half of the century, by which time some signs of decline had become apparent.

This period from the end of the fourth century also saw military events on the continent which increased the magnitude of state expenditure. After the reversion to a division between East and West in 395, the bulk of the threat lay in the West, as did 41 per cent of the whole army, but 55 per cent of the *comitatenses*. Thus the weaker half of the Empire, with its smaller tax base, inherited a disproportionately heavy fiscal load. The effect of this on the taxpayers cannot be adequately assessed, as most of the evidence for a really severe taxation is later and comes from the East (Wickham 1984, 11). However, given that military costs represented the largest single item of state expenditure, the rise in army activity in the West may have become a major and increasing burden on a province like Britain.

Given this increasing burden, the attack on Britain in 408 and the failure of the military to cope with it may have forced the élite to take control of their own destiny, removing first the barbarians and then the Roman government in 409. The suggestion by Thompson (1984, 34) that this revolt was one of peasants (*bacaudae*) is difficult to accept, unless one takes Wood's view (1984, 3–4) that the *bacaudae* included any who were politically oppressed whatever their class. Whether the revolt was of the established élite, a dissatisfied underclass or even peasants (as Thompson maintains), we can be certain that the structure of the government which followed was new. If we accept the revolt of 409 as a coup involving the removal of the existing power (that is, the Roman bureaucracy and perhaps members of the dominant élite), it is reasonable to attribute it to those who had most to gain: those paying taxes for a defence and administration which no longer served their needs.

Such an explanation of the revolt has several consequences. First, as Evans has pointed out (1983; 1985; forthcoming), since such a revolt was partly against taxation, this would presumably have ceased, removing any primary function from bronze coinage. This in turn would have had an impact on trade as the province's economy may have benefited to a large measure from the multiplier effect of the coinage which circulated at the state's behest. The end of coinage and pottery manufacture is independently attested; that of taxation and military pay seems certain, so a tax revolt associated with 409 is a reasonable inference. Secondly, the revolt against the centralized Roman administrative system apparently resulted in a fragmentation into a series of smaller units. These may still have borne some relationship to the administrative districts of the Principate, since Thompson (1984, 33) suggests that the letter of Honorius was addressed to the *civitates* in the sense of city-states. This fragmentation allowed powerful individuals to take control of different areas which were henceforth quasi-independent, and seem not to have acted together except in times of emergency like the 440s, 480s and 490s (table 9.2). More often we can suggest that the leaders (*tyranni*) of individual territories undertook their own defence, bringing in barbarian federates where necessary to help. Even the cost of this will presumably have been less than the level of taxation needed to help support the defence of the whole of the West, especially when land grants were used in lieu of cash payments. It is questionable whether these territories continued the boundaries which had dominated Roman Britain, but I suspect that they did, although in the absence of distribution evidence we cannot know. Nonetheless, acting alone these individual territories were more exposed to defeat by barbarians, with the result that much of Roman

Table 9.2. *The end of Roman Britain*

Date	Roman source	Saxon source	Reference
401–2	Stilicho withdraws some troops from Britain to defend Italy		Claudian (416–18)
406	Usurper Marcus takes power in Britain		Zosimus (6.2,1)
407	Usurper Gratian replaces Marcus		Zosimus (6.2,1)
407	Constantine III replaces Gratian and leaves Britain to campaign on continent		Zosimus (6.2,1) Orosius (7.40,4)
408–9	Britain attacked by Saxons		Zosimus (6.5,2)
410	Honorius responds to appeal from Britain by telling the cities to look to their own defence		Zosimus 6.10,2) Gildas (1.18)
411	Rome unable to recover Britain from rebels		Procopius (1.2,37)
418–	Pelagianism outlawed at Ravenna		
429	St Germanus visits Britain to counter Pelagianism; fights skirmish against Saxons		Constantius (*Vita*)
435–7	St Germanus visits Britain again		Constantius (*Vita*)
440, 442 or 445/6	'Britain . . . passed under the control of the Saxons'	Arrival of Saxons	Gallic Chronicle of 452 and 511 Bede (1.23; V.23–24)
446	Britons appeal to Count Aetius for help		Gildas (1,20)
447		*Adventus Saxonum*	Bede (11.14)
449[a]		Hengist and Horsa invited to Britain by Vortigern and given Thanet, then revolt	Anglo-Saxon Chronicle
450–5	Warfare between Britons and Saxons		Gildas (1,20)
455–80	Peace and establishment of kingship		Gildas (1,21)
477		Aelle comes to settle Sussex	Anglo-Saxon Chronicle
480–90	Renewed Saxon invasions; *superbus tyranus* appointed to lead Britons; invites Saxon mercenaries, who revolt		Gildas (1,23)
490–5	Ambrosius Aurelianus reorganizes Britons		Gildas (1,24–5)
495		Cerdic and Cynric come to settle Wessex	Anglo-Saxon Chronicle
495–500	Warfare culminates in British victory at *Mons Badonicus*		Gildas (1,26)
500–50	Peace leading to time of Gildas' writing		Gildas (1,26)

Note:
[a] Nennius (IV.31) gives a date of 428 for this invitation and this is followed by Morris (1973, 38). The date of 449 is preferred as it does not conflict with Constantius (*Vita*) in the way that Nennius' 428 appears to do. (On the veracity of Nennius see Dumville 1977, 176ff.)
Source: adapted from Dumville 1984.

Britain disappeared piecemeal. Once an administrative and military unity had gone, so too did the ability to maintain the whole. As Thompson notes (1984, 110), this handover to the barbarians is very different from that seen in Gaul, where much land was given to the barbarians by treaty. There some Germans became partially Romanized by accepting many elements of the system into which they became incorporated and this acted to continue a mutated *Romanitas* into the Middle Ages. As earlier with the Gauls, the vested interest of the barbarians in the Romanized state guaranteed its maintenance, albeit in a different form.

The British experience was different. The territory taken by the Saxons was rarely ceded peacefully; more often it was taken by force and thus the new élite had no need to conform with existing structures and organization. As areas came under Saxon control one assumes that most of the previous Romanized élite fled or were slaughtered, although the remainder of the population may well have remained to work the land under their new masters. These people henceforth came to emulate Germanic customs and habits, so their Romanization was replaced by what we may call Germanization. We can thus see the new culture as the result of positive choices, resulting in a fusion of Romano-British and Saxon elements to produce something new and Anglo-Saxon. To be understood, the development of this cultural fusion also needs to be examined with the social, political and economic pressures of that period.

References

Ancient sources cited have all been used in translation since I am not a classicist. The abbreviations used in the text should make the source clear. In general I have relied on J. C. Mann and R. G. Penman (eds.), *Literary Sources for Roman Britain*, London Association of Classical Teachers (1978). Where other works are cited, the standard texts from Loeb have generally been used.

The following abbreviations have been used:

CIL   *Corpus Inscriptionum Latinarum* (Berlin, 1863–)

CSIR *Corpus Signorum Imperii Romani*, vol. 1: *Great Britain* (British Academy, Oxford, 1977–)

DBG   Caesar, *De Bello Gallico*

RIB   *The Roman Inscriptions of Britain*, vol. 1 (eds. R. G. Collingwood and R. P. Wright, Oxford, 1965)

Modern works cited

Abbott, F. F. and A. C. Johnson. 1926. *Municipal Administration in the Roman Empire*, Princeton

Agache, R. 1970. *Détection aérienne de vestiges protohistoriques Gallo-Romains et Médiévaux dans le bassin de la Somme et ses abords*, Amiens

Alföldi, G. 1974. *Noricum*, London

Anderson, A., M. G. Fulford, H. Hatcher and A. M. Pollard. 1982. Chemical Analysis of Hunt Cups and Allied Wares from Britain, *Britannia* 13, 229–43

Applebaum, S. 1953. The Distribution of the Romano-British Population in the Basingstoke Area, *Proc. Hampshire Field Club and Archaeol. Society* 18, 119–38

1972. Roman Britain, *The Agrarian History of England and Wales*, vol. 1/2, ed. H. P. R. Finberg, Cambridge, 3–277

Archer, S. 1979. Late Roman Gold and Silver Hoards in Britain: a gazetteer, *The End of Roman Britain*, ed. P. J. Casey, Oxford, 29–64

Arnold, C. J. 1984. *Roman Britain to Saxon England*, London

Arthur, P. 1986. Roman Amphorae from Canterbury, *Britannia* 17, 239–58

Atkinson, D. 1942. *Report on the Excavations at Wroxeter, 1923–1927*, Oxford

Baatz, D. 1983. Town Walls and Defensive Weapons, Roman Urban Defences in the West, eds. J. Maloney and B. Hobley, London, 136–40

Badian, E. 1968. *Roman Imperialism in the Late Republic*, Oxford

Baldwin, R. 1985. Intrusive Burial Groups in the late Roman Cemetery of Lankhills, Winchester, *Oxford J. Archaeol.* 4 (1), 93–104

Barker, P. 1981. *Wroxeter Roman City: Excavations 1966–1980*, London

Bennett, P. 1984. The Topography of Roman Canterbury: a brief reassessment, *Archaeologia Cantiana* 100, 47–56

Bennett, P., S. S. Frere and S. Stow. 1982. *Excavations at Canterbury Castle*, Maidstone

Benson, D. and D. Miles. 1974. *The Upper Thames Valley: an archaeological survey of the river gravels*, Oxford

Biddle, M. 1975. Excavations at Winchester 1971, tenth and final interim report. Part 1, *Antiq. J.* 55, 96–126

1983. The Study of Winchester: archaeology and history in a British town, 1961–1983, *Proc. British Academy* 69, 93–135

Bidwell, P. 1979. *Exeter Archaeological Reports*, vol. 1: *The Legionary Bath-House and Basilica and Forum*, Exeter

Birchall, A. 1965. The Aylesford-Swarling Culture: the problem of the Belgae reconsidered, *Proc. Prehistoric Soc.* 31, 241–367

Bird, J. 1977. African Red Slip Ware in Roman Britain, *Roman Pottery Studies in Britain and Beyond*, eds. J. Dore and K. Greene, Oxford, 269–77

Birley, A. R. 1981a. The Economic Effects of Roman Frontier Policy, *The Roman West in the Third Century*, eds. A. C. King and M. Henig, Oxford, 39–53
  1981b. *The Fasti of Roman Britain*, Oxford
Birley, E. 1953. *Roman Britain and the Roman Army*, Kendall
Biró, M. 1975. The Inscriptions of Roman Britain, *Acta Archaeologica Academiae Scientiarum Hungariae* 27, 13–58
Blackmore, C., M. Braithwaite and I. R. Hodder. 1979. Social and Cultural Patterning in the Late Iron Age of Southern Britain, *Space, Hierarchy and Society*, eds. B. C. Burnham and J. Kingsbury, Oxford, 93–112
Blagg, T. F. C. 1979. The Date of the Temple at Bath, *Britannia* 10, 101–8
  1980. Roman Civil and Military Architecture in the Province of Britain, *World Archaeol.* 12 (1), 27–42
  1984. An Examination of the Connexions Between Military and Civilian Architecture in Roman Britain, *Military and Civilian in Roman Britain*, eds. T. F. C. Blagg and A. C. King, Oxford, 249–63
  forthcoming. Architectural Benefaction: the evidence of inscriptions
Blagg, T. F. C. and M. Millett (eds.) in press. *The Early Roman Empire in the West*, Oxford
Blockley, R. C. 1980. The Date of the 'Barbarian Conspiracy', *Britannia* 11, 223–5
Bloemers, J. H. F. 1983. Acculturation in the Rhine/Meuse Basin in the Roman Period: a preliminary survey, *Roman and Native in the Low Countries*, eds. R. Brandt and J. Slofstra, Oxford, 159–210
  in press. Lower Germany: Plura consilio quam vi, *The Early Roman Empire in the West*, eds. T. F. C. Blagg and M. Millett, Oxford
Bogaers, J. E. 1967. Review of Wacher 1966, *J. Roman Stud.* 57, 230–4
  1979. King Cogidubnus: another reading of R.I.B. 91, *Britannia* 10, 243–54.
Boon, G. C. 1974. *Silchester: the Roman town of Calleva*, Newton Abbot
  1975. Segontium Fifty Years on: 1, *Archaeologia Cambrensis* 124, 52–67
Bowen, H. C. and P. J. Fowler. 1966. Romano-British Rural Settlements in Dorset and Wiltshire, *Rural Settlement in Roman Britain*, ed. A. C. Thomas, London, 43–67
Bowman, A. K. and J. D. Thomas. 1983. *Vindolanda: the Latin writing-tablets*, London
Bradley, R. 1978. *The Prehistoric Settlement of Britain*, London
  1984. *The Social Foundations of Prehistoric Britain*, London
Branigan, K. 1972. The End of the Roman West, *Trans. Bristol Gloucestershire Archaeol. Society* 91, 117–28
  1973. Gauls in Gloucestershire, *Trans. Bristol Gloucestershire Archaeol. Society* 92, 82–94
  1977. *Gatcombe: the excavation and study of a Romano-British villa estate, 1967–1976*, Oxford
  1985. *The Catuvellauni*, Gloucester
Braund, D. C. 1984. *Rome and the Friendly King: the character of client kingship*, London
Breeze, D. 1982. *The Northern Frontiers of Roman Britain*, London
  1984. Demand and Supply on the Northern Frontier, *Between and Beyond the Walls*, eds. R. Miket and C. Burgess, Edinburgh, 264–86
Breeze, D. and B. Dobson. 1985. Roman Military Deployments in North England, *Britannia* 16, 1–20
  1987. *Hadrian's Wall* (3rd edn), Harmondsworth
Brendel, O. 1979. *Prolegomena to the Study of Roman Art*, New Haven
Brickstock, R. 1987. *Copies of Fel Temp Reparatio Coinage in Britain*, Oxford
Brodribb, A. C. C., A. R. Hands and D. R. Walker. 1978. *Excavations at Shakenoak V*, Oxford
Brooks, D. A. 1986. A Review of the Evidence for Continuity in British Towns in Fifth and Sixth Centuries, *Oxford J. Archaeol.* 5 (1), 77–102
  1988. The Case for Continuity in Fifth Century Canterbury Re-examined, *Oxford J. Archaeol.* 7 (1), 99–114
Brown, P. 1971. *The World of Late Antiquity from Marcus Aurelius to Muhammad*, London
Brown, P. D. C. 1974. Problems of Continuity, *Anglo-Saxon Settlement and Landscape*, ed. T. Rowley, Oxford, 16–19
Bulleid, A. and H. St George Gray. 1911. *The Glastonbury Lake Village*, vol. 1, Taunton
Burnham, B. C. 1986. The Origins of Romano-British Small Towns, *Oxford J. Archaeol.* 5 (2), 185–203
  1987. The Morphology of Romano-British Small Towns, *Archaeol. J.* 144, 156–90
Burrows, I. C. G. 1979. Roman Materials in Hillforts, *The End of Roman Britain*, ed. P. J. Casey, Oxford, 212–29
Bury, J. B. 1923. *History of the Later Roman Empire from the Death of Theodosius I to the Death of Justinian*, New York
Butler, R. M. 1971. The Defences of the Fourth-Century Fortress at York, *Soldier and Civilian in Roman Yorkshire*, ed. R. M. Butler, Leicester, 97–105
Carandini, A. and C. Panella. 1981. The Trading Connections of Rome and Central Italy in the Late Second

and Third Centuries, *The Roman West in the Third Century*, eds. A. C. King and M. Henig, Oxford, 487–503

Carver, M. O. H. 1987. *Underneath English Towns*, London

Carver, M. O. H., S. Donaghy and A. B. Sumpter. 1978. *Riverside Structures and a Well in Skeldergate and Buildings in Bishopshill*, London

Casey, P. J. 1979. Magnus Maximus in Britain: a reappraisal, *The End of Roman Britain*, ed. P. J. Casey, Oxford, 66–79

1983. Imperial Campaigns and Fourth Century Defences in Britain, *Roman Urban Defences in the West*, eds. J. Maloney and B. Hobley, London, 121–4

Champion, T. C. 1976. Britain in the European Iron Age, *Archaeologia Atlantica* 1 (2), 127–45

Chapman, H. and T. Johnson. 1973. Excavations at Aldgate and Bush Lane 1972, *Trans. London and Middlesex Archaeol. Society* 24, 1–72

Childe, V. G. 1956. *Piecing Together the Past: the interpretation of archaeological data*, London

Clack, P. and S. Haselgrove (eds.) 1981. *Rural Settlement in the Roman North*, Durham

Clarke, G. N. 1979. *Pre-Roman and Roman Winchester*, part 2: *The Roman Cemetery at Lankhills*, Oxford

1982. The Roman Villa at Woodchester, *Britannia* 13, 197–228

Clay, P. and J. E. Mellor. 1985. *Excavations in Bath Lane, Leicester*, Leicester

Cocks, A. H. 1921. A Romano-British Homestead in the Hambledon Valley, Bucks., *Archaeol. J.* 71, 141–98

Collingwood, R. G. 1924. The Fosse, *J. Roman Stud.* 14, 252–6

1929. Town and Country in Roman Britain, *Antiquity* 3, 261–76

1939. *An Autobiography*, Oxford

Collingwood, R. G. and J. N. L. Myres. 1937. *Roman Britain and the English Settlements*, Oxford

Collingwood, R. G. and I. A. Richmond. 1969. *The Archaeology of Roman Britain*, London

Collis, J. R. 1973. Burials with Weapons in Iron Age Britain, *Germania* 51, 121–33

1977. An Approach to the Iron Age, *The Iron Age: a review*, ed. J. R. Collis, Sheffield, 1–7

1984. *Oppida: earliest towns north of the Alps*, Sheffield

1985. Review of Cunliffe 1984b, *Proc. Prehistoric Soc.* 51, 348–9

Crawford, D. J. 1976. Imperial Estates, *Studies in Roman Property*, ed. M. Finley, Cambridge, 35–70

Crawford, M. H. 1978. *The Roman Republic*, Hassocks

Crickmore, J. 1984. *Romano-British Urban Defences*, Oxford

Crouch, K. and S. Shanks. 1984. *Excavations in Staines, 1975–1976*, London

Crowther, D. R. 1987. Redcliff, *Current Archaeol.* 104, 284–5

Crummy, P. 1977. Colchester, Fortress and Colonia, *Britannia* 8, 65–106

1982a. The Origins of Some Major Romano-British Towns, *Britannia* 13, 125–34

1982b. The Roman Theatre at Colchester, *Britannia* 13, 299–303

1984. *Excavations at Lion Walk, Balkerne Lane and Middleborough*, Colchester

unpublished. Lecture at Durham University, 30 October 1985

Cunliffe, B. W. 1968. *Fifth Report on the Excavations of the Roman Fort at Richborough, Kent*, London

1971. *Excavations at Fishbourne 1961–1971*, Leeds

1973a. Chalton, Hants.: the Evolution of a Landscape, *Antiq. J.* 53, 173–90

1973b. *The Regni*, London

1976. The Origins of Urbanization in Britain, *Oppida in Barbarian Europe*, eds. B. Cunliffe and T. Rowley, Oxford, 135–61

1977. The Romano-British Village at Chalton, Hants., *Proc. Hants. Field Club Archaeol. Society* 33, 45–67

1978a. *Iron Age Communities in Britain* (2nd edn), London

1978b. Settlement and Population in the British Iron Age: some facts, figures and fantasies, *Lowland Iron Age Communities in Europe*, eds. B. W. Cunliffe and T. Rowley, Oxford, 3–24

1981. Money and Society in Pre-Roman Britain, *Coinage and Society in Britain and Gaul*, ed. B. W. Cunliffe, London, 29–39

1983. *Danebury: anatomy of an Iron Age hillfort*, London

1984a. Relations between Britain and Gaul in the First Century B.C. and the First Century A.D., *Cross Channel Trade between Gaul and Britain in the Pre-Roman Iron Age*, eds. S. Macready and F. H. Thompson, London, 3–23

1984b. *Danebury: an Iron Age hillfort in Hampshire*, London

1987. *Hengistbury Head, Dorset*, vol. 1: *The Prehistoric and Roman Settlement 3500 B.C.–A.D. 500*, Oxford

Cunliffe, B. W. and P. Davenport. 1985. *The Temple of Sulis Minerva at Bath*, vol. 1: *The Site*, Oxford

Daniels, C. M. 1978. *J. Collingwood Bruce's Handbook to the Roman Wall*, Newcastle upon Tyne

Dannell, G. B. 1981. The Italian and Gaulish Samian, *Skeleton Green: an Iron Age and Romano-British Site*, ed. C. Partridge, London, 152–8

Dannell, G. B. and J. P. Wild. 1987. *Longthorpe II: the military works depot*, London

Darvill, T. 1979. A Petrological Study of LHS and TPF Stamped Tiles from the Cotswold Region, *Roman Brick and Tile*, ed. A. D. McWhirr, Oxford

Davies, J. L. 1980. Roman Military Deployments in Wales and the Marches from Claudius to the Antonines, *Roman Frontier Studies 1979*, eds. W. S. Hanson and L. J. F. Keppie, Oxford, 255–77

Davies, R. W. 1971. The Roman Military Diet, *Britannia* 2, 122–42

de Brisay, K. W. and K. A. Evans (eds.) 1975. *Salt: the study of an ancient industry*, Colchester

Dent, J. 1984. Two Chariot Burials at Wetwang Slack, *Current Archaeol.* 93, 302–6

1985. Wetwang: a third chariot, *Current Archaeol.* 95, 360–1

Detsicas, A. 1983. *The Cantiaci*, Gloucester

Didsbury, P. n.d. *The Finds from the 1986 Excavations at Redcliff*, unpublished interim report, Hull Museums

Dobson, B. and J. C. Mann. 1973. The Roman Army in Britain and Britons in the Roman Army, *Britannia* 4, 191–205

Down, A. 1978. *Chichester Excavations III*, Chichester

Downey, R., G. Soffe and A. King. 1980. The Hayling Island Temple and Religious Connections across the Channel, *Temples, Churches and Religion in Roman Britain*, ed. W. Rodwell, Oxford, 289–304

Drinkwater, J. F. 1979. A Note on Local Careers in the Three Gauls under the Early Empire, *Britannia* 10, 89–100

1983. *Roman Gaul: the three provinces 58 BC–AD 260*, London

1985. Urbanization in the Three Gauls: some observations, *Roman Urban Topography in Britain and the Western Empire*, eds. F. Grew and B. Hobley, London, 39–55

Drury, P. 1975. Roman Chelmsford: Caesaromagus, *The Small Towns of Roman Britain*, eds. W. Rodwell and T. Rowley, Oxford, 159–73

1984. The Temple of Claudius at Colchester Reconsidered, *Britannia* 15, 7–50

Dudley, D. R. and G. Webster. 1965. *The Roman Conquest of Britain*, London

Dumville, D. N. 1977. Sub-Roman Britain: history and legend, *History* 62, 173–92

1984. The Chronology of de Excidio Britanniae, Book 1, *Gildas: New Approaches*, eds. M. Lapidge and D. N. Dumville, Woodbridge, 61–84

Duncan-Jones, R. P. 1985. Who Paid for Public Buildings in Roman Cities, *Roman Urban Topography in Britain and the Western Empire*, eds. F. Grew and B. Hobley, London, 28–33

Dunnett, R. 1971. The Excavation of the Roman Theatre at Gosbecks, *Britannia* 2, 27–47

Dyson, T. (ed.) 1986. *The Roman Quay at St Magnus House, London*, London

Ebel, C. 1976. *Transalpine Gaul: the emergence of a Roman Province*, Leiden

Edwards, A. M. and G. P. Wibberley. 1971. *An Agricultural Land Budget for Britain 1965–2000*, London

Ekwall, E. 1960. *The Concise Oxford Dictionary of English Placenames* (4th edn), Oxford

Ellis, P. 1984. *Catsgore 1979*, Bristol

1987. Sea Mills, Bristol: the 1965–1968 excavations, *Trans. Bristol Gloucestershire Archaeol. Society* 105, 15–108

Ellmers, D. 1978. Shipping on the Rhine during the Roman Period: the pictorial evidence, *Roman Shipping and Trade: Britain and the Rhine Provinces*, eds. J. du Platt Taylor and H. Cleere, London, 1–14

Erim, K. T. and J. Reynolds. 1973. The Aphrodisias Copy of Diocletian's Edict on Maximum Prices, *J. Roman Stud.* 63, 99–100

Esmonde-Cleary, S. 1987. *Extra-Mural Areas of Romano-British Towns*, Oxford

Evans, J. 1983. Towns and the End of Roman Britain in Northern England, *Scottish Archaeol. Review* 2, 144–9

1984. Settlement and Society in North-East England in the Fourth Century, *Settlement and Society in the Roman North*, eds. P. R. Wilson, R. F. Jones and D. M. Evans, Bradford, 43–8

1985. Aspects of Later Roman Pottery Assemblages in Northern England, unpublished Ph.D. thesis, University of Bradford

1987. Graffiti and the Evidence of Literacy and Pottery Use in Roman Britain, *Archaeol. J.* 144, 191–204

1988. Crambeck: the development of a major northern pottery industry, *The Crambeck Roman Pottery Industry*, ed. P. R. Wilson, Leeds, 43–90

forthcoming. When the Brightest Light of the Whole Earth is Extinguished, from Roman Britain to gathering gloom, *Oxford J. Archaeol.*, 1988

Fasham, P. J. 1985. *The Prehistoric Settlement at Winnall Down, Winchester*, Gloucester

Fentress, E. 1981. African Buildings: money, politics and crisis in Auzia, *The Roman West in the Third Century*, eds. A. C. King and M. Henig, Oxford, 199–201

Finley, M. I. 1973. *The Ancient Economy*, London

Fishwick, D. 1972. Templum Divio Claudio Constitutum, *Britannia* 3, 164–81

Fitzpatrick, A. P. 1984. The Deposition of La Tène Iron Age Metalwork in Watery Contexts in Southern England, *Aspects of the Iron Age in Central Southern Britain*, eds. B. Cunliffe and D. Miles, Oxford, 178–90

1985. The Distribution of Dressel 1 amphorae in North-West Europe, *Oxford J. Archaeol.* 4 (3), 305–40

1986. Camulodunum and the Early Occupation of South-East England: some reconsiderations, *Studien zu den Militärgrenzen Roms III, 13 Internationaler Limeskongress, Aalen 1983*, ed. C. Unz, Stuttgart, 35–41

Foster, J. 1986. *The Lexden Tumulus: a re-appraisal of an Iron Age burial from Colchester, Essex*, Oxford

Fowler, P. J. 1972. Field Archaeology in the Future, *Archaeology and the Landscape*, ed. P. J. Fowler, London, 96–126

1978. Lowland Landscapes: culture, time and personality, *The Effect of Man on the Landscape: the lowland zone*, eds. S. Limbrey and J. G. Evans, London, 1–12

1981. Later Prehistory, *The Agrarian History of England and Wales*, vol. 1 (1), ed. J. Thirsk, Cambridge, 63–298

Fox, A. and W. Ravenhill. 1972. The Roman Fort at Nanstallon, Cornwall, *Britannia* 3, 56–111

Fox, C. 1933. *The Personality of Britain: its influence on inhabitant and invader in prehistoric and early historic times* (2nd edn), Cardiff

1958. *Pattern and Purpose: a survey of early Celtic art in Britain*, Cardiff

Frank, T. 1940. *An Economic Survey of Ancient Rome*, vol. 5: *Rome and Italy of the Empire*, Baltimore

Frere, S. S. 1966. The End of the Towns in Roman Britain, *The Civitas Capitals of Roman Britain*, ed. J. S. Wacher, Leicester, 87–100

1967. *Britannia: a history of Roman Britain* (1st edn), London

1972. *Verulamium Excavations*, vol. 1, Oxford

1981. Verulamium in the Third Century, *The Roman West in the Third Century*, eds. A. C. King and M. Henig, Oxford, 383–92

1982. The Bignor Villa, *Britannia* 13, 135–95

1983. *Verulamium Excavations*, vol. II, London

1984a. British Urban Defences in Earthwork, *Britannia* 15, 63–74

1984b. Excavations at Dorchester on Thames 1963, *Archaeol. J.* 141, 91–174

1985. Civic Pride: a factor in Roman town planning, *Roman Urban Topography in Britain and the Western Empire*, eds. F. Grew and B. Hobley, London, 34–6

1987. *Britannia: a history of Roman Britain* (3rd edn), London

Frere, S. S. and J. K. St Joseph. 1974. The Roman Fortress at Longthorpe, *Britannia* 5, 1–129

Frere, S. S., S. Stow and P. Bennett. 1982. *Excavations on the Roman Defences of Canterbury*, Maidstone

Frézouls, E. 1984. Evergétisme et construction urbaine dans les Trois Gaules et les Germanies, *Revue de Nord* 64, no. 260, 27–54

Fuentes, N. 1985. Of Castles and Elephants, *London Archaeologist* 5 (4), 90–4

Fulford, M. G. 1975. *New Forest Roman Pottery*, Oxford

1977a. Pottery and Britain's Foreign Trade in the Later Roman Period, *Pottery and Early Commerce*, ed. D. P. S. Peacock, London, 35–84

1977b. The Location of Romano-British Pottery Kilns: institutional trade and the market, *Roman Pottery Studies in Britain and Beyond*, eds. J. Dore and K. Greene, Oxford, 301–6

1978a. The Interpretation of Britain's Late Roman Trade: the scope of medieval historical and archaeological analogy, *Roman Shipping and Trade: Britain and the Rhine Provinces*, eds. J. du Platt Taylor and H. Cleere, London, 59–69

1978b. Coin Circulation and Mint Activity in the Late Roman Empire: some economic implications, *Archaeol. J.* 135, 67–114

1979. Pottery Production and Trade at the End of Roman Britain: the case against continuity, *The End of Roman Britain*, ed. P. J. Casey, Oxford, 120–32

1981. Roman Pottery: towards the investigation of economic and social change, *Production and Distribution: a ceramic viewpoint*, eds. H. Howard and E. Morris, Oxford, 195–208

1982. Town and Country in Roman Britain – a Parasitical Relationship?, *The Romano-British Countryside*, ed. D. Miles, Oxford, 403–19

1984. Demonstrating Britannia's Economic Dependence in the First and Second Centuries, *Military and Civilian in Roman Britain*, eds. T. F. C. Blagg and A. C. King, Oxford, 129–42

1985. Excavations on the Sites of the Amphitheatre and Forum-Basilica at Silchester, Hampshire: an interim report, *Antiq. J.* 65, 39–81

1986. *Silchester Excavations 1986*, Reading

1987. Calleva Atrebatum: an interim report on the excavation of the oppidum 1980–1986, *Proc. Prehistoric Soc.* 53, 271–8

Fulford, M. G. and J. Bird. 1975. Imported Pottery from Germany in Late Roman Britain, *Britannia* 6, 171–81

Fulford, M. G. and I. R. Hodder. 1975. A Regression Analysis of Some Late Romano-British Pottery: a case study, *Oxoniensia* 39, 26–33

Fulford, M. G. and D. W. A. Startin. 1984. The Building of Town Defences in Earthwork in the Second Century A.D., *Britannia* 15, 240–2

Gaffney, C., V. Gaffney and M. Tingle. 1985. Settlement, Economy or Behaviour?, *Archaeology From the Ploughsoil*, eds. C. Haselgrove, M. Millett and I. M. Smith, Sheffield, 95–107

Galliou, P., M. G. Fulford and M. Clément. 1980. La Diffusion de la céramique 'à l'éponge' dans le nord-ouest de l'empire romain, *Gallia* 38 (2), 265–78

Garnsey, P. D. A. 1978. Rome's African Empire under the Principate, *Imperialism in the Ancient World*, eds. P. D. A. Garnsey and C. R. Whittaker, Cambridge, 223–54

1983. Grain for Rome, *Trade in the Ancient Economy*, eds. P. Garnsey, K. Hopkins and C. R. Whittaker, London, 118–30

Garnsey, P. D. A. and R. Saller. 1987. *The Roman Empire: economy, society and culture*, London

Gillam, J. P. 1979. Romano-Saxon Pottery: an alternative interpretation, *The End of Roman Britain*, ed. P. J. Casey, Oxford, 103–18

Gillam, J. P. and K. Greene. 1981. Roman Pottery and the Economy, *Roman Pottery Studies in Britain and North-West Europe*, eds. A. C. and A. S. Anderson, Oxford, 1–24

Goffart, W. 1974. *Caput and Colonate: towards a history of Late Roman taxation*, Toronto

Going, C. 1987. *The Mansio and Other Sites in the South-Eastern Sector of Caesaromagus: the Roman pottery*, London

Goodburn, R. 1972. Review of Cunliffe 1971, *Britannia* 3, 368–71

1979. *Chedworth: the Roman villa*, London

Goodburn, R. and P. Bartholomew (eds.) 1976. *Aspects of the Notitia Dignitatum*, Oxford

Goodchild, R. G. 1946. The Origins of the Romano-British Forum, *Antiquity* 20, 70–7

Grant, A. 1984. Animal Husbandry in Wessex and the Thames Valley, *Aspects of the Iron Age in Central Southern Britain*, eds. B. Cunliffe and D. Miles, Oxford, 102–19

Green, C. 1980. Roman Pottery, *Excavations at Billingsgate Buildings, 'Triangle', Lower Thames Street, 1974*, by D. M. Jones, London, 39–71

Green, C. and J. Draper. 1978. The Mileoak Roman Villa, Hanley, Towcester, Northants, *Northants Archaeol.* 13, 28–66

Green, C. J. S. 1982. The Cemetery of a Romano-British Christian Community at Poundbury, Dorchester, Dorset, *The Early Church in Western Britain and Ireland*, ed. S. M. Pearce, Oxford, 61–76

Greene, J. P. 1975. Bath and Other Small Western Towns, *The Small Towns of Roman Britain*, eds. W. Rodwell and T. Rowley, Oxford, 131–8

Greene, K. 1973. The Pottery from Usk, *Current Research in Romano-British Coarse Pottery*, ed. A. Detsicas, London, 25–37

1986. *The Archaeology of the Roman Economy*, London

Gregson, M. 1982a. The Villa as Private Property, *Young Archaeologist: collected unpublished papers, contributions to archaeological thinking and practice*, ed. K. Ray, Cambridge, 143–91

1982b. Linear Archaeology: the case of gas pipelines, *Young Archaeologist: collected unpublished papers, contributions to archaeological thinking and practice*, ed. K. Ray, Cambridge, 215–37

unpublished. Appendices to Gregson 1982a in undergraduate dissertation submitted to Cambridge University in 1980

Grimes, W. F. 1968. *The Excavation of Roman and Medieval London*, London

Groenman-van Waateringe, W. 1980. Urbanization and the North-West Frontier of the Roman Empire, *Roman Frontier Studies 1979*, eds. W. S. Hanson and L. J. F. Keppie, Oxford, 1037–44

Hachmann, R. 1976. The Problem of the Belgae seen from the Continent, *Bulletin Univ. London Inst. Archaeol.* 13, 117–37

Hadfield, C. 1966. *British Canals: an illustrated history* (2nd edn), Newton Abbot

REFERENCES

Hadman, J. 1978. Aisled Buildings in Roman Britain, *Studies in the Romano-British Villa*, ed. M. Todd, Leicester, 187–95

Halkon, P. 1987. Aspects of the Romano-British Landscape around Holme-on-Spalding Moor, East Yorkshire, unpublished M.A. thesis, University of Durham

Hallam, S. 1964. Villages in Roman Britain: some evidence, *Antiq. J.* 44, 19–32

1970. Settlement Around the Wash, *The Fenland in Roman Times*, ed. C. W. Phillips, London, 22–113

Halphen, L. 1939. The Barbarian Background, *Cambridge Ancient History* 12, 96–107

Hanson, W. S. 1986. Rome, the Cornovii and the Ordovices, *Studien zu den Militärgrenzen Roms III, 13 Internationaler Limeskongress Aalen 1983*, ed. C. Unz, Stuttgart, 47–52

1987. *Agricola and the Conquest of the North*, London

Harris, E. 1986. Words and Meaning: ACCIPE ET VTERE FELIX, *Pagan Gods and Shrines of the Roman Empire*, eds. M. Henig and A. C. King, Oxford, 105–11

Harris, W. V. 1979. *War and Imperialism in Republican Rome 327–70 B.C.*, Oxford

Harrison, K. 1976. *Framework of Anglo-Saxon History*, Cambridge

Hartley, B. R. 1960. *Notes on the Roman Pottery Industry in the Nene Valley*, Peterborough

1983. The Enclosure of Romano-British Towns in the Second Century A.D., *Rome and her Northern Provinces*, eds. B. R. Hartley and J. S. Wacher, Gloucester, 84–95

Hartley, B. R. and K. F. Hartley. 1970. Pottery in the Romano-British Fenland, *The Fenland in Roman Times*, ed. C. W. Phillips, London, 165–9

Haselgrove, C. C. 1982. Wealth, Prestige and Power: the dynamics of late Iron Age political centralization in South East England, *Ranking, Resource and Exchange*, eds. C. Renfrew and S. Shennan, Cambridge, 79–88

1984a. The Later Pre-Roman Iron Age between the Humber and the Tyne, *Settlement and Society in the Roman North*, eds. P. R. Wilson, R. F. Jones and D. M. Evans, Bradford, 9–25

1984b. Romanization before the Conquest: Gaulish precedents and British consequences, *Military and Civilian in Roman Britain*, eds. T. F. C. Blagg and A. C. King, Oxford, 1–64

1986a. Central Places in British Iron Age Studies: a review and some problems, *Central Places, archaeology and history*, ed. E. Grant, Sheffield, 3–12

1986b. An Iron Age Community and its Hillfort: the excavations at Danebury 1969–1979. A review, *Archaeol. J.* 143, 363–8

1987a. *Iron Age Coinage in South East England: the archaeological context*, Oxford

1987b. Culture Process on the Periphery: Belgic Gaul and Rome during the late Republic and early Empire, *Centre and Periphery in the Ancient World*, eds. M. Rowlands, M. Larsen and K. Kristiansen, Cambridge, 104–24

Haselgrove, C. C. and P. Turnbull. 1987. *Stanwick: excavations and research interim report 1985–1986*, Durham

Haselgrove, S. 1979. Romano-Saxon Attitudes, *The End of Roman Britain*, ed. P. J. Casey, Oxford, 4–13

Hassall, M. W. C. 1973. Roman Soldiers in Roman London, *Archaeologica, Theory and Practice*, ed. D. E. Strong, London, 231–7

1979. The Impact of Mediterranean Urbanism on Indigenous Nucleated Centres, *Invasion and Response: the case of Roman Britain*, eds. B. C. Burnham and H. B. Johnson, Oxford, 241–54

Hassan, F. A. 1981. *Demographic Archaeology*, London

Haverfield, F. 1912. *The Romanization of Roman Britain* (2nd edn), Oxford

Hawkes, S. C. 1974. Some Recent Finds of Late Roman Buckles, *Britannia* 5, 386–93

Hawkes, S. C. and G. C. Dunning. 1961. Soldiers and Settlers in Britain, Fourth to Fifth Century, *Medieval Archaeol.* 5, 1–70

Hayes, P. 1981. New Approaches to Ancient Fields, *Prehistoric Communities in Northern England*, ed. G. Barker, Sheffield, 105–18

Hayfield, C. 1987. *An Archaeological Survey of the Parish of Wharram Percy, East Yorkshire, 1: The evolution of the Roman landscape*, Oxford

Hebditch, M. and J. Mellor. 1973. The Forum and Basilica of Roman Leicester, *Britannia* 4, 1–83

Hemp, W. J. and C. Gresham. 1943. Park, Llanfrothen and the Unit System, *Archaeologia Cambriensis* 97, 98–112

Henig, M. 1978. A Cube of Bronze, *The Chessals Excavation, Kingscote*, ed. E. J. Swain, Stroud, 17–18

1984. *Religion in Roman Britain*, London

Heslop, D. 1987. *The Excavation of an Iron Age Settlement at Thorpe Thewles, Cleveland, 1980–1982*, London

Hingley, R. 1981. Roman Britain: the structure of Roman Imperialism and the consequences of imperialism on the development of a peripheral province, *The Romano-British Countryside*, ed. D. Miles, Oxford, 17–52

Hingley, R. and D. Miles. 1984. Aspects of Iron Age Settlement in the Upper Thames Valley, *Aspects of the Iron Age in Central Southern Britain*, eds. B. Cunliffe and D. Miles, Oxford, 52–71

Hobley, B. 1969. A Neronian-Vespasianic Military Site at The Lunt, Baginton, Warwicks, *Trans. Birmingham Archaeol. Soc.* 83, 65–129

Hodder, I. R. 1974a. The Distribution of Savernake Ware, *Wilts. Archaeol. Natural History Magazine*, 69, 67–84

1974b. Regression Analysis of Some Trade and Marketing Patterns, *World Archaeol.* 6 (2), 172–89

1975. The Spatial Distribution of Romano-British Small Towns, *The Small Towns of Roman Britain*, eds. W. Rodwell and T. Rowley, Oxford, 67–74

1977. How are We to Study Distributions of Iron Age Material?, *The Iron Age: a review*, ed. J. R. Collis, Sheffield, 8–16

1978. The Human Geography of Roman Britain, *An Historical Geography of England and Wales*, eds. R. A. Dodgson and R. A. Butlin, London, 29–55

1979. Pre-Roman and Romano-British Tribal Economies, *Invasion and Response: the case of Roman Britain*, eds. B. C. Burnham and H. B. Johnson, Oxford, 189–96

1982. *Symbols in Action*, Cambridge

Hodder, I. R. and M. W. C. Hassall. 1971. The Non-random Spacing of Romano-British Walled Towns, *Man* 6, 391–407

Hodder, I. R. and M. Millett. 1980. Romano-British Villas and Towns: a systematic analysis, *World Archaeol.* 12 (1), 69–76

Hodder, I. R. and C. R. Orton. 1976. *Spatial Analysis in Archaeology*, Cambridge

Hodson, F. R. 1962. Some Pottery from Eastbourne; the 'Marnians' and the pre-Roman Iron Age in Southern England, *Proc. Prehistoric Soc.* 28, 140–55

1964. Cultural Groupings within the British pre-Roman Iron Age, *Proc. Prehistoric Soc.* 30, 99–110

Holder, P. A. 1980. *Studies in the Auxilia of the Roman Army from Augustus to Trajan*, Oxford

Hopkins, K. 1978. *Conquerors and Slaves*, Cambridge

1980. Taxes and Trade in the Roman Empire 200 B.C.–A.D. 400, *J. Roman Stud.* 70, 101–25

1983a. *Death and Renewal*, Cambridge

1983b. Introduction, *Trade in the Ancient Economy*, eds. P. Garnsey, K. Hopkins and C. R. Whittaker, London, ix–xxv

Horne, P. 1981. Romano-Celtic Temples in the Third Century, *The Roman West in the Third Century*, eds. A. C. King and M. Henig, Oxford, 21–6

Howe, M., J. R. Perrin and D. F. Mackreth. n.d. *Roman Pottery from the Nene Valley: a guide*, Peterborough

Hull, M. R. 1963. *The Roman Potters' Kilns of Colchester*, London

Hurst, H. R. 1974. Excavations at Gloucester 1971–1973: second interim report, *Antiq. J.* 54, 8–52

1985. *Kingsholm*, Gloucester

Jackson, K. 1953. *Language and History in Early Britain*, Edinburgh

James, S. T. 1984. Britain and the Late Roman Army, *Military and Civilian in Roman Britain*, eds. T. F. C. Blagg and A. C. King, Oxford, 161–86

1988. The Fabricae: state arms factories of the later Roman Empire, *Roman Military Equipment and the Identity of Roman Soldiers*, ed. J. C. Coulston, Oxford, 257–331

James, S. T., A. Marshall and M. Millett. 1985. An Early Medieval Building Tradition, *Archaeol. J.* 141, 182–215

Jobey, I. 1979. Housesteads Ware – a Frisian tradition on Hadrian's Wall. *Archaeol. Aeliana* (5th series) 7, 127–43

Johnson, S. 1975. Vici in Lowland Britain, *Small Towns of Roman Britain*, eds. W. Rodwell and T. Rowley, Oxford, 75–83

1976. *The Roman Forts of the Saxon Shore*, London

1983. *Late Roman Fortifications*, London

Johnston, D. E. (ed.) 1977. *The Saxon Shore*, London

Jones, A. H. M. 1973. *The Later Roman Empire AD 284–602: a social, economic and administrative survey* (2nd edn), Oxford

1974. Taxation in Antiquity, *The Roman Economy: studies in ancient economic and administrative history*, ed. P. A. Brunt, Oxford, 151–86

Jones, A. H. M., J. R. Martindale and J. Morris. 1971. *The Prosopography of the Later Roman Empire*, vol. 1, 260–395, Cambridge

REFERENCES

Jones, M. J. 1975. *Roman Fort Defences to A.D. 117*, Oxford

    1981. Excavations at Lincoln: third interim report, *Antiq. J.* 61, 83–114

    1985. New Streets for Old: the topography of Roman Lincoln, *Roman Urban Topography in Britain and the Western Empire*, eds. F. Grew and B. Hobley, London, 86–93

Jones, M. K. 1981. The Development of Crop Husbandry, *The Environment of Man: the Iron Age to the Anglo-Saxon period*, eds. G. Dimbleby and M. K. Jones, Oxford, 95–128

    1982. Crop Production in Roman Britain, *The Romano-British Countryside*, ed. D. Miles, Oxford, 97–108

Keay, S. 1984. *Late Roman Amphorae in the Western Mediterranean*, Oxford

    1988. *Roman Spain*, London

Kent, J. P. C. 1978. The London Area in the Late Iron Age: an interpretation of the earliest coins, *Collectiana Londiniensis: studies presented to Ralph Merrifield*, ed. J. Bird, London, 53–8

    1979. The End of Roman Britain: the literary and numismatic evidence reviewed, *The End of Roman Britain*, ed. P. J. Casey, Oxford, 15–28

Kimes, T., C. C. Haselgrove and I. R. Hodder. 1982. A Method for the Identification of the Location of Regional Cultural Boundaries, *J. Anthropological Archaeol.* 1, 113–31

King, A. C. 1978. A Comparative Survey of Bone Assemblages from Roman Sites in Britain, *Bulletin Univ. London Inst. Archaeol.* 15, 207–32

    1981. The Decline of Samian Manufacture in the North West Provinces: problems of chronology and interpretation, *The Roman West in the Third Century*, eds. A. C. King and M. Henig, Oxford, 55–78

    1984. Animal Bones and the Dietary Identity of Military and Civilian Groups in Roman Britain, Germany and Gaul, *Military and Civilian in Roman Britain*, eds. T. F. C. Blagg and A. C. King, Oxford, 187–218

Krautheimer, R. 1983. *Three Christian Capitals: topography and politics*, Berkeley

Lambrick, G. 1984. Pitfalls and Possibilities in Iron Age Pottery Studies, *Aspects of the Iron Age in Central Southern Britain*, eds. B. Cunliffe and D. Miles, Oxford, 162–77

Lawrence, T. E. 1939. The Evolution of a Revolt, *Oriental Assembly*, ed. A. W. Lawrence, London, 103–34

Leech, R. H. 1976. Larger Agricultural Settlements in the West Country, *The Roman West Country*, ed. K. Branigan and P. J. Fowler, Newton Abbot, 142–61

    1982a. *Excavations at Catsgore 1970–1973*, Bristol

    1982b. *Ilchester*, vol. 1: *Excavations 1974–1975*, Bristol

Lewis, M. J. T. 1965. *Temples in Roman Britain*, Cambridge

Lewis, N. and M. Reinhold (eds.) 1955. *Roman Civilization Sourcebook II: the Empire*, Columbia

Lingren, C. 1980. *Classical Art Forms and Celtic Mutations: figural art in Roman Britain*, Park Ridge, N.J.

Liversidge, J. 1969. Furniture and Interior Decoration, *The Roman Villa in Britain*, ed. A. L. F. Rivet, London, 127–72

Loewenstein, K. 1973. *The Governance of Rome*, The Hague

Luttwak, E. N. 1976. *The Grand Strategy of the Roman Empire*, Baltimore

Lyne, M. A. B. and R. S. Jefferies. 1979. *The Alice Holt/Farnham Roman Pottery Industry*, London

McCarthy, M. 1984. Roman Carlisle, *Settlement and Society in the Roman North*, eds. P. R. Wilson, R. F. Jones and D. M. Evans, Bradford, 65–74

McGrail, S. 1983. Cross Channel Seamanship and Navigation in the Late First Millennium BC, *Oxford J. Archaeol.* 2 (3), 299–38

    1987. *Ancient Boats in NW Europe*, London

Macgregor, M. 1976. *Early Celtic Art in North Britain*, Leicester

Mackie, N. 1983. *Local Administration in Roman Spain, A.D. 14–211*, Oxford

    in press. Urban Munificence and the Growth of Urban Consciousness in Roman Spain, *The Early Roman Empire in the West*, eds. T. F. C. Blagg and M. Millett, Oxford

Mackreth, D. 1978. Orton Hall Farm, Peterborough: a Roman and Saxon settlement, *Studies in the Romano-British Villa*, ed. M. Todd, Leicester, 209–28

    1987. Roman Public Building, *Urban Archaeology in Britain*, eds. J. Schofield and R. Leech, London, 133–46

MacMullen, R. 1959. Roman Imperial Building in the Provinces, *Harvard Stud. in Classical Philology* 64, 207–35

    1970. Market-days in the Roman Empire, *Phoenix* 24, 333–41

    1982. The Epigraphic Habit in the Roman Empire, *American J. Philology* 103, 233–46

Macphail, R. 1981. Soil and Botanical Studies of the 'Dark Earth', *The Environment of Man: the Iron Age to the Anglo-Saxon period*, Oxford, 309–32

McWhirr, A. D. 1979. Tile-kilns in Roman Britain, *Roman Brick and Tile*, ed. A. D. McWhirr, Oxford, 97–189

1986. *Houses in Roman Cirencester*, Cirencester

McWhirr, A. D., L. Viner and C. Wells. 1982. *Romano-British Cemeteries at Cirencester*, Cirencester

Maloney, J. 1983. Recent Work on London's Defences, *Roman Urban Defences in the West*, eds. J. Maloney and B. Hobley, London, 96–117

Maloney, J. and B. Hobley. 1983. *Roman Urban Defences in the West*, London

Maltby, M. 1979. *Exeter Archaeological Reports, 2: The Animal Bones from Exeter 1971–1975*, Sheffield

1981. Iron Age, Romano-British and Anglo-Saxon Animal Husbandry: a review of the faunal evidence, *The Environment of Man: the Iron Age to the Anglo-Saxon period*, eds. G. Dimbleby and M. K. Jones, Oxford, 155–203

Mann, J. C. 1961. The Administration of Roman Britain, *Antiquity* 35, 316–20

1965. City Foundations in Gaul and Britain, *Britain and Rome: essays presented to Eric Birley*, ed. M. G. Jarrett and B. Dobson, Kendal, 109–13

1971. Spoken Latin in Britain as Evidenced in Inscriptions, *Britannia* 2, 218–24

1974. The Frontiers of the Principate, *Aufsteig und Niedergang der römischen Welt*, II/1, ed. H. Temporini, Berlin, 508–33

1976. What Was the Notitia Dignitatum For?, *Aspects of the Notitia Dignitatum*, eds. R. Goodburn and P. Bartholomew, Oxford, 1–10

1979. Power, Force and the Frontiers of the Empire, *J. Roman Stud.* 69, 175–83

1983. *Legionary Recruitment and Veteran Settlement during the Principate*, London

1985a. Two Topoi in the Agricola, *Britannia* 16, 21–4

1985b. Epigraphic Consciousness, *J. Roman Stud.* 75, 204–6

Mann, J. C. and R. G. Penman (eds.) 1978. *Literary Sources for Roman Britain*, London

Manning, W. H. 1975. Economic Influences on Land Use in the Military Areas of the Highland Zone during the Roman Period, *The Effect of Man on the Landscape: the highland zone*, eds. J. G. Evans, S. Limbrey and H. Cleere, London, 112–16

Manning, W. H. 1981. *Report on the Excavations at Usk 1965–1976: the fortress excavations 1968–1971*, Cardiff

Marsden, P. 1975. The Excavation of a Roman Palace Site in London, 1961–1972, *Trans. London and Middlesex Archaeol. Society* 26, 1–102

1980. *Roman London*, London

1987. *The Roman Forum Site in London: discoveries before 1985*, London

Maxfield, V. A. 1986. Pre-Flavian Forts and their Garrisons, *Britannia* 17, 59–72

May, J. 1984. The Major Settlements of the Later Iron Age in Lincolnshire, *A Prospect of Lincolnshire*, eds. N. Field and A. White, Lincoln, 18–22

Merrifield, R. 1983. *London: City of the Romans*, London

Merriman, N. 1987. A Prehistory for Central London?, *London Archaeologist* 5 (12), 318–26

Middleton, P. S. 1977. Review of D. Nikolou, *The Thraco-Roman Villa Rustica near Chatalka, Stara Zagora, Bulgaria*, in *J. Roman Stud.* 67, 228–9

1979. Army Supply in Roman Gaul: an hypothesis for Roman Britain, *Invasion and Response: the case of Roman Britain*, eds. B. C. Burnham and H. B. Johnson, Oxford, 81–98

Miles, D. 1982a. Confusion in the Countryside: some comments from the Upper Thames region, *The Romano-British Countryside*, ed. D. Miles, Oxford, 53–79

(ed.) 1982b. *The Romano-British Countryside*, Oxford

1984. *Archaeology at Barton Court Farm, Abingdon, Oxon*, London

Miles, D. and S. Palmer. 1982. *Archaeological Investigations at Claydon Pike, Fairford/Lechlade: an interim report 1979–1982*, Oxford

Millar, F. G. B. 1977. *The Emperor in the Roman World 31 B.C.–A.D. 337*, London

1982. Emperors, Frontiers and Foreign Relations, 31 B.C. to A.D. 378, *Britannia* 13, 1–24

Miller, E. and J. Hatcher. 1978. *Medieval England: rural society and economic change 1086–1348*, London

Miller, S. V. 1935. *The Roman Empire in the First Three Centuries*, Cambridge

Millett, M. 1979. The Dating of Farnham Pottery, *Britannia* 10, 121–38

1981. An Approach to the Romano-British Pottery of West Sussex, *Sussex Archaeol. Collect.* 118, 57–68

1983a. Excavations at Cowdery's Down, Basingstoke, 1978–1981, *Archaeol. J.* 140, 151–279

1983b. A Comparative Study of Some Contemporaneous Pottery Assemblages from Roman Britain, unpublished D.Phil. thesis, Oxford University

REFERENCES

1984. Forts and the Origin of Towns: cause or effect?, *Military and Civilian in Roman Britain*, eds. T. F. C. Blagg and A. C. King, Oxford, 65–75

1987a. An Early Roman Burial Tradition in Central Southern England, *Oxford J. Archaeol*. 6, 63–8

1987b. A Question of Continuity: Rivenhall Reviewed, *Archaeol. J*. 144, 434–8

in press (a). Pottery: population or supply pattern?, *La Struttura Agricola Romana nel Mediterranea: il contribuo della ricognizone archeologia*, ed. G. Barker, London

in press (b). Romanization: historical issues and archaeological interpretation, *The Early Roman Empire in the West*, eds. T. F. C. Blagg and M. Millett, Oxford

in press (c). The Southern Vale of York 500 B.C.–A.D. 500, *The Humber and its Environs in History and Prehistory*, eds. D. Crowther and S. Ellis, Hull

Millett, M. and D. Graham. 1986. *Excavations on the Romano-British Small Town at Neatham, Hampshire, 1969–1979*, Winchester

Millett, M. and S. McGrail. 1987. The Archaeology of the Hasholme Logboat, *Archaeol. J*. 144, 69–155

Millett, M. and D. Russell. 1984. Excavation of an Iron Age and Romano-British Site at Viables Farm, Basingstoke, *Proc. Hants. Field Club Archaeol. Society* 40, 49–60

Milne, G. 1985. *The Port of Roman London*, London

Monaghan, J. 1987. *Upchurch and Thameside Roman Pottery*, Oxford

Morris, J. 1973. *The Age of Arthur; a history of the British Isles from 350 to 650*, London

1974. Review of Myres and Green 1973, *Medieval Archaeol*. 18, 225–32

1975. London's Decline A.D. 150–250, *London Archaeologist* 2 (13), 343–4

Morris, P. 1979. *Agricultural Buildings in Roman Britain*, Oxford

Myres, J. N. L. and B. Green. 1973. *The Anglo-Saxon Cemeteries at Caister-by-Norwich and Markshall, Norfolk*, Oxford

Nash, D. 1978a. Territory and State Formation in Central Gaul, *Social Organization and Settlement*, eds. D. Green, C. Haselgrove and M. Spriggs, Oxford, 455–75

1978b. *Settlement and Coinage in Central Gaul c. 200–50 B.C.*, Oxford

1987. Imperial Expansion under the Roman Republic, *Centre and Periphery in the Ancient World*, eds. M. Rowlands, M. Larsen and K. Kristiansen, Cambridge, 87–103

Neal, D. S. 1978. The Growth and Decline of Villas in the Verulamium Area, *Studies in the Romano-British Villa*, ed. M. Todd, Leicester, 33–58

1987. Stanwick, *Current Archaeol*. 106, 334–5

O'Neil, H. E. 1945. The Roman Villa at Park Street near St Albans, Herts. Report on the excavations of 1943–45, *Archaeol. J*. 102, 21–110

Parnell, G. 1985. The Roman and Medieval Defences and Later Development of the Inmost Ward, Tower of London: excavations 1955–1977, *Trans. London and Middlesex Archaeol. Society* 36, 1–79

Partridge, C. 1981. *Skeleton Green: a late Iron Age and Romano-British site*, London

Peacock, D. P. S. 1969. A Contribution to the Study of Glastonbury Ware from Southwest Britain, *Antiq. J*. 49, 41–61

1978. The Rhine and the Problem of Gaulish Wine in Roman Britain, *Roman Shipping and Trade: Britain and the Rhine Provinces*, eds. J. du Platt Taylor and H. Cleere, London, 49–51

1982. *Pottery in the Roman World: an ethnoarchaeological approach*, London

1984. Amphorae in Iron Age Britain: a reassessment, *Cross Channel Trade between Gaul and Britain in the Pre-Roman Iron Age*, eds. S. Macready and F. H. Thompson, London, 37–42

Peacock, D. P. S. and D. F. Williams. 1986. *Amphorae and the Roman Economy; an introductory guide*, London

Percival, J. 1976. *The Roman Villa: an historical introduction*, London

Perring, D. 1981. Excavations at Watling Court. Part 1: Roman, *London Archaeologist* 4 (4), 103–8

1987. Domestic Buildings in Romano-British Towns, *Urban Archaeology in Britain*, eds. J. Schofield and R. Leech, London, 147–55

Phillips, E. J. 1977. The Classical Tradition in the Popular Sculpture of Roman Britain, *Roman Life and Art in Britain*, eds. J. Munby and M. Henig, Oxford, 35–50

Pitts, M. W. 1979. A Gazetteer of Roman Sites and Finds on the West Sussex Coastal Plain, *Sussex Archaeol. Collect*. 117, 63–83

Platt, C. 1976. *The English Medieval Town*, London

Polanyi, K. 1963. Ports of Trade in Early Societies, *J. Economic History* 23, 30–45

Pomel, M. G. 1984. A Study of Later Roman Pottery Groups in Southern Britain: fabrics, forms and chronology, unpublished M.Phil. thesis, University of London

Potter, T. W. 1981. The Roman Occupation of the Central Fenland, *Britannia* 12, 79–133

241

Potter, T. W. and R. P. J. Jackson. 1982. *The Roman Site of Stonea, Cambs., Antiquity* 217, 111–20

Potter, T. W. and C. F. Potter. 1982. *A Romano-British Village at Grandford, March, Cambridgeshire*, London

Pucci, G. 1983. Pottery and Trade in the Roman Period, *Trade in the Ancient Economy*, eds. P. Garnsey, K. Hopkins and C. R. Whittaker, London, 105–17

Rainey, A. 1973. *Mosaics in Roman Britain*, Newton Abbot

RCHM. 1962. *Eburacum: Roman York*, London

  1976. *Iron Age and Romano-British Monuments in the Gloucestershire Cotswolds*, London

  1983. West Park Roman Villa, Rockbourne, Hants., *Archaeol. J.* 140, 129–50

Redknap, M. and M. Millett. 1980. Excavations on a Romano-British farmstead at Elsted, West Sussex, *Sussex Archaeol. Collect.* 118, 197–229

Reece, R. M. 1970. *Roman Coins*, London

  1972. A Short Survey of the Roman Coins found on Fourteen Sites in Britain, *Britannia* 3, 269–76

  1979a. Roman Monetary Impact, *Invasion and Response: the case of Roman Britain*, eds. B. C. Burnham and H. B. Johnson, Oxford, 211–17

  1979b. Romano-British Interaction: a summary, *Space, Hierarchy and Society*, eds. B. C. Burnham and J. Kingsbury, Oxford, 229–40

  1980. Town and Country: the end of Roman Britain, *World Archaeol.* 12 (1), 77–92

  1981. The Third Century: crisis or change, *The Roman West in the Third Century*, eds. A. C. King and M. Henig, Oxford, 27–38

  1984. Mints, Markets and the Military, *Military and Civilian in Roman Britain*, eds. T. F. C. Blagg and A. C. King, Oxford, 143–60

  1985. Roman Towns and their Plans, *Roman Urban Topography in Britain and the Western Empire*, eds. F. Grew and B. Hobley, London, 37–40

  1987. *Roman Coinage in Britain*, London

Rees, S. E. 1979. *Agricultural Implements in Prehistoric and Roman Britain*, Oxford

Renfrew, A. C. 1979. Systems Collapse as Social Transformation, *Transformations: mathematical approaches to culture change*, eds. A. C. Renfrew and K. L. Cooke, London, 481–506

Reynolds, P. J. 1979. *Iron Age Farm: the Butser experiment*, London

Reynolds, P. J. and J. K. Langley. 1979. The Romano-British Corn-drying Oven: an experiment, *Archaeol. J.* 136, 27–42

Richardson, B. 1986. Pottery, *The Roman Quay at St Magnus House, London*, ed. A. Dyson, London, 96–138

Richardson, B. and Tyers, P. A. 1984. North Gaulish Pottery in Britain, *Britannia* 15, 133–41

Richmond, I. A. 1955. *Roman Britain*, Harmondsworth

  1966. Industry in Roman Britain, *The Civitas Capitals of Roman Britain*, ed. J. S. Wacher, Leicester, 76–86

  1968. *Hod Hill, vol. 2: Excavations carried out between 1951 and 1958*, London

Rigby, V. 1978. The Early Roman Fine Wares, *Chichester Excavations III*, ed. A. Down, Chichester, 190–201

  1981. The Gallo-Belgic Wares, *Skeleton Green: a late Iron Age and Romano-British site*, ed. C. Partridge, London, 159–95

Rigby, V. and I. Freestone. 1986. The Petrology and Typology of the Earliest Identified Central Gaulish Imports, *J. Roman Pottery Studies* 1, 6–20

Riley, D. N. 1980. *Early Landscape from the Air*, Sheffield

Rivet, A. L. F. 1955. The Distribution of Villas in Roman Britain, *Archaeological Newsletter* 6, 29–34

  1958. *Town and Country in Roman Britain*, London

  1966. Summing-up: some historical aspects of the civitates of Roman Britain, *The Civitas Capitals of Roman Britain*, ed. J. S. Wacher, Leicester, 101–13

  1969. Social and Economic Aspects, *The Roman Villa in Britain*, ed. A. L. F. Rivet, London, 173–216

  1974. A Comment, *Britannia* 5, 284

  1975. Summing Up: the classification of minor towns and related settlements, *The Small Towns of Roman Britain*, eds. W. Rodwell and T. Rowley, Oxford, 111–14

  1977. The Origins of Cities in Roman Britain, *Thèmes de recherche sur les villes antiques de l'Occident*, eds. P. M. Duval and E. Frézouls, Paris 161–72

Rivet, A. L. F. and C. Smith. 1979. *The Place-names of Roman Britain*, London

Roberts, W. I. 1982. *Romano-Saxon Pottery*, Oxford

Rodwell, W. 1978. Rivenhall and the Emergence of First Century Villas in Northern Essex, *Studies in the Romano-British Villa*, ed. M. Todd, Leicester, 11–32

242

Rodwell, W. and K. Rodwell. 1986. *Rivenhall: investigations of a villa, church and village 1950–1977*, London

Roskams, S. 1980. GPO Newgate Street, 1975–9: the Roman levels, *London Archaeologist* 3 (15), 403–7

1986. *Later Roman Towns*, paper presented to Conference, Rewley House, Oxford, 19/1/86

Rowley, T. 1974. Early Saxon Settlements in Dorchester on Thames, *Anglo-Saxon Settlement and Landscape*, ed. T. Rowley, Oxford, 42–50

1975. Roman Towns in Oxfordshire, *The Small Towns of Roman Britain*, eds. W. Rodwell and T. Rowley, Oxford, 115–23

Ryder, M. L. 1981. Livestock, *The Agrarian History of England and Wales*, vol. 1 (1), ed. J. Thirsk, Cambridge, 301–410

Saller, R. P. and B. D. Shaw. 1984. Tombstones and Roman Family Relations in the Principate: civilians, soldiers and slaves, *J. Roman Stud.* 74, 124–56

Salmon, E. T. 1969. *Roman Colonization under the Republic*, London

Salway, P. 1967. *The Frontier People of Roman Britain*, Cambridge

1970. The Roman Fenland, *The Fenland in Roman Times*, ed. C. W. Phillips, London, 1–21

1981, *Roman Britain*, Oxford

Sanders, J. 1973. Late Roman Shell Gritted Ware in Southern Britain, unpublished B.A. dissertation, University of London

Saunders, L. 1986. A Study of the Distribution of Romano-British Pottery Kilns with Respect to the Major Settlements of the Province, unpublished B.Sc. dissertation, University of Durham

Schadla-Hall, R. T. 1978. *Winchester District: the archaeological potential*, Winchester

Schönberger, H. 1969. The Roman Frontier in Germany: an archaeological survey, *J. Roman Stud.* 59, 144–97

Sealey, P. R. 1985. *Amphoras from the 1970 Excavations at Colchester Sheepen*, Oxford

Selkirk, A. 1969. York Minster, *Current Archaeol.* 17, 162–6

1979. Kingscote, *Current Archaeol.* 69, 294–9

1983. Gorhambury, *Current Archaeol.* 87, 115–21

Sellwood, L. 1984. Tribal Boundaries Viewed from the Perspective of Numismatic Evidence, *Aspects of the Iron Age in Central Southern Britain*, eds. B. Cunliffe and D. Miles, Oxford, 191–204

Sheldon, H. 1975. A Decline in the London Settlement A.D. 150–250?, *London Archaeologist* 2 (11), 278–84

1978. The 1972–1974 Excavations: their contribution to Southwark's history, *Southwark Excavations 1972–1974*, eds. J. Bird, A. H. Graham, H. Sheldon and P. Townend, London, 11–49

Sheldon, H. and I. Tyers. 1983. Recent Dendrochronological work in Southwark and its Implications, *London Archaeologist* 4 (13), 355–61

Simco, A. 1984. *Survey of Bedfordshire: the Roman period*, Bedford

Simpson, C. J. 1976. Belt-Buckles and Strap-Ends of the Later Roman Empire, *Britannia* 7, 192–223

Sitch, B. 1987. Faxfleet 'B': a Romano-British site near Broomfleet, North Humberside, unpublished M.A. thesis, University of Durham

Slofstra, J. 1983. An Anthropological Approach to the Study of Romanization Processes, *Roman and Native in the Low Countries*, eds. R. Brandt and J. Slofstra, Oxford, 71–104

Smith, C. 1977. The Valleys of the Tame and the Middle Trent – their populations and ecology, *The Iron Age: a review*, ed. J. R. Collis, Sheffield, 51–61

Smith, D. J. 1969. The Mosaic Pavements, *The Roman Villa in Britain*, ed. A. L. F. Rivet, London, 71–125

1984. Roman Mosaics in Britain: a synthesis, *Atti del III Colloquio Internazionale sul Mosaico Antico, Ravenna, 1980*, ed. F. Campanati, Ravenna, 357–80

Smith, J. T. 1964. Romano-British Aisled Houses, *Archaeol. J.* 120, 1–30

1978a. Villas as a Key to Social Structure, *Studies in the Romano-British Villa*, ed. M. Todd, Leicester, 149–86

1978b. Halls or Yards? a problem in villa interpretation, *Britannia* 9, 349–58

1983. Flight of Capital or Flight of Fancy?, *Oxford J. Archaeol.* 2 (2), 239–46

1984. Villa Plans and Social Structure in Britain and Gaul, *Caesarodunum* 17, 321–36

1985. Barnsley Park Villa: its interpretation and implications, *Oxford J. Archaeol.* 4 (3), 341–51

1987. The Social Structure of a Roman Villa: Marshfield – Ironmongers Piece, *Oxford J. Archaeol.* 6 (2), 243–55

Smith, R. F. 1987. *Roadside Settlement in Lowland Roman Britain*, Oxford

Spratling, M. G. 1972. Southern British Decorated Bronzes of the Late Pre-Roman Iron Age, unpublished Ph.D. thesis, University of London

1979. The Debris of Metal Working, *Gussage All Saints: an Iron Age settlement in Dorset*, by G. J. Wainwright, London, 125–49

Stead, I. M. 1967. A La Tène III Burial at Welwyn Garden City, *Archaeologia* 101, 1–62

1976a. The Earliest Burials of the Aylesford Culture, *Problems in Economic and Social Archaeology*, eds. G. de G. Sieveking, I. H. Longworth and K. E. Wilson, London, 401–16

1976b. *Excavations at Winterton Roman Villa*, London

1979. *The Arras Culture*, York

1987. Garton Station, *Current Archaeol.* 103, 234–7

Stead, I. M. and V. Rigby. 1986. *Baldock: the excavation of a Roman and Pre-Roman settlement 1968–1972*, London

Stevens, C. E. 1933. *Sidonius Apollinaris and his Age*, Oxford

1947. A Possible Conflict of Laws in Roman Britain, *J. Roman Stud.* 37, 132–4

1951. Britain Between the Invasions (B.C. 54–A.D. 43), *Aspects of Archaeology in Britain and Beyond*, ed. W. F. Grimes, London, 332–44

1966. The Social and Economic Aspects of Rural Settlement, *Rural Settlement in Roman Britain*, ed. A. C. Thomas, London, 108–28

Strong, D. E. 1968. The Monument, *Fifth Report on the Excavations of the Roman Fort at Richborough, Kent*, ed. B. W. Cunliffe, Oxford, 40–73

1971. Corinthian Capitals, *Excavations at Fishbourne 1961–1969*, vol. 2, by B. W. Cunliffe, Leeds, 11–14

Sutherland, C. H. V. 1939. *The Romans in Spain*, London

Swain, E. J. and R. J. Ling. 1981. The Kingscote Wall Paintings, *Britannia* 12, 167–75

Swan, V. G. 1984. *The Pottery Kilns of Roman Britain*, London

Tatton-Brown, T. 1974. Excavations at the Custom House Site, City of London, 1973, *Trans. London and Middlesex Archaeol. Society* 25, 117–219

Taylor, C. C. 1975. Roman Settlements in the Nene Valley: the impact of recent archaeology, *Recent Work in Rural Archaeology*, ed. P. J. Fowler, London, 107–20

1987. *Fields in the English Landscape*, Gloucester

Tchernia, A. 1983. Italian Wine in Gaul at the End of the Republic, *Trade in the Ancient Economy*, eds. P. Garnsey, K. Hopkins and C. R. Whittaker, London, 87–104

Thomas, A. C. 1981. *Christianity in Roman Britain to A.D. 500*, London

Thompson, E. A. 1977. Britain A.D. 406–410, *Britannia* 8, 303–18

1983. Fifth Century Facts?, *Britannia* 14, 272–4

1984. *St Germanus of Auxerre and the End of Roman Britain*, Woodbridge

Thompson, F. H. 1983. Excavations at Bigberry near Canterbury 1978–1980, *Antiq. J.* 63, 237–78

Todd, M. (ed.) 1968. *The Roman Fort at Great Casterton, Rutland*, Nottingham

1970. The Small Towns of Roman Britain, *Britannia* 1, 114–30

1975. Margidunum and Ancaster, *The Small Towns of Roman Britain*, eds. W. Rodwell and T. Rowley, Oxford, 211–23

1978a. *The Walls of Rome*, London

1978b. Villas and Romano-British Society, *Studies in the Romano-British Villa*, ed. M. Todd, Leicester, 197–208

1984. Excavations at Hembury, Devon, 1980–1983, a summary report, *Antiq. J.* 64, 251–68

1985a. Oppida and the Roman Army. A review of recent evidence, *Oxford J. Archaeol.* 4 (2), 187–99

1985b. The Roman Fort at Bury Barton, Devonshire, *Britannia* 16, 49–56

1987. *The South-West to A.D. 1000*, London

Tomlin, R. S. O. 1974. The Date of the 'Barbarian Conspiracy', *Britannia* 5, 303–9

1976. Notitia Dignitatum Omnium, Tam Civilium Quam Militarium, *Aspects of the Notitia Dignitatum*, eds. R. Goodburn and P. Bartholomew, Oxford, 189–209

1983. Non Coritani sed Corieltauvi, *Antiq. J.* 63, 353–5

Trow, S. D. in press. By the Northern Shore of Ocean. Some observations on acculturation process at the edge of the Roman world, *The Early Roman Empire in the West*, eds. T. F. C. Blagg and M. Millett, Oxford

Turner, E. G. 1956. A Writing Tablet from Somerset, *J. Roman Stud.* 46, 115–18

Turner, J. 1979. The Environment of North-East England during Roman Times as Shown by Pollen Analysis, *J. Archaeol. Science* 6, 285–90

Tyers, P. 1981. A Note on the Mica Dusted Vessels, *Skeleton Green: a late Iron Age and Romano-British site*, by C. Partridge, London, 102–3

Veen, M. van der. 1988. Romans, Natives and Cereal Consumption – food for thought, *First Millennium*

REFERENCES

Papers: Western Europe in the first millennium A.D., eds. R. F. Jones, J. H. F. Bloemers, S. L. Dyson and M. Biddle, Oxford, 99–107

Wacher, J. S. (ed.) 1966. *The Civitas Capitals of Roman Britain*, Leicester

   1975a. *The Towns of Roman Britain*, London

   1975b. Village Fortifications, *The Small Towns of Roman Britain*, eds. W. Rodwell and T. Rowley, Oxford, 51–2

Wacher, J. S. and A. D. McWhirr. 1982. *Early Roman Occupation of Cirencester*, Cirencester

Walker, S. 1981. The Burden of Roman Grandeur: aspects of public building in the cities of Asia and Achaea, *The Roman West in the Third Century*, eds. A. C. King and M. Henig, Oxford, 189–98

Walthew, C. V. 1975. The Town House and Villa House in Roman Britain, *Britannia* 6, 189–205

Ward-Perkins, J. B. 1970. From Republic to Empire: reflections on the early provincial architecture of the Roman west, *J. Roman Stud.* 60, 1–19

   1974. *Cities of Ancient Greece and Italy*, London

Watson, G. 1969. *The Roman Soldier*, London

Webster, G. 1958. The Roman Military Advance under Ostrius Scapula, *Archaeol. J.* 115, 49–98

   1966. Fort and Town in Early Roman Britain, *The Civitas Capitals of Roman Britain*, ed. J. S. Wacher, Leicester, 31–45

   1970. The Military Situations in Britain between A.D. 43 and 71, *Britannia* 1, 179–97

   1975. *The Cornovii*, London

   1979. Final Report on the Excavations of the Roman Fort at Waddon Hill, Stoke Abbott, 1963–1969, *Proc. Dorset Natur. Hist. Archaeol. Soc.* 101, 51–90

   1980. *The Roman Invasion of Britain*, London

   1987. Wroxeter, *Current Archaeology* 107, 364–8

Wedlake, W. J. 1958. *Excavations at Camerton, Somerset*, Bath

   1982. *The Excavation of the Shrine of Apollo at Nettleton, Wiltshire, 1956–1971*, London

Wells, C. M. 1972. *The German Policy of Augustus: an examination of the archaeological evidence*, Oxford

Wheeler, R. E. M. 1930. Mr Collingwood and Mr Randall: a note, *Antiquity* 4, 91–5

   1943. *Maiden Castle, Dorset*, Oxford

Wheeler, R. E. M. and T. V. Wheeler. 1936. *Verulamium: a Belgic and two Roman cities*, Oxford

Whittaker, C. R. 1983. Late Roman Trade and Traders, *Trade in the Ancient Economy*, eds. P. Garnsey, K. Hopkins and C. R. Whittaker, London, 163–80

Whittick, G. C. 1982. Roman Lead-Mining on Mendip and in North Wales, *Britannia* 13, 113–23

Wickham, C. 1984. The Other Transition: from the ancient world to feudalism, *Past and Present* 103, 3–36

Wightman, E. M. 1970. *Roman Trier and the Treveri*, London

Wild, J. P. 1974. Roman Settlement in the Lower Nene Valley, *Archaeol. J.* 131, 140–70

Wilkes, J. J. 1969. *Dalmatia*, London

Wilkes, J. J. and C. R. Elrington. 1978. *Roman Cambridgeshire: Victoria county history of the county of Cambridgeshire and the Isle of Ely*, vol. VII, Oxford

Willems, W. J. H. 1983. Romans and Batavians: regional developments at the Imperial frontier, *Roman and Native in the Low Countries*, eds. R. Brandt and J. Slofstra, Oxford, 105–28

Williams, D. F. 1987. Amphorae, *Hengistbury Head, Dorset*, vol. 1, B. W. Cunliffe, Oxford, 271–7

Williamson, T. M. 1984. The Roman Countryside: settlement and agriculture in N.W. Essex, *Britannia* 15, 225–30

Willis, S. H. 1986. The Roman Site at Fingringhoe Wick, near Colchester, During the First Century AD. An examination of the material culture, unpublished M.A. thesis, University of Durham

Wilmott, T. 1982. Excavations at Queen Street, City of London, 1953 and 1960 and Roman Timber Lined Wells in London, *Trans. London and Middlesex Archaeol. Society* 33, 1–78

Wilson, D. R. (ed.) 1969. Roman Britain in 1968, *J. Roman Stud.* 59, 198–246

Wood, I. 1984. The End of Roman Britain: continental evidence and parallels, *Gildas: new approaches*, eds. M. Lapidge and D. Dumville, Woodbridge, 1–25

   1987. The Fall of the Western Empire and the End of Roman Britain, *Britannia* 18, 251–62

Woodman, A. J. 1985. *Tacitus and Tiberius: the alternative annales*, Durham

Young, C. J. 1977. *The Roman Pottery Industry of the Oxford Region*, Oxford

Index